Maker Innovations Series

Jump start your path to discovery with the Apress Maker Innovations series! From the basics of electricity and components through to the most advanced options in robotics, Machine Learning, and even the metaverse, you'll forge a path to building ingenious hardware and controlling it with cutting-edge software. All while gaining new skills and experience with common toolsets you can take to new projects or even into a whole new career.

The Apress Maker Innovations series offers project-based learning with a strong foundation in theory and best practices. So you get hands-on experience while also learning the key concepts, terminology, and creative processes that professionals such as entrepreneurs, inventors, and engineers, use when developing and executing hardware projects. You can learn to design circuits, program AI, create IoT systems for your home or even city, or build immersive environments for the Metaverse. Each book provides the building blocks to bring your ideas to life, and so much more!

Whether you're a beginning hobbyist or a seasoned entrepreneur working out of your basement or garage, you'll scale up your skillset to become a hardware design and engineering pro. And often using low-cost and open-source software such as Raspberry Pi, Arduino, PIC microcontroller, and Robot Operating System (ROS). Programmers and software engineers will also find opportunities to expand their skills, as many projects use popular languages and operating systems like Python and Linux.

If you want to build a robot, set up a smart home, assemble a weather-ready meteorology system, create a brand-new circuit using breadboards and design software, or even build anything with LEGO, this series has all that and more! Written by creative and seasoned Makers, every book tackles both tested and leading-edge approaches and technologies, for bringing your visions and projects to life.

More information about this series at https://link.springer.com/bookseries/17311.

LLVM Compiler for RISC-V Architecture

A Unique Approach to Vectorization

Alexey Bataev

Apress®

LLVM Compiler for RISC-V Architecture: A Unique Approach to Vectorization

Alexey Bataev
NY, NY, USA

ISBN-13 (pbk): 979-8-8688-2168-4 ISBN-13 (electronic): 979-8-8688-2169-1
https://doi.org/10.1007/979-8-8688-2169-1

Copyright © 2025 by Alexey Bataev

This work is subject to copyright. All rights are reserved by the Publisher, whether the whole or part of the material is concerned, specifically the rights of translation, reprinting, reuse of illustrations, recitation, broadcasting, reproduction on microfilms or in any other physical way, and transmission or information storage and retrieval, electronic adaptation, computer software, or by similar or dissimilar methodology now known or hereafter developed.

Trademarked names, logos, and images may appear in this book. Rather than use a trademark symbol with every occurrence of a trademarked name, logo, or image we use the names, logos, and images only in an editorial fashion and to the benefit of the trademark owner, with no intention of infringement of the trademark.

The use in this publication of trade names, trademarks, service marks, and similar terms, even if they are not identified as such, is not to be taken as an expression of opinion as to whether or not they are subject to proprietary rights.

While the advice and information in this book are believed to be true and accurate at the date of publication, neither the authors nor the editors nor the publisher can accept any legal responsibility for any errors or omissions that may be made. The publisher makes no warranty, express or implied, with respect to the material contained herein.

>Managing Director, Apress Media LLC: Welmoed Spahr
>Acquisitions Editor: Miriam Haidara
>Coordinating Editor: Jessica Vakili

Cover image by eStudioCalamar

Distributed to the book trade worldwide by Springer Science+Business Media New York, 1 New York Plaza, New York, NY 10004. Phone 1-800-SPRINGER, fax (201) 348-4505, e-mail orders-ny@springer-sbm.com, or visit www.springeronline.com. Apress Media, LLC is a Delaware LLC and the sole member (owner) is Springer Science + Business Media Finance Inc (SSBM Finance Inc). SSBM Finance Inc is a **Delaware** corporation.

For information on translations, please e-mail booktranslations@springernature.com; for reprint, paperback, or audio rights, please e-mail bookpermissions@springernature.com.

Apress titles may be purchased in bulk for academic, corporate, or promotional use. eBook versions and licenses are also available for most titles. For more information, reference our Print and eBook Bulk Sales web page at http://www.apress.com/bulk-sales.

Any source code or other supplementary material referenced by the author in this book is available to readers on GitHub (https://github.com/Apress). For more detailed information, please visit https://www.apress.com/gp/services/source-code.

If disposing of this product, please recycle the paper

To my beloved wife, Yulia, and my daughter, Stephanie, whose encouragement and support made this book possible.

Table of Contents

About the Author ix

About the Technical Reviewer xi

Introduction xiii

Chapter 1: Introduction 1

    RISC-V Vector Extension Introduction 2

    Evolution of the Vector Extensions 6

    Technical Details of the Vector Extension 8

    Summary 20

Chapter 2: RISC-V RVV Support in Clang-Based Compiler 21

    What Is lang/LLVM? 21

    Clang Compilation Pipeline 26

    RISC-V Support in LLVM-Based Toolchains 30

    RISC-V Vector Language Extensions 43

    Summary 57

Chapter 3: Vector Extensions in Clang-Based Compilers 59

    Extensions for Loop Hint Optimizations 59

    Compatibility with OpenMP 91

        Vector Function Application Binary Interface 122

    SiFive Extension for Loop Vectorization 128

    Common Recommendations for Successful Code Vectorization 136

    Summary 138

TABLE OF CONTENTS

Chapter 4: RISC-V RVV Specific LLVM-Based Optimizations 141
RISC-V Vector Extension Support in LLVM..141
Optimizations and Target-Specific Information..146
RISC-V RVV Code Generation 157
Summary..166

Chapter 5: LLVM Loop Vectorizer..169
Design of the Loop Vectorizer 178
Legality Checks and Analysis 182
Loop Vectorization Planner..207
Loop Vectorization Generation 227
Summary..230

Chapter 6: LLVM SLP Vectorizer 233
Design of SLP Vectorizer 238
Analysis Phase..240
Reduction Analysis Phase..254
Tree Building and Legality Checks Phase 261
Transformation Phase 273
    Tree Nodes Reordering 275
    Target-Specific Tree Nodes Transformation...284
    External Uses Analysis...295
    Minimal Bitwidth Analysis 297
    Cost Estimation Phase...304
    Vector Code Emission Phase 307
Summary..310

Index...313

About the Author

Alexey Bataev is an experienced compiler developer, researcher, and leader with a Ph.D. in Computer Science and about two decades of experience in LLVM, Clang, and OpenMP. He is a maintainer of OpenMP in Clang and SLP vectorizer in LLVM as well as a published researcher.

About the Technical Reviewer

Massimo Nardone has more than 29 years of experience in information and cybersecurity for IT/OT/IoT/IIoT, web/mobile development, cloud, and IT architecture. His true IT passions are security and Android. He holds an M.Sc. degree in computing science from the University of Salerno, Italy. Throughout his working career, he has held various positions, starting as a programming developer, and then security teacher, PCI QSA, auditor, assessor, lead IT/OT/SCADA/cloud architect, CISO, BISO, executive, program director, OT/IoT/IIoT security competence leader, VP OT Security, etc. In his last working engagement, he worked as a seasoned cyber and information security executive, CISO, and OT, IoT, and IIoT security competence leader helping many clients to develop and implement cyber, information, OT, and IoT security activities. He is currently working as Vice President of OT Security for SSH Communications Security. He is a co-author of numerous Apress books, including *Pro Spring Security*, *Pro JPA 2 in Java EE 8*, and *Pro Android Games*, and has reviewed more than 70 titles.

Introduction

The rapid evolution of computer architectures has fundamentally reshaped compiler technology. Modern processors are no longer designed around scalar execution alone—they rely on parallelism, vectorization, and specialized extensions to deliver performance across workloads. Among the open instruction set architectures, RISC-V stands out for its clean design and modular extensibility, allowing implementers to combine a stable base with standardized and vendor-specific extensions. This openness has enabled RISC-V to grow from a research project into a mainstream architecture, competing directly with entrenched proprietary ISAs.

The LLVM compiler framework has become the backbone of this transformation. Its modular structure, powerful optimization infrastructure, and multitarget backend make it the de facto choice for supporting emerging architectures. LLVM's intermediate representation and its ability to host both static and just-in-time compilation have created an ecosystem where industry, academia, and open source communities converge to push forward compiler research and production-quality toolchains.

Vectorization represents the most critical frontier in this landscape. The RISC-V Vector Extension (RVV) introduces a scalable vector programming model, capable of adapting to hardware with different vector lengths while maintaining a consistent software interface. This flexibility demands a sophisticated compiler strategy. LLVM addresses this with scalable vector types, specialized intrinsics, and advanced passes that bridge the gap between abstract IR and efficient hardware-specific code.

INTRODUCTION

This book examines the integration of RISC-V vector support into LLVM and Clang. It begins by explaining the RISC-V and its extensions taxonomy, LLVM toolchain and RISC-V backend support, then analyzes the challenges of mapping RVV semantics onto LLVM's IR, followed by a detailed exploration of vector-specific optimizations. The later chapters investigate the design and implementation of LLVM's Loop and SLP vectorizers.

By combining the theory of compiler construction with practical details from real-world implementations, this text provides a comprehensive view of how vectorization transforms high-level code into efficient RISC-V executables. It is intended for compiler engineers, researchers, and practitioners working at the intersection of programming languages and hardware design, where the ability to translate scalable abstractions into raw performance defines the future of computing.

This book is based on open source Clang/LLVM version 21.1.0 and considers some features for clang, being part of SiFive Freedom Tools.

CHAPTER 1

Introduction

RISC-V Vector Extension Introduction

The RISC-V instruction set architecture (ISA) represents an important step in processor design, focusing on simplicity, modularity, and openness. It was part of the research conducted at the University of California, Berkeley. RISC-V follows the Reduced Instruction Set Computer (RISC) approach to ISA development, in contrast to the more complex instruction sets like x86.

RISC-V defines base set of instructions, which can be expanded with optional extensions. This modularity improves the flexibility, enabling support for the whole range of cores, from minimalistic embedded systems to high-performance computing platforms. The base instruction sets are available in several variants:

- RV32I: 32-bit integer base
- RV32E: 32-bit integer base for embedded applications
- RV64I: 64-bit integer base
- RV64E: 64-bit integer base for embedded applications
- RV128I: 128-bit integer base (currently under development)

CHAPTER 1   INTRODUCTION

These base instruction sets are intentionally minimal, covering fundamental operations such as branching, basic integer arithmetic, logic, and memory access. Complex operations like multiplication and division are part of extensions, thus preserving the simplicity of the base ISA.

One of the important design decisions in RISC-V is the exclusion of condition flags in the processor status register. Instead, comparison results are directly stored in integer registers, reducing inter-instruction dependencies and enabling more efficient hardware implementations.

As it was said before, RISC-V's extensibility is achieved by using standardized and custom extensions.

Table 1-1. *RISC-V Standard Extensions*

Extension	Description	Notes
I	Base integer instructions	
M	Integer multiplication and division	
A	Atomic operations	
F	Single-precision floating-point	Requires Zicsr and implies IEEE-754 compliance
D	Double-precision floating-point	Implies F
P	Packed SIMD	Targets short-vector/SIMD workloads
V	Vector operations	Generalizes to scalable vector processing

This extension mechanism allows RISC-V to adapt to a wide range of computational needs while maintaining a clean, fundamental ISA. Additionally, the open nature of the architecture benefits the creation of custom extensions, driving innovation and specialization. Extensions are modular and particular ISA is defined using the following format: RV[XLEN] + extensions (e.g. RV64IMAFDV).

A nonprofit RISC-V International organization supports the development and standardization of RISC-V. This collaborative approach has attracted considerable interest from both academia and industry, positioning RISC-V as a potential breakthrough technology in the processor market.

In summary, RISC-V's modular design philosophy and open source nature offer a distinctive approach to ISA design. By offering a simple yet extensible base set, RISC-V supports diverse computing environment, from embedded systems to high-performance computing.

However, the modularity of RISC-V could lead to fragmentation, where applications compiled for one vendor equipment might not run on another vendor's hardware. To address this issue, the RISC-V standard defines so-called profiles. These profiles are standardized configurations of the RISC-V ISA, enhancing software compatibility and minimizing fragmentation within the ecosystem. Each profile specifies a combination of the base ISA and extensions, customized for specific application domains.

Profiles typically include the following:

- Base ISA, usually RV32I (32-bit) or RV64I (64-bit).

- Standard extensions, such as "M" for integer multiplication/division, "A" for atomic operations, "F" for single-precision floating-point, etc.

- A distinction between mandatory and optional features, providing a clear separation of required and optional components.

Common profiles include the following:

- RVA20 (Application). Aimed at general-purpose computing, includes RV64I base with M, A, F, D, and C extensions.

- RVI20 (Integer). Base unprivileged profile, which provides generic target for software toolchain and represent the minimum level of compatibility with RISC-V standards.

- RVA22 (Application). Further evolution of RVA20, adds some extra standard extensions, including V extension as an optional extension in RVA22U64 profile (user-mode execution).

- RVA23 (Application). Further evolution of RVA22, adds some extra standard extensions, including V extension as mandatory extension in RVA23U64 profile (user-mode execution).

The naming convention typically includes the year of ratification (e.g., "20" for 2020) to differentiate between various versions. Latest RVA23 profiles now add mandatory vector extension "V". Latest profiles family also adds support for RVB23 (customized 64-bit application processors) and RVM23 (microcontrollers) profiles families.

These profiles receive ratification from RISC-V International to guarantee industry-wide standardization. They contribute to the simplification of hardware design decisions and improve software portability, which are essential elements for the widespread adoption and expansion of the RISC-V architecture across different computing domains.

Evolution of the Vector Extensions

The development of Single Instruction, Multiple Data (SIMD) and vector extensions for RISC-V represents a major progression in its Instruction Set Architecture (ISA), emphasizing both flexibility and the cooperative nature of its development process.

CHAPTER 1 INTRODUCTION

At the time of RISC-V's initial concept, vector operations were not included in the base specification. The initial focus was on creating a clean, efficient base ISA. However, as RISC-V gained more popularity and attraction, the necessity for improved parallel processing capabilities became clear.

In approximately 2015, the first major proposal for vector extensions was introduced, inspired by earlier vector work in Berkeley's RISC-V implementations. This proposal set the stage for developing a comprehensive vector extension.

In acknowledgement of the necessity for standardized vector operations, the RISC-V Foundation (now RISC-V International) formed the Vector Extension Task Group in 2017. This group was responsible for creating a robust, scalable vector extension suitable for a wide range of applications, ranging from embedded systems to high-performance computing.

Between 2018 and 2019, the task group released several draft specifications, which passed extensive review and rework based upon responses from academia and industry. A key milestone was reached in 2019 with version 0.7.1, which resulted in a stable version for initial implementations and compiler support.

In 2020, version 0.9 was frozen for public review, and this was a major step in the standardization process. Preliminary broad review helped to identify and address potential issues, ensuring the extension's robustness and usability. In December 2021, the RISC-V Vector Extension (RVV) version 1.0 was officially ratified. This ratification marked a critical milestone, offering a stable and standardized vector extension for RISC-V.

The transition from version 0.7.1 to 1.0 of the RISC-V Vector (RVV) extension represents a dedicated effort to improve and advance RISC-V's vector processing capabilities. This effort addresses modern computational challenges while maintaining the architecture's core simplicity and flexibility. Version 1.0 introduces a more comprehensive and coherent instruction set, adding new instructions for vector

CHAPTER 1   INTRODUCTION

reductions, permutations, and advanced mask manipulations. These additions expand the range of the efficient vector operations, particularly improving scientific computing and signal processing areas. Some instructions from version 0.7.1 were removed or replaced based on practical implementation experience and performance evaluations.

The instruction encoding scheme in version 1.0 has been revised to improve extensibility and future-proofing, ensuring that RVV can progress in future to meet new computational needs without disruptive changes. The assembly language syntax has also been refined for consistency and readability, aiding both programmers and automated tools.

Significant efforts have been invested in enhancing the overall performance and energy efficiency of vector operations in version 1.0. These optimizations play a critical role in assisting the adoption of RVV in areas that are sensitive to power consumption, and in high-performance computing environments.

Technical Details of the Vector Extension

Key features of the RISC-V Vector Extension include

- Scalable vector length, which allows implementations to choose appropriate vector sizes

- Support for various data types, including integer and floating-point

- Mask registers for predicated execution, enhancing efficiency in conditional operations

- Configurable vector register grouping, offering flexibility in resource utilization

CHAPTER 1   INTRODUCTION

Parallel to the vector extension development, some internal development of the SIMD-related approach started ("P" extension). This extension did not gain a lot of attention and still does not have officially ratified version.

The RISC-V Vector Extension (RVV) version 1.0 introduces a set of vector registers and associated instructions. The key architectural elements include

- Vector Registers (v0-v31): 32 vector registers, each capable of holding multiple elements.

- Vector Length Register (vl): Specifies the number of elements to be processed in a vector operation.

- Vector Type Register (vtype): Defines the data type and grouping of elements within vector registers.

- Vector Mask Register (v0): Enables predicated execution of vector operations.

A fundamental concept in RVV is vectors with variable length. Unlike fixed-width SIMD architectures, RVV allows the vector length to be determined by the hardware implementation, with software ability to change it dynamically during execution. This approach, known as "vector-length agnostic" (VLA) programming, enhances portability across different implementations.

The vector extension defines several instructions categories.

1. Vector Arithmetic Operations

    a. Integer Addition/Subtraction: vadd, vsub, vrsub

    b. Integer Multiplication: vmul, vmulh, vmulhu, vmulhsu

    c. Integer Division: vdiv, vdivu, vrem, vremu

    d. Floating-point Arithmetic: vfadd, vfsub, vfmul, vfdiv, vfmin, vfmax

7

e. Fused Multiply-Add: vfmacc, vfnmacc, vfmsac, vfnmsac

f. Bitwise Operations: vand, vor, vxor

g. Shift Operations: vsll, vsrl, vsra

2. Vector Reduction Operations

   a. Integer Reductions: vredsum, vredand, vredor, vredxor, vredmin, vredmax, vredminu, vredmaxu

   b. Floating-point Reductions: vfredosum, vfredusum, vfredmin, vfredmax

3. Vector Load/Store Instructions

   a. Unit-stride: vle8, vle16, vle32, vle64, vse8, vse16, vse32, vse64

   b. Strided: vlse8, vlse16, vlse32, vlse64, vsse8, vsse16, vsse32, vsse64

   c. Indexed: vluxei8, vluxei16, vluxei32, vluxei64, vsuxei8, vsuxei16, vsuxei32, vsuxei64

   d. Segmented: vlseg<nf>e8, vlseg<nf>e16, vlseg<nf>e32, vlseg<nf>e64, vsseg<nf>e8, vsseg<nf>e16, vsseg<nf>e32, vsseg<nf>e64 (nf—number of fields)

   e. Strided segmented: vlsseg<nf>e8, vlsseg<nf>e16, vlsseg<nf>e32, vlsseg<nf>e64, vssseg<nf>e8, vssseg<nf>e16, vssseg<nf>e32, vssseg<nf>e64 (nf—number of fields)

   f. Indexed segmented: vluxseg<nf>e8, vluxseg<nf>e16, vluxseg<nf>e32, vluxseg<nf>e64, vsuxseg<nf>e8, vsuxseg<nf>e16, vsuxseg<nf>e32, vsuxseg<nf>e64 (nf—number of fields)

4. Vector Permutation Instructions

    a. Scalar-to-vector move: vmv, vfmv

    b. Slide vector elements up or down: vslideup, vslidedown, vslide1up, vfslide1up, vslide1down, vfslide1down

    c. Gather elements from a source vector using indices: vrgather

    d. Vector compress: vcompress

5. Vector Fixed-Point Instructions

    a. Saturating Add/Subtract: vsaddu, vsadd, vssubu, vssub

    b. Averaging Add/Subtract: vaaddu, vaadd, vasubu, vasub

    c. Rounding Add/Subtract: vnclipu, vnclip

6. Vector Mask Instructions

    a. Bitwise operations: vmand, vmnand, vmandn, vmxor, vmor, vmnor, vmorn, vmxnor

    b. Vector count population: vcpop

    c. Find-first-set mask bit: vfirst

    d. Set-before-rst mask bit: vmsbf

    e. Set-including-rst mask bit: vmsif

    f. Set-only-rst mask bit: vmsof

7. Vector Cryptography Instructions (AES, SHA2, SM3, SM4, GCM)

    a. vaes...family of instructions (Zvkned extension)

    b. vsha...family of instructions (Zvknha, Zvkmhb extensions)

    c. vsm...family of instructions (Zvksh, Zvksed extensions)

CHAPTER 1   INTRODUCTION

The RISC-V Vector Extension (RVV) provides a flexible and extensive approach to the data type support. It supports the following standard and fundamental data types:

1. RVV supports signed and unsigned integers of various widths:

    a. 8-bit (byte)

    b. 16-bit (halfword)

    c. 32-bit (word)

    d. 64-bit (doubleword)

2. The extension incorporates IEEE 754-2008 compliant floating-point formats:

    a. 16-bit half-precision (binary16). This support is enabled in Zvfh and Zvfhmin extensions. Zvfh enables support for all floating-point instructions with 16-bit half-precision operands, while Zvfhmin defines a reduced support, which only includes conversion between half-precision and single- and double-precision data types, and memory operations with 16-bit floating point data types.

    b. 16-bit BFloat16. The support for this data type is very limited. It is enabled in Zvfbfmin and Zvfbfwma extensions. These extensions include only type conversions (Zvfbfmin) and widening FMA (Zvfbfma) operations.

    c. 32-bit single-precision (binary32)

    d. 64-bit double-precision (binary64)

3. Fixed-Point Types. While not explicitly defined, fixed-point arithmetic can be implemented using integer types with appropriate scaling.

CHAPTER 1   INTRODUCTION

One of the important features of RVV is its support for operations across different data widths:

1. Same-Width Operations. Most arithmetic and logical operations can be performed on operands of the same width (e.g., 32-bit + 32-bit).

2. Widening Operations. These operations produce results wider than their input operands:

    a. Integer: e.g., 16-bit * 16-bit → 32-bit product

    b. Floating-point: e.g., single-precision to double-precision conversion

3. Narrowing Operations. These reduce the width of operands or results:

    a. Integer: e.g., 64-bit to 32-bit with optional saturation

    b. Floating-point: e.g., double-precision to single-precision conversion

4. Mixed-Width Operations. Some instructions allow operands of different widths:

    a. Integer: e.g., 32-bit + 64-bit → 64-bit sum

    b. Floating-point: e.g., fused multiply-add with different precisions

RVV uses the concept of Effective Element Width (EEW) to specify the width of vector elements. This approach allows for vectors to contain elements of varying widths, thereby providing flexibility and efficiency in computation. The RVV supports a range of element widths, typically including 8-bit, 16-bit, 32-bit, and 64-bit.

CHAPTER 1   INTRODUCTION

The Selected Element Width (SEW) is a parameter that defines the width of each element within a vector. The SEW can vary, and common values include 8, 16, 32, and 64 bits. The SEW is crucial for defining how data is loaded, stored, and processed within the vector registers. The RVV includes instructions to set and query the current SEW, allowing dynamic adjustment based on the workload requirements.

The Vector Register File (VRF) in RVV is composed of a set of vector registers, each capable of holding multiple elements. The size of these registers is implementation-dependent but must be a multiple of the standard vector length (VLEN). The element width encoding determines how these registers are partitioned into individual elements.

RVV introduces the concept of register groups, controlled by the LMUL (Length Multiplier) setting:

- LMUL can be 1, 2, 4, or 8
- LMUL can also be fractional: 1/2, 1/4, or 1/8

The Length Multiplier (LMUL) parameter specifies the effective vector length relative to the base vector length (VLEN). This multiplier allows increasing or decreasing the number of elements processed in a single instruction. For example, an LMUL value of 1 means the vector length is equal to VLEN, while an LMUL value of 2 doubles the number of elements, grouping registers into groups of 2 registers. It allows, in some sense, "gluing" (or splitting, for fractional LMULs) consecutive (relatively) "small" registers into larger register (groups).

Most of these parameters are controlled by the special family of the instructions—Configuration—Setting Instructions (vsetvli/vsetivli/vsetvl). These instructions allow to set/control Effective Vector Length based on the Application Vector Length (AVL), which defines the maximum number ofelements, required processing, data type, and length multiplier. Also, it allows to control mask and tail policies.

The format of these instructions is described in Listing 1-1.

CHAPTER 1   INTRODUCTION

Listing 1-1. Formats of the vsetvl instructions.

```
vsetvli rd, rs1, vtypei ; rd = new vl, rs1 = AVL, vtypei = new vtype setting
vsetivli rd, uimm, vtypei ; rd = new vl, uimm = AVL, vtypei = new vtype setting
vsetvl rd, rs1, rs2 ; rd = new vl, rs1 = AVL, rs2 = new vtype value
```

rd here specifies the destination general purpose register, and rs1 and rs2—source general purpose registers. The vtypei, marked here as a "new vtype setting", represents some complex description of the Selected Element Width (SEW), Length Multiplier (LMUL), and tail and mask policies.

SEW in the assembly can be expressed using symbolic names such as e8, e16, e32, and e64 for 8 bit, 16 bits, 32 bits, and 64 bits, correspondingly. LMUL can be specified as one of the values: mf8, mf4, mf2, m1, m2, m4, and m8 for multipliers 1/8, 1/4, 1/2, 1, 2, 4, and 8 correspondingly. Tail policy might be encoded either as ta (Tail Agnostic) or tu (Tail Undisturbed). Similarly, mask policy can be specified either as ma (Mask Agnostic) or mu (Mask Undisturbed), as shown in Listing 1-2 and Figure 1-1.

Listing 1-2. Vector length adjustment example.

```
vsetvli a3, a0, e32, m4, ta, ma
vadd.vv v4, v12, v8, v0.t
```

13

CHAPTER 1   INTRODUCTION

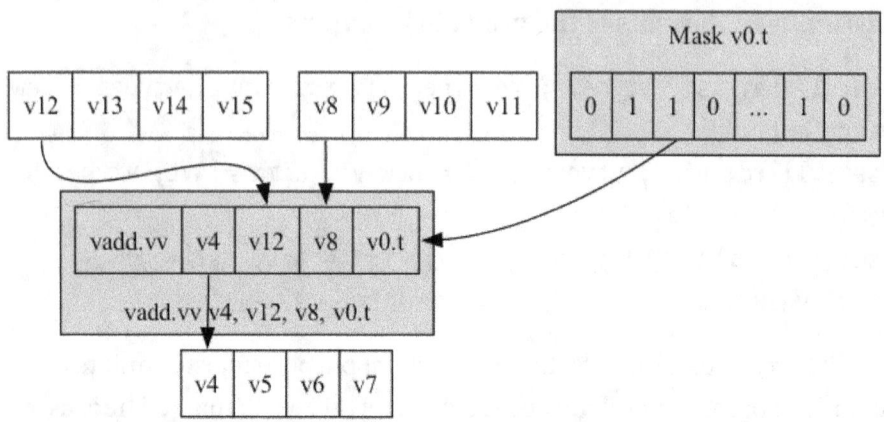

Figure 1-1. *Vector length adjustment example*

In the example above, AVL is stored in a0, SEW is 32 bits, LMUL is set to 4, and tail and mask policies are set to agnostic. a3 gets the value of the Effective Vector Length after the vsetvli instruction and the following vadd. vv instruction is executed, returning the sum of the vectors of 32-bit integer element vector. Since the LMLU is set to 4, it adds the vector registers [v12:v15] and [v8:v11], storing the result in the vector registers [v4:v7]. The addition operation is masked; the mask is stored in the vector register v0. All elements, for which the bit value in a mask is set to 1, are added. The elements, with corresponding bits in v0 set to 0, might be set to all-one value in the resulting [v4:v7] register group.

The RISC-V Vector Extension (RVV) supports complex mechanism for vector masking and predication, which is important for the flexibility and efficiency of vector operations. This feature is particularly valuable in scientific computing, where complex conditional operations and sparse data structures are common.

CHAPTER 1   INTRODUCTION

RISC-V Vector extension follows several fundamental concepts. RVV designates the v0 register as the implicit vector mask register. This register contains a bit vector, where each bit corresponds to an element in a vector operation. A '1' bit indicates that the corresponding element operation should be executed. A '0' bit indicates that the operation should be suppressed for that element.

RVV supports two primary masking modes (for both tail and masking policies):

- Agnostic execution, where masked-off elements are handled in a way that may be most efficient for the hardware.

- Undisturbed execution, where masked-off elements retain their original values in the destination register.

RVV provides several instructions for generating and manipulating mask registers:

1. Comparison Instructions, e.g., vmseq, vmsne, vmslt, vmsle. These compare vector elements and produce a mask based on the comparison results.

2. Logical Mask Operations, e.g., vmand, vmor, vmxor. These perform logical operations on mask registers, allowing for complex condition composition.

3. Population Count, vcpop. This instruction counts the number of set bits in a mask, useful for determining the number of active elements.

CHAPTER 1 INTRODUCTION

Vector masking enables efficient handling of loops with conditional execution:

1. Tail Handling. For loops where the vector length doesn't evenly divide the data size, masking allows processing of the remaining elements without separate scalar code.

2. In iterative algorithms, masking allows updating vector elements based on previously calculated conditions.

3. For operations on sparse data structures, masking can be used to correctly process nonzero elements.

The following example in Listing 1-3 and Figure 1-2 shows how the values are calculated for the tail undisturbed and mask agnostic policies, if the mask is provided and Application Vector Length is not divisible by the total number of elements with the given SEW.

Listing 1-3. Tail elements calculation example.

```
vsetivli a3, 6, e32, m1, tu, ma
vadd.vv v4, v12, v8, v0.t
```

CHAPTER 1 INTRODUCTION

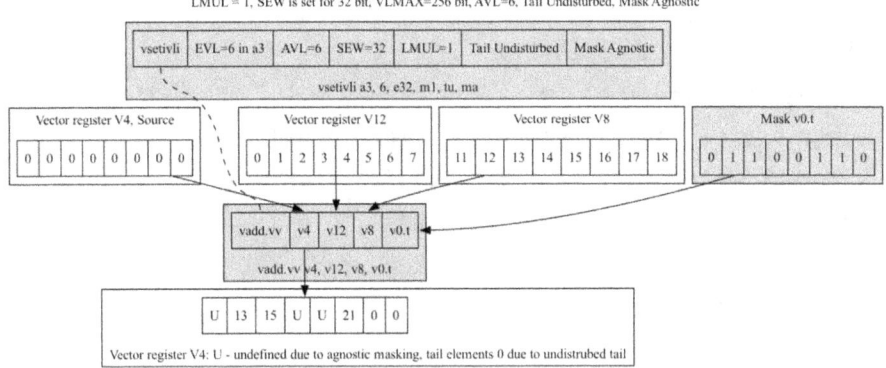

Figure 1-2. *Tail elements calculation example*

Listing 1-4 and Listing 1-5 provide a more advanced example, demonstrating the abilities of RVV extension.

Listing 1-4. SAXPY example.

```
void saxpy(size_t n, const float a, const float * __restrict x,
float * __restrict y) {
  size_t i;
  for (i=0; i<n; i++)
    y[i] = a * x[i] + y[i];
}
```

Listing 1-5. SAXPY example, RVV assembly.

```
saxpy: # @saxpy
  beqz a0, .LBB0_3 ; n == 0? Exit
  li a3, 0 ; i = 0
.LBB0_2: # %vector.body
  sh2add a5, a3, a1 ; a5=i+x
  sub a4, a0, a3 ; a4=n-i
  vsetvli a4, a4, e32, m8, ta, ma ; a4(AVL) = vset a4(n-i),
LMUL 8, SEW is e32 (float), tail-mask agnostic
```

17

CHAPTER 1   INTRODUCTION

```
  vle32.v v8, (a5)   ; [v8:v15] = load 0[a5]
  sh2add a5, a3, a2  ; a5=i+y
  add a3, a3, a4     ; a3+=a4(AVL)
  vle32.v v16, (a5)  ; [v16:v23] = load 0[a5]
  vfmacc.vf v16, fa0, v8 ; v[16:v23]+=a*[v8:v15]
  vse32.v v16, (a5)  ; store [v16:v23], 0[a5]
  bne a3, a0, .LBB0_2 ; a3 != n? Repeat
.LBB0_3: # %for.end
  ret
```

The RISC-V Vector Extension (RVV) offers an advanced ISA for integrating both vector and scalar operations, which is essential for effective scientific computing. This integration allows flexible manipulation of vector data and enables seamless transitions between vector and scalar data processing. Many vector instructions in RVV can accept scalar operands from the general-purpose register file. This ability enables cross operations such as vector-scalar addition, multiplication, and comparison without the need to replicate the scalar value across a vector register. RVV also includes instructions for moving data between scalar and vector registers, e.g., vmv.x.s (move the first element of a vector register to a scalar register) or vmv.s.x (move a scalar value to the first element of a vector register). These instructions enhance data exchange efficiency between scalar and vector processing units.

The vector length agnostic design of RVV provides significant implementation flexibility. Hardware designers can choose appropriate vector lengths based on their target applications and hardware constraints. This scalability also applies to the number of vector registers that can be used simultaneously, allowing efficient utilization of hardware resources. The full technical description of RISC-V Vector extension (RVV) can be found in the official RISC-V repository https://github.com/riscv/riscv-v-spec.

Future development of RISC-V Vector extensions includes better support for BFloat16 data type (Zvfbfa extension), support for Open Compute 8-bit floating point data types (OFP8 E5M2 and E4M3 formats, Zvfofp8min/ Zvfmx8min extensions), special extensions for DSP and video processing (instructions for the sum of absolute differences, zip/unzip-like instructions), and extended support for Matrix data types and operations (https://fprox.substack.com/p/taxonomy-of-risc-v-vector-extensions).

Summary

In this chapter, you learned

- That RISC-V is built around a minimal base ISA, extended through standardized and custom modules for greater flexibility.

- How standardized extensions expand capabilities while keeping the base clean.

- That standardized profiles (e.g., RVA20, RVA22, RVA23) are defined to prevent fragmentation, ensuring software portability and compatibility across vendors.

- The concept of vector-length agnostic (VLA) programming, which allows software to remain portable across implementations with different hardware vector lengths.

- The core elements of RVV, the categories of RVV instructions and the supported data types.

- How RVV handles masking and predication for tail processing, sparse data, and conditional execution and the role of configuration instructions (vsetvl family) in dynamically setting effective vector length, element width, LMUL, and execution policies.

CHAPTER 2

RISC-V RVV Support in Clang-Based Compiler

What Is lang/LLVM?

Clang can be viewed from two distinct perspectives. First, clang is a comprehensive toolchain, which supports compilation of C/C++/CUDA/Objective-C/Objective-C++/HIP source code into a machine code for a wide range of platforms. These include, but are not limited to, x86 (32/64-bit), ARM (32/64-bit), RISC-V(32/64-bit), Power PC (32/64-bit), as well as GPU architectures such as NVPTX (NVIDIA) and AMDGCN (AMD), both supporting 32-bit and 64-bit execution. Clang is designed to be highly portable and is compatible with multiple operating systems, including Linux, Windows, macOS, iOS, Android, FreeBSD, OpenBSD, and more. It offers competitive compile time/memory consumption/optimization level/feature set, making it a strong alternative to GCC-based toolchains. It provides extensive support for modern programming language standards, including full support for C99 and partial support for C11, C17, C23, and the evolving C2y standard. Similarly, for C++, it fully supports C++17, with partial implementations of C++20, C++23, and the upcoming C++2c standard. Clang also includes comprehensive support for OpenMP (fully implementing version 5.0 and partially supporting versions 5.1, 5.2, and 6.0). Additionally, it supports many nonstandard GCC extensions, making it a viable drop-in replacement for GCC-based compilers in numerous development environments.

The second aspect of clang is its frontend component, which is part of the clang toolchain compilation pipeline. It serves as translator, converting high-level source code into LLVM Intermediate Representation (LLVM IR). LLVM IR is a low-level, typed, SSA-based representation that serves as the central data structure in LLVM's compilation process. It is independent of any specific hardware, making it suitable for cross-compilation and platform portability.

Key characteristics of LLVM IR:

- SSA (Static Single Assignment) Form. It is widely used in modern compilers, including LLVM/GCC(GIMPLE)/Go/etc. SSA enforces a strict rule where each variable is assigned a value only once, a constraint that significantly enhances optimization opportunities.

- Three Representations. LLVM IR can be stored in textual form, binary bitcode, or in-memory representation.

- Target Independence. Code can be optimized and transformed before being lowered to machine-specific instructions.

The examples in Listing 2-1 and Listing 2-2 demonstrate the main principles and ideas of the LLVM IR.

Listing 2-1. SAXPY example.

```
void saxpy(size_t n, const float a, const float * __restrict x,
float * __restrict y) {
  size_t i;
  for (i=0; i<n; i++)
    y[i] = a * x[i] + y[i];
}
```

Listing 2-2. SAXPY example, LLVM IR.

```
; Function definition
define dso_local void @saxpy(i64 noundef %n, float noundef
nofpclass(nan inf) %a, ptr noalias nocapture noundef readonly
%x, ptr noalias nocapture noundef %y) local_unnamed_addr {
; Basic block named %entry
entry:
; %n == 0? Exit, otherwise goto %vector.ph block
  %cmp8.not = icmp eq i64 %n, 0
  br i1 %cmp8.not, label %for.end, label %vector.ph
vector.ph:
; %brodcast.splat = <%a, %a, …, %a> of type <vscale x 16
x float>
  %broadcast.splatinsert = insertelement <vscale x 16 x float>
poison, float %a, i64 0
  %broadcast.splat = shufflevector <vscale x 16 x float>
%broadcast.splatinsert, <vscale x 16 x float> poison, <vscale x
16 x i32> zeroinitializer
  br label %vector.body

vector.body:
; i is 0, if the control from %vector.ph block, or %index.evl.
next, if the control from block %vector.body
```

```
  %evl.based.iv = phi i64 [ 0, %vector.ph ], [ %index.evl.next,
  %vector.body ]
  %avl = sub i64 %n, %evl.based.iv ; %avl = %n-i
; vsetvli %0, %avl, vscale x 16 (represents LMUL m8, SEW e32 if
last arg is true)
  %0 = tail call i32 @llvm.experimental.get.vector.length.
  i64(i64 %avl, i32 16, i1 true)
; %1 = x+i
  %1 = getelementptr inbounds nuw float, ptr %x, i64 %evl.
  based.iv
; [v8:v15]=load 0[%1]
  %vp.op.load = tail call <vscale x 16 x float> @llvm.vp.load.
  nxv16f32.p0(ptr align 4 %1, <vscale x 16 x i1> splat (i1
  true), i32 %0)
; [v8:v15]*=%br.splat
  %vp.op = tail call fast <vscale x 16 x float> @llvm.vp.fmul.
  nxv16f32(<vscale x 16 x float> %vp.op.load, <vscale x 16
  x float> %broadcast.splat, <vscale x 16 x i1> splat (i1
  true), i32 %0)
; %2 = y+i
  %2 = getelementptr inbounds nuw float, ptr %y, i64 %evl.
  based.iv
; [v16:v23]=load 0[%2]
  %vp.op.load10 = tail call <vscale x 16 x float> @llvm.
  vp.load.nxv16f32.p0(ptr align 4 %2, <vscale x 16 x i1> splat
  (i1 true), i32 %0)
; [v8:v15]+=[v16:23]
  %vp.op11 = tail call fast <vscale x 16 x float> @llvm.
  vp.fadd.nxv16f32(<vscale x 16 x float> %vp.op, <vscale x
  16 x float> %vp.op.load10, <vscale x 16 x i1> splat (i1
  true), i32 %0)
```

CHAPTER 2 RISC-V RVV SUPPORT IN CLANG-BASED COMPILER

```
; store [v8:v15], 0[%2]
  tail call void @llvm.vp.store.nxv16f32.p0(<vscale x 16 x
  float> %vp.op11, ptr align 4 %2, <vscale x 16 x i1> splat (i1
  true), i32 %0)
; %3 = (uint64_t)%0
  %3 = zext i32 %0 to i64
; %index.evl.next = i+%3
  %index.evl.next = add nuw i64 %evl.based.iv, %3
; %index.evl.next == %n? Exit, otherwise repeat
  %4 = icmp eq i64 %index.evl.next, %n
  br i1 %4, label %for.end, label %vector.body

for.end:
  ret void
}

; LLVM intrinsics declarations
declare i32 @llvm.experimental.get.vector.length.i64(i64, i32
immarg, i1 immarg) #1

declare <vscale x 16 x float> @llvm.vp.load.nxv16f32.p0(ptr
nocapture, <vscale x 16 x i1>, i32) #2

declare <vscale x 16 x float> @llvm.vp.fmul.nxv16f32(<vscale x
16 x float>, <vscale x 16 x float>, <vscale x 16 x i1>, i32) #1

declare <vscale x 16 x float> @llvm.vp.fadd.nxv16f32(<vscale x
16 x float>, <vscale x 16 x float>, <vscale x 16 x i1>, i32) #1

declare void @llvm.vp.store.nxv16f32.p0(<vscale x 16 x float>,
ptr nocapture, <vscale x 16 x i1>, i32) #3
```

More information about LLVM IR can be found in LLVM Language Reference Manual (https://llvm.org/docs/LangRef.html).

The LLVM backend is responsible for further optimizing the IR and translating it into highly efficient, target-specific assembly or machine code. This backend operates as a target-independent optimizer and code generator, ensuring that Clang delivers high-performance executables across diverse hardware architectures.

LLVM is a versatile, modular, and highly extensible compiler infrastructure that has revolutionized compiler design. Through its intermediate representation, optimization framework, and multitarget backend support, LLVM serves as a foundation for modern compilers and runtime systems. Its ability to support static, JIT, and dynamic compilation makes it an essential tool in both industry and academia for developing high-performance, cross-platform software.

Clang Compilation Pipeline

Clang/LLVM-based compilers have straightforward execution pipeline. The clang compiler itself consists of two high-level components: the driver and the frontend. The driver itself does not compile anything; it just generalizes the options, prepares the environment, identifies required flags, and calls the clang frontend. The clang frontend includes several phases.

1. Lexical analysis. Its primary function is to transform the preprocessed source code into a sequence of tokens, which form the atomic units of the language's grammar. This process, called lexical analysis or tokenization, prepares the data for the following phases (see the content of the clang/lib/Lex directory). The clang lexer also performs preprocessing. The preprocessing is a very specific phase for C-like languages. It does file inclusion, where the preprocessor handles #include directives

CHAPTER 2   RISC-V RVV SUPPORT IN CLANG-BASED COMPILER

by recursively processing the contents of the specified files, macro expansion, and conditional compilation of the constructs surrounded by #if-#endif like directives.

2. Parsing. Clang implements a hand-written recursive descent parser, chosen for its flexibility, error recovery capabilities, and performance characteristics. This approach allows to control the parsing process and facilitates the generation of high-quality error messages (see clang/lib/Parse directory).

3. Semantic analysis. This stage is responsible for enforcing the language's semantic rules, performing type checking, and emission of the Abstract Syntax Tree (AST) with semantic information. At this stage, the compiler performs name lookup and scope resolution, type checking, template instantiation, access control, exception checking, etc. (see clang/lib/Sema directory). The AST, in turn, serves as a hierarchical representation of the program's structure in a form that facilitates further analysis and transformation (see clang/lib/AST directory). In clang, the AST is designed to follow several principles:

    a. Fidelity. The AST closely mirrors the structure of the source code, preserving information about the original syntax.

    b. Completeness. It captures all relevant syntactic and semantic information, including comments and preprocessing directives.

CHAPTER 2 RISC-V RVV SUPPORT IN CLANG-BASED COMPILER

    c. Immutability. Once constructed, the AST nodes are immutable, enhancing thread safety and simplifying analysis.

    d. Memory Efficiency. Extensive use of memory pooling and careful design of node structures to minimize memory footprint.

It supports serialization/deserialization (see clang/lib/Serialization directory), recursive traversal and provides excessive data for the following analysis (see clang/lib/Analysis, clang/lib/StaticAnalyzer directories) and transformation to the intermediate representation.

4. IR generation. This phase translates the language-specific constructs from the AST representation into LLVM IR. At this stage, the clang CodeGen performs traversal of the AST nodes, which is translated to the corresponding LLVM IR code, translates the type from AST representation to LLVM IR representation, meanwhile managing the context, including data locality, control flow, and exception handling (see clang/lib/CodeGen directory), as shown in Figure 2-1.

CHAPTER 2 RISC-V RVV SUPPORT IN CLANG-BASED COMPILER

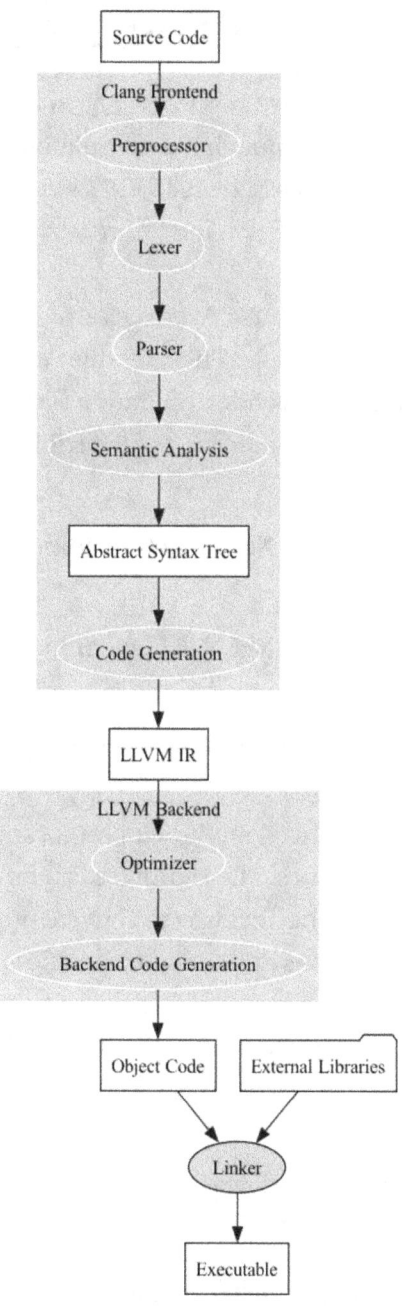

Figure 2-1. *Clang compilation pipeline*

RISC-V Support in LLVM-Based Toolchains

Currently, LLVM offers extensive support for both RV32I and RV64I. The RV32E and RV64E variants, although not completely integrated into the compiler backend, can be accessed via LLVM's assembly-based toolchain. Support for RV128I is anticipated in the future, as its practical applications continue to develop.

To use LLVM's support for RISC-V effectively, developers must accurately specify the target triple. This identifier informs the compiler about the target architecture, vendor, operating system, and environment. For RISC-V, the architecture component of the triple is particularly significant:

- riscv32. RISC-V with XLEN=32 (encompassing RV32I and RV32E)

- riscv64. RISC-V with XLEN=64 (encompassing RV64I and RV64E)

XLEN, in this context, refers to the width of integer registers and the size of the address space.

LLVM presents an advanced method for target specification through the utilization of profile names. These profiles can be defined using the -march flag, offering a succinct way to activate predefined sets of extensions and configurations designed for specific applications. This methodology simplifies the process of targeting distinct RISC-V variants, eliminating the necessity for detailed ISA string specifications.

LLVM's RISC-V backend recognizes several ratified profiles, each designed to meet different computational needs:

1. rvi20u32: 32-bit unprivileged integer profile (2020 specification)

2. rvi20u64: 64-bit unprivileged integer profile (2020 specification)

CHAPTER 2 RISC-V RVV SUPPORT IN CLANG-BASED COMPILER

3. rva20u64: 64-bit unprivileged application profile (2020 specification)

4. rva20s64: 64-bit supervisor-mode application profile (2020 specification)

5. rva22u64: 64-bit unprivileged application profile (2022 specification)

6. rva22s64: 64-bit supervisor-mode application profile (2022 specification)

7. rva23u64: 64-bit unprivileged application profile (2023 specification)

8. rva23s64: 64-bit supervisor-mode application profile (2023 specification)

9. rvb23u64: 64-bit unprivileged custom application profile (2023 specification)

10. rvb23s64: 64-bit supervisor-mode custom application profile (2023 specification)

One of the most powerful features of LLVM's profile system is its extensibility. Developers can modify profile specifications with additional extensions to fine-tune the target architecture. For instance, specifying rva20u64_zicond as the -march value will enable the zicond (conditional operations) extension in addition to all extensions included in the rva20u64 profile. This flexibility allows better selection of the target architecture features to meet specific project requirements.

LLVM also provides support for advanced RISC-V profiles that are currently undergoing the ratification process. These experimental profiles provide an insight into the future RISC-V capabilities but require explicit opt-in due to their potentially unstable nature. To enable these profiles, developers must specify the -menable-experimental-extensions flag (or its equivalent in other LLVM tools).

Currently experimental profiles include only rvm23u32: 32-bit unprivileged microcontroller profile (2023 draft).

These experimental profiles are subject to change and should be used with caution in production environments. However, they provide an excellent opportunity for early users to explore upcoming RISC-V features and prepare their codebases for the future developments.

The profile-based approach to RISC-V target specification in LLVM offers several advantages:

- Simplification of toolchain configuration
- Standardization of feature sets across different projects
- Easy adoption of well-tested combinations of RISC-V extensions
- Future-proofing of build systems through profile-based specifications

By understanding and using these profiles, developers can improve their RISC-V development workflows, ensure consistency across builds, and take full advantage of the RISC-V ecosystem's flexibility.

The following detailed description clarifies the status of RISC-V extension support in LLVM, focusing on ratified extensions with ratified specifications. LLVM provides three different levels of support of the extensions:

1. Assembly Support. LLVM recognizes and processes the extension's instructions in assembly code. This includes support in assemblers, disassemblers, and tools like llvm-objdump. The compiler and linker accept extension names, and resulting binaries contain appropriate ELF flags and attributes.

CHAPTER 2 RISC-V RVV SUPPORT IN CLANG-BASED COMPILER

2. Fully Supported. These extensions have full compiler support. This includes all features of Assembly Support, plus C language intrinsics (where applicable) and compiler pattern matching for efficient instruction lowering.

3. Partially Supported. Some aspects of the extension are implemented, but full functionality may not be available.

Supported extensions and their support level is described in Table 2-1. This support may change with time; the updated status can be seen in `https://llvm.org/docs/RISCVUsage.html#riscv-profiles-extensions-note`.

Table 2-1. *RISC-V support status in LLVM.*

Category	Fully Supported	Assembly Support	Partially Supported	Notes
Base ISA	A, B, C, D, F, M	H	E	E support is experimental
Vector	V, Zve64x/f/d, Zvfbfmin, Zvfbfwma, Zvfh, Zvbb, Zvfhmin, Zvkb, Zvkt, Zvl64b, Zvl128b, Zvl256b, Zvl512b, Zvl1024b, Zvl2048b, Zvl4096b, Zvl8192b, Zvl16384b, Zvl32768b, Zvl65536b	-	Zvbc, Zve32x, Zve32f, Zvbc, Zvkg, Zvkn, Zvknc, Zvkned, Zvkng, Zvknha, Zvknhb, Zvks, Zvksc, Zvksed, Zvksg, Zvksh, Zvl32b	VLEN>=64 required for Zve32x/f and Zvl32b, not pattern matching for partially supported extensions
Bit Manipulation	Zba, Zbb, Zbc, Zbkc, Zbs	-	Zbkb, Zbkx	Incomplete pattern matching for Zbkb/x

(*continued*)

Table 2-1. (*continued*)

Category	Fully Supported	Assembly Support	Partially Supported	Notes
Crypto	Zkn, Zk, Zkr, Zks, Zkt	-	Zknd, Zkne, Zknh, Zksed, Zksh	No pattern matching for partially supported extensions
Compressed	Zca, Zcb, Zcd, Zcf, Zcmop, Zcmp	Zcmt	-	-
Floating-Point	Zfh, Zfhmin, Zfinx, Zhinx, Zhinxmin, Zdinx, Zfa, Zfbfmin	-	-	-
Integer	Zmmul, Zimop	-	-	-
Memory Model	Ziccamoa, Ziccif, Zicclsm, Ziccrse, Ztso	-	-	-

(*continued*)

Table 2-1. (*continued*)

Category	Fully Supported	Assembly Support	Partially Supported	Notes
Privileged	Smaia, Smcdeleg, Smcsrind, Smdbltrp, Smepmp, Smmpm, Smnpm, Ssaia, Ssccfg, Sscsrind, Ssdbltrp, Ssnpm, Sspm, Supm, Svpbmt, Svvptc	Smrnmi, Smstateen, Ssccptr, Sscofpmf, Sscounterenw, Ssqosid, Ssstateen, Ssstrict, Sstc, Sstvala, Sstvecd, Ssu64xl, Svade, Svadu, Svbare, Svinval, Svnapot	-	-
Atomic	Za128rs, Za64rs, Zabha, Zacas, Zama16b	Zaamo, Zalrsc, Zawrs	-	The compiler will not generate amocas.d on RV32 or amocas.q on RV64 due to ABI compatibilty.
Cache Management	Zicbop, Zic64b	Zicbom, Zicboz	-	-

(*continued*)

Table 2-1. (*continued*)

Category	Fully Supported	Assembly Support	Partially Supported	Notes
Other	Zabha, Zicond, Zihintntl, Sha, Zicsr, Zifencei, Zihintntl, Zihpm, Zimop	Zihintpause, Shcounterenw, Shgatpa, Shtvala, Shvsatpa, Shvstvala, Shvstvecd	-	-

LLVM also supports some number of the experimental extensions. These extensions usually have special "experimental-" prefix. This naming convention serves as a clear indicator of the extension's developmental status, indicating to users and developers that they are working with potentially unstable features.

It is important to understand that experimental extensions come with no guarantees of backward or forward compatibility between different versions of the LLVM toolchain. This intentional design decision assists the quick development and improvement of suggested extensions. It does so without the limitations imposed by the need to maintain compatibility with earlier versions.

The main goals of supporting experimental features are as follows:

1. Ratification Facilitation. By providing a working implementation, LLVM accelerates the ratification process for proposed extensions.

2. Large-scale Validation. Experimental support enables comprehensive testing against extensive codebases, uncovering potential issues or benefits that may not be apparent in smaller-scale tests.

3. Proof-of-Concept Demonstration. This feature allows extension designers to showcase the practical viability of their proposals.

Experimental extensions in LLVM typically follow one of two paths:

1. Ratification. Successful extensions transition to officially ratified status, becoming part of the standard RISC-V specification.

2. Deprecation. Extensions that fail to gain traction or prove impractical are eventually removed from the LLVM codebase.

To use the experimental extensions, users and developers must use special options.

1. For Clang Users

    - Employ the -menable-experimental-extensions flag to activate support for experimental features.

    - Explicitly specify the version of the experimental extension in use (format is <main_version>p<subversion>).

    - Omit the experimental "-" prefix when referencing the extension.

    ```
    clang -march=rv64gczbb0p92 -menable-experimental-extensions source.c
    ```

2. For LLVM Internal Tool Users (e.g., llc, llvm-objdump, llvm-mc).

    - Prepend the experimental "-" prefix to the extension name.

CHAPTER 2   RISC-V RVV SUPPORT IN CLANG-BASED COMPILER

- Version specification is not required for these tools.

  ```
  llc -march=riscv64 -mattr=+experimental-zxxx
  source.ll
  ```

LLVM provides support for a set of vendor extensions. This support is pivotal for developers working with specialized RISC-V hardware, enabling them to leverage vendor-specific optimizations and features.

The integration of vendor extensions into LLVM follows a meticulous process:

- Proposal Review. Each extension undergoes scrutiny during bi-weekly RISC-V synchronization calls, ensuring community involvement and technical viability.

- Naming Standards. Extensions generally adhere to the conventions outlined in the riscv-toolchain-conventions document, promoting consistency across the ecosystem. Deviations from these standards require strong justification.

- Case-by-Case Evaluation. The LLVM community assesses each proposed extension individually, considering factors such as broader applicability, implementation complexity, and potential impact on the existing codebase.

LLVM currently supports several vendor extensions, each bringing unique capabilities to the RISC-V platform. Here's an overview of some key extensions:

1. T-HEAD Extensions (Alibaba).

   - XTHeadBa, XTHeadBb, XTHeadBs: Address generation and bit manipulation instructions.

- XTHeadCondMov: Conditional move operations.
- XTHeadCmo: Cache management optimizations.
- XTHeadFMemIdx, XTHeadMemIdx: Indexed memory operations for both floating-point and general-purpose registers.
- XTheadMac: Multiply-accumulate instructions for enhanced DSP capabilities.
- XTHeadMemPair: Efficient two-GPR memory operations.
- XTHeadSync: Multicore synchronization primitives.
- XTHeadVdot: Vector dot product operations (v 1.0.0).

2. Ventana Micro Systems Extensions.

- XVentanaCondOps: Conditional operations for RISC-V 64-bit architectures (v 1.0.0).

3. SiFive Extensions.

- XSfvcp: Vector Coprocessor Interface (VCIX) for enhanced vector processing (v 1.1.0).
- XSfvqmaccdod, XSfvqmaccqoq: Int8 matrix multiplication extensions (v 1.1.0).
- Xsfvfnrclipxfqf: FP32-to-int8 ranged clip instructions (v 1.0.0).
- Xsfvfwmaccqqq: Matrix multiply-accumulate instructions (v 1.0.0).

CHAPTER 2   RISC-V RVV SUPPORT IN CLANG-BASED COMPILER

- XSiFivecdiscarddlone, XSiFiveflushdlone: Cache management instructions.
- XSfcease: System control instruction.

4. OpenHW Group (CORE-V) Extensions.

- XCVbitmanip: Bit manipulation instructions (v 1.0.0).
- XCVelw: Event load instructions for RISC-V 32-bit (v 1.0.0).
- XCVmac: Multiply-accumulate operations for RISC-V 32-bit (v 1.0.0).
- XCVmem: Post-increment load and store instructions for RISC-V 32-bit (v 1.0.0).
- XCValu: Custom ALU instructions for RISC-V 32-bit (v 1.0.0).
- XCVsimd: SIMD instructions for enhanced parallel processing (v 1.0.0).
- XCVbi: Immediate branching instructions for RISC-V 32-bit (v 1.0.0).

5. WCH / Nanjing Qinheng Microelectronics:

- Xwchc: Custom compressed opcodes for QingKe cores.

6. Qualcomm

- experimental-Xqccmp: 16-bit push/pop instructions and double moves extension (v 0.1)
- experimental-Xqcia: uC Arithmetic extension (v 0.4)

CHAPTER 2   RISC-V RVV SUPPORT IN CLANG-BASED COMPILER

- experimental-Xqciac: uC Load-Store Address Calculation (v 0.3)
- experimental-Xqcibm: uC Bit Manipulation (v 0.4)
- experimental-Xqcicli: uC Conditional Load Immediate (v 0.2)
- experimental-Xqcicm: uC Conditional Move (v 0.2)
- experimental-Xqcics: uC Conditional Select (v 0.2)
- experimental-Xqcicsr: uC CSR (v 0.2)
- experimental-Xqciint: uC Interrupts (v 0.2)
- experimental-Xqcilia: uC Large Immediate Arithmetic (v 0.2)
- experimental-Xqcilo: uC Large Offset Load Store (v 0.2)
- experimental-Xqcilsm: uC Load Store Multiple (v 0.2)
- experimental-Xqcisls: uC Scaled Load Store (v 0.2)

7. MIPS p8700

    - Xmipscmove: conditional move
    - Xmipslsp: load/store pair instructions

8. Rivos

    - experimental-XRivosVisni: Vector Integer Small New Instructions (v 0.1)
    - experimental-XRivosVizip: Vector Register Zips (v 0.1)

These extensions provide several important features and some corner stones:

1. Enhanced Performance. These extensions often provide significant performance improvements for specific workloads.

2. Hardware-Software Co-optimization. Leveraging vendor extensions allows for tighter integration between hardware capabilities and software optimization.

3. Portability Considerations. Code utilizing vendor extensions may have reduced portability across different RISC-V implementations.

4. Toolchain Compatibility. Ensure your entire toolchain supports the necessary vendor extensions for your target hardware.

LLVM's support for vendor extensions will likely expand, providing the developers a full support for optimizing their applications on specialized RISC-V hardware.

RISC-V Vector Language Extensions

Clang's support for the RISC-V Vector (RVV) extension is implemented via whole set of different language extensions and compiler features. These features let developers to leverage the power of vector processing in RISC-V architectures efficiently.

The compiler introduces an RVV specific option, -mrvv-vector-bits=<num_bits|zvl>, which allows developers to specify the bit-width of RVV vector registers. This flexibility is very important for tuning code generation for a specific hardware. When 'zvl' is provided instead of a numeric value, the compiler tries to define the appropriate size from the -march or -mcpu options, ensuring consistency with the target architecture specifications.

As it was mentioned before, RVV introduces a set of 32 vector registers, each of size VLEN. The unique aspect of this design is that VLEN is not a compile-time constant. To handle this correctly and efficiently, Clang uses scalable vector types represented in the form <vscale x n x ty>. This notation describes a vector containing a multiple of 'n' elements of type 'ty'.

In the RISC-V context, 'n' and 'ty' correspond to LMUL (register group size) and SEW (element width), respectively. The 'vscale' factor is a runtime value, defined as VLEN/64 (see RISCV::RVVBitsPerBlock). This definition implies that the minimum supported VLEN is 64 bits, as LLVM's implementation currently supports only ELEN (element length) values of 32 or 64 bits for floating-point data types and up to 64 bits for integer types. It means that each vector register/instruction can operate with vectors and each single element cannot be larger than the given maximum ELEN size.

To provide a robust interface for vector operations, Clang defines a comprehensive set of RVV-specific types. These types are defined in the clang/include/clang/Basic/RISCVVTypes.def file and are exposed as built-in types recognized by the compiler. The type system includes several categories:

1. RVV_VECTOR_TYPE_INT. Defines integer vector types.

2. RVV_VECTOR_TYPE_FLOAT. Specifies floating-point vector types.

3. RVV_VECTOR_TYPE_BFLOAT. Represents bfloat vector types, catering to specific numerical precision requirements.

4. RVV_PREDICATE_TYPE. Defines masking types, represented as vector boolean types.

CHAPTER 2 RISC-V RVV SUPPORT IN CLANG-BASED COMPILER

These type definitions are highly parametrizable, allowing developers to specify

- The name of the vector type
- The number of elements (which encodes LMUL)
- The size of individual elements (corresponding to SEW)
- Additional parameters such as the number of fields for segmented loads/stores and signedness

The example of the type definition system for RV extension is provided in Listing 2-3.

Listing 2-3. RISC-V RVV type definition.

```
// Integer vector types
#define RVV_VECTOR_TYPE_INT(Name, Id, SingletonId, NumEls, ElBits, NF, IsSigned)

// Specifies integer vector type __rvv_int8mf8_t, signed, with number of elements 1 (LMUL is mf8) and SEW 8
RVV_VECTOR_TYPE_INT("__rvv_int8mf8_t", RvvInt8mf8, RvvInt8mf8Ty, 1,  8, 1, true)
// Specifies integer vector type __rvv_uint32m4_t, unsigned, with number of elements 16 (LMUL is m4) and SEW 32
RVV_VECTOR_TYPE_INT("__rvv_uint32m4_t", RvvUint16m4, RvvUint16m4Ty, 16, 32, 1, false)

// Float vector types
#define RVV_VECTOR_TYPE_FLOAT(Name, Id, SingletonId, NumEls, ElBits, NF)

// Specifies float vector type __rvv_float16m2_t, with number of elements 8 (LMUL is m2) and SEW 16
```

CHAPTER 2 RISC-V RVV SUPPORT IN CLANG-BASED COMPILER

```
RVV_VECTOR_TYPE_FLOAT("__rvv_float16m2_t", RvvFloat16m2,
RvvFloat16m2Ty, 8,  16, 1)

// BFloat vector types
#define RVV_VECTOR_TYPE_BFLOAT(Name, Id, SingletonId, NumEls,
ElBits, NF)

// Specifies bfloat vector type __rvv_bfloat16m8_t, with number
of elements 32 (LMUL is m8) and SEW 16
RVV_VECTOR_TYPE_BFLOAT("__rvv_bfloat16m8_t", RvvBFloat16m8,
RvvBFloat16m8Ty, 32, 16, 1)

// Predicated (mask) vector types
#define RVV_PREDICATE_TYPE(Name, Id, SingletonId, NumEls)

// Specifies bool vector type __rvv_bool2_t, with the SEW/
LMUL ratio 2
RVV_PREDICATE_TYPE("__rvv_
bool2_t",  RvvBool2,  RvvBool2Ty,  32)
```

The Clang/LLVM compiler introduces C/C++ language extensions to provide efficient support for vector programming in the context of RISC-V Vector architectures. One particularly powerful extension is the 'riscv_rvv_vector_bits' attribute, which closes the gap between scalable vector types and fixed-length vector types support, as shown in Listing 2-4.

Listing 2-4. RISC-V RVV type definition for fixed vector length.

```
#include <riscv_vector.h>

#if defined(__riscv_v_fixed_vlen)
typedef vint8m1_t fixed_vint8m1_t __attribute__((riscv_rvv_
vector_bits(__riscv_v_fixed_vlen)));
#endif
```

CHAPTER 2   RISC-V RVV SUPPORT IN CLANG-BASED COMPILER

This declaration creates 'fixed_vint8m1_t', a fixed-length variant of 'vint8m1_t'. The size of this new type is determined by the __riscv_v_fixed_vlen macro, which is typically set to 512 bits when enabled. Unlike its scalable counterpart, 'fixed_vint8m1_t' can be used in contexts that require fixed sizes, such as:

- Global variables
- Structures
- Unions
- Arrays

These use cases are not supported for scalable vector types due to their dynamic nature.

The 'riscv_rvv_vector_bits' attribute can only be applied to individual RVV vector types. The compiler enforces a strict size requirement:

N == __riscv_v_fixed_vlen * LMUL
where

- N is the specified bit length
- __riscv_v_fixed_vlen is a macro enabled by the -mrvv-vector-bits compiler flag
- LMUL is the register group size multiplier for the vector type

The __riscv_v_fixed_vlen macro must be a power of 2, ranging from 64 to 65536.

For vector types where LMUL != 1, __riscv_v_fixed_vlen needs to be scaled by the LMUL of the type before passing to the attribute.

Mask types (vbool*_t) require special processing due to their compact representation. For size calculation, __riscv_v_fixed_vlen needs to be divided by the number from the type name and the resulting value must be a multiple of 8. For example, vbool8_t needs to use __riscv_v_fixed_vlen / 8.

Different vector configurations can lead to the same internal representation for mask types. For instance, two different comparisons—one under SEW=16, LMUL=2 and the other under SEW=8, LMUL=1—will both generate a mask <vscale x 8 x i1> (which is the internal representation of vbool8_t).

The Clang compiler performs rigorous checks to ensure the correctness of fixed-length vector declarations:

1. It validates that the specified size matches the calculated size based on __riscv_v_fixed_vlen and LMUL.

2. For mask types, it verifies that the resulting size is a multiple of 8.

3. If these conditions are not met, the compiler rejects the attribute, ensuring type safety and consistency.

Clang provides a powerful mechanism for RISC-V Vector programming through a set of built-in functions, also known as intrinsics. These built-ins offer a high-level interface to RVV instructions, allowing developers to use vector operations without relying on assembly. The compiler translates these built-ins directly to compiler intrinsics, which are low-level, compiler-specific functions that provide direct access to machine instructions.

The translation mechanism for these built-ins is primarily implemented in the clang/lib/CodeGen/CGBuiltin.cpp file. This component of Clang's code generation process is responsible for

1. Recognizing built-in function calls in the AST nodes

2. Generating the appropriate LLVM IR intrinsics and instructions

3. Handling any necessary type conversions or special cases

The RVV intrinsics are defined in clang/include/clang/Basic/BuiltinsRISCVVector.def. This file is simple as shown in Listing 2-5.

Listing 2-5. RISC-V RVV intrinsics definition file.

```
//==- BuiltinsRISCVVector.def - RISC-V Vector Builtin Database
---*- C++ -*-==//
//
// Part of the LLVM Project, under the Apache License v2.0 with
LLVM Exceptions.
// See https://llvm.org/LICENSE.txt for license information.
// SPDX-License-Identifier: Apache-2.0 WITH LLVM-exception
//
//===----------------------------------------------------------===//
//
// This file defines the RISC-V-specific builtin function
database.  Users of
// this file must define the BUILTIN macro to make use of this
information.
//
//===----------------------------------------------------------===//

#if defined(BUILTIN) && !defined(TARGET_BUILTIN)
#   define TARGET_BUILTIN(ID, TYPE, ATTRS, FEATURE) BUILTIN(ID, TYPE, ATTRS)
#endif

#include "clang/Basic/riscv_vector_builtins.inc"
#include "clang/Basic/riscv_sifive_vector_builtins.inc"

#undef BUILTIN
#undef TARGET_BUILTIN
```

Instead of explicitly defining each intrinsic, it includes two auto-generated header files that contain the actual definitions.

The compiler utilizes TableGen, LLVM's domain-specific language for code generation, to automate the creation of intrinsic variants. This approach relies on three main source files:

1. clang/include/clang/Basic/riscv_vector.td, which defines the standard RVV intrinsics as specified in the RISC-V Vector Extension.

2. clang/include/clang/Basic/riscv_sifive_vector.td, which specifies intrinsics for SiFive's implementation of RVV, accommodating vendor-specific extensions.

3. clang/include/clang/Basic/riscv_vector_common.td, which contains base classes and common definitions used across all RVV intrinsic descriptions.

Each C/C++ built-in function in these TableGen files is described using two primary components:

1. Base Instruction. Represents the fundamental operation of the intrinsic.

2. Base Class. Describes variants and semantic requirements for the instruction.

This structure supports comprehensive description of each intrinsic, from which multiple variants can be generated. Advantages of this approach are as follows:

1. Reduced Manual Support. By generating variants automatically, this system significantly reduces the amount of hand-written code required to support all possible combinations of SEW, LMUL, tail handling, and masking policies.

2. Consistency. Automated generation ensures that all variants of an intrinsic are consistently implemented and documented.

3. Extensibility. New intrinsics or variants can be added by modifying the TableGen files, rather than writing numerous individual function definitions.

4. Vendor-Specific Support. The separation of standard RVV intrinsics (riscv_vector.td) from vendor-specific ones (e.g., riscv_sifive_vector.td) allows for easy integration of custom extensions.

5. Maintainability. Centralizing the intrinsic definitions in TableGen files makes it easier to update and maintain the RVV support as the specification evolves.

The TableGen files describe each intrinsic's characteristics, including its operands, return type, and any special handling required, as shown in Listing 2-6.

Listing 2-6. RISC-V RVV intrinsics specification file.

```
/// clang/include/clang/Basic/riscv_vector.td

// Definition of the builtin functions for vadd instruction.
defm vadd : RVVIntBinBuiltinSet;

/// clang/include/clang/Basic/riscv_vector_common.td
// Defines signed/unsigned int set of builtins
multiclass RVVIntBinBuiltinSet
       : RVVSignedBinBuiltinSet,
         RVVUnsignedBinBuiltinSet;

multiclass RVVSignedBinBuiltinSet
```

```
    : RVVOutOp1BuiltinSet<NAME, "csil",
                         [["vv", "v", "vvv"],
                          ["vx", "v", "vve"]]>;

multiclass RVVUnsignedBinBuiltinSet
    : RVVOutOp1BuiltinSet<NAME, "csil",
                         [["vv", "Uv", "UvUvUv"],
                          ["vx", "Uv", "UvUvUe"]]>;

// IntrinsicTypes is output, op1 [-1, 1]
multiclass RVVOutOp1BuiltinSet<string intrinsic_name, string type_range,
                               list<list<string>> suffixes_prototypes>
    : RVVBuiltinSet<intrinsic_name, type_range, suffixes_prototypes, [-1, 1]>;

multiclass RVVBuiltinSet<string intrinsic_name, string type_range,
                        list<list<string>> suffixes_prototypes,
                        list<int> intrinsic_types> {
  let IRName = intrinsic_name, MaskedIRName = intrinsic_name # "_mask",
      IntrinsicTypes = intrinsic_types in {
    foreach s_p = suffixes_prototypes in {
      let Name = NAME # "_" # s_p[0] in {
        defvar suffix = s_p[1];
        defvar prototype = s_p[2];
        def : RVVBuiltin<suffix, prototype, type_range>;
      }
    }
  }
}
```

The RVVEmitter (see clang/utils/TableGen/RISCVEmitter.cpp) translates the TableGen descriptions into .inc files containing C preprocessor macros and code. For the vadd family of instructions, it generates code as shown in Listing 2-7.

Listing 2-7. RISC-V RVV vadd builtins definition.

```
#if defined(TARGET_BUILTIN) && !defined(RISCVV_BUILTIN)
#define RISCVV_BUILTIN(ID, TYPE, ATTRS) TARGET_BUILTIN(ID, TYPE, ATTRS, "zve32x")
#endif
RISCVV_BUILTIN(__builtin_rvv_vadd_vv,"", "n")
RISCVV_BUILTIN(__builtin_rvv_vadd_vv_tu,"", "n")
RISCVV_BUILTIN(__builtin_rvv_vadd_vv_m,"", "n")
RISCVV_BUILTIN(__builtin_rvv_vadd_vv_tum,"", "n")
RISCVV_BUILTIN(__builtin_rvv_vadd_vv_tumu,"", "n")
RISCVV_BUILTIN(__builtin_rvv_vadd_vv_mu,"", "n")
...
// Other builtins for other instructions
```

Different variants of vadd are generated, covering various masking and tail handling policies (e.g., _tu for tail-undisturbed, _m for mask agnostic operations, etc.).

Instead of generating separate intrinsics for each SEW and LMUL combination, the compiler builds special tables of valid SEW/LMUL combinations supported by the specification. When the compiler encounters a use of these built-ins in the code, it performs an automatic check during the semantic analysis phase to ensure the correctness of the specified SEW/LMUL combination. This approach offers several benefits:

- Reduced Compiler Size. By not generating separate intrinsics for each SEW/LMUL combination, the compiler binary size is kept smaller.

CHAPTER 2   RISC-V RVV SUPPORT IN CLANG-BASED COMPILER

- Improved Compile Time. The semantic analysis check is faster than having to match against a larger set of distinct intrinsics.

- Reduced Memory Consumption. Fewer intrinsic definitions mean less memory usage during compilation.

These generated built-ins, along with other C/C++ language extensions, provide programmers with a direct interface to RVV-specific operations. You can find some extra info about adding new built-ins here: https://llvm.org/devmtg/2023-10/slides/tutorials/Chen-Cheng-HowToAddCInstrinsucAndCodeGenIt.pdf and https://www.youtube.com/watch?v=t17O_bU1jks. The comprehensive list of the built-ins can be found in the official documentation repository (https://github.com/riscv-non-isa/rvv-intrinsic-doc). The example of lowering built-in function into actual RVV code is shown in Listing 2-8, Listing 2-9, Listing 2-10, Listing 2-11, and Listing 2-12.

Listing 2-8. RISC-V RVV builtins source code example.

```
#include <riscv_vector.h>

void *memcpy_rvv(void *restrict dst, const void *restrict src, size_t n) {
  // copy data byte by byte
  for (size_t vl, i = 0; i < n; i += vl) {
   // Calculate vector length
    vl = __riscv_vsetvl_e8m8(n - i);
   // Load src[0..vl]
    vint8m8_t vec_src = __riscv_vle8_v_i8m8(src + i, vl);
   // Store src[0..vl] to dst[0..vl]
    __riscv_vse8_v_i8m8(dst + i, vec_src, vl);
  }
```

```
    return dst;
}
```

Listing 2-9. Command to compile to LLVM IR.

```
clang --target=riscv64-unknown-linux -mcpu=sifive-x280 test.c
-O3 -c -S -emit-llvm
```

Listing 2-10. Resulting LLVM IR code.

```
define ptr @memcpy_rvv(ptr noalias writeonly %dst, ptr noalias
nreadonly %src, i64 %n) {
entry:
  %cmp10.not = icmp eq i64 %n, 0
  br i1 %cmp10.not, label %for.cond.cleanup, label %for.body

for.body:
; preds = %entry, %for.body
  %i = phi i64 [ %add, %for.body ], [ 0, %entry ]
  %sub = sub i64 %n, %i
  %0 = tail call i64 @llvm.riscv.vsetvli.i64(i64 %sub, i64 0,
i64 3)   ; Calculate vector length
  %add.ptr = getelementptr inbounds i8, ptr %src, i64 %i
  %1 = tail call <vscale x 64 x i8> @llvm.riscv.vle.nxv64i8.
i64(<vscale x 64 x i8> poison, ptr %add.ptr, i64 %0) ; Load
src[0..vl)
  %add.ptr1 = getelementptr inbounds i8, ptr %dst, i64 %i
    tail call void @llvm.riscv.vse.nxv64i8.i64(<vscale x 64 x i8>
%1, ptr %add.ptr1, i64 %0) ; Store src[0..vl) to dst[0..vl)
  %add = add i64 %0, %i
  %cmp = icmp ult i64 %add, %n
  br i1 %cmp, label %for.body, label %for.cond.cleanup
```

```
for.cond.cleanup:
; preds = %for.body, %entry
  ret ptr %dst
}
```

Listing 2-11. Command to compile to assembly.

```
clang --target=riscv64-unknown-linux -mcpu=sifive-x280 test.
c -O3 -c -S
```

Listing 2-12. Resulting RISC-V RVV assembly code.

```
memcpy_rvv:                             # @memcpy_rvv
        .cfi_startproc
# %bb.0:                                # %entry
        beqz    a2, .LBB0_3
# %bb.1:                                # %for.body.preheader
        li      a3, 0
.LBB0_2:                                # %for.body
                                        # =>This Inner Loop
Header: Depth=1
        add     a4, a1, a3
        sub     a5, a2, a3
        vsetvli a5, a5, e8, m8, ta, ma  # Calculate
vector length
        vle8.v  v8, (a4)                #Load src[0..vl)
        add     a4, a0, a3
        add     a3, a3, a5
        vse8.v  v8, (a4)                # Store src[0..vl) to
                                        dst[0..vl)
        bltu    a3, a2, .LBB0_2
.LBB0_3:                                # %for.cond.cleanup
        ret
```

Summary

In this chapter you learned

- How the LLVM/Clang compiler framework is structured and how target-specific support in LLVM relies on a modular backend.

- How the RISC-V backend implements both the base ISA and optional standardized extensions, while also allowing experimental and vendor-specific extensions.

- That standardized profiles provide consistent configurations of base ISAs and extensions, improving portability and reducing fragmentation in the ecosystem.

- The difference between scalable vector types (which map directly to RVV's vector-length agnostic model) and fixed-length vector types, and how LLVM represents both.

- How the compiler lowers high-level vector constructs into LLVM IR, and from there into RVV-specific instructions through the backend.

- That LLVM's extensibility enables experimentation with new ISA features, vendor extensions, and evolving RISC-V standards.

CHAPTER 3

Vector Extensions in Clang-Based Compilers

Extensions for Loop Hint Optimizations

Clang provides support for special #pragma clang loop directive, which allows developers to use special high-level hints for the compiler, potentially improving performance without the need for low-level code modifications. This directive allows to specify several key categories of loop hints:

1. Transformation Control Hints. These directly enable or disable specific optimizations.

    - vectorize(enable|disable)
    - interleave(enable|disable)
    - unroll(enable|disable|full)
    - unroll_and_jam(enable|disable)
    - distribute(enable|disable)

CHAPTER 3 VECTOR EXTENSIONS IN CLANG-BASED COMPILERS

2. Transformation Option Hints. These set specific parameters for the optimizations.

    - vectorize_width(n[, fixed|scalable])
    - interleave_count(n)
    - unroll_count(n)
    - unroll_and_jam_count(n)

3. Additional Hints. These allow to enable or disable predicated vectorization.

    - vectorize_predicate(enable|disable)

The directive is placed immediately before a loop construct (for, while, do-while, or C++11 range-based for) to provide optimization hints specific to that loop. These hints are treated as suggestions by the programmer and compiler may reject them in some cases. The example below (Listing 3-1, Listing 3-2, Listing 3-3, and Listing 3-4) is one where the code cannot be vectorized because it is not profitable. In this case, the code should be compiled at -O1 optimization level, which should make the executable code as compact as possible.

Listing 3-1. Non-vectorizable source code example.

```
void foo(float *restrict a, float *restrict b, int N) {
  for (int i = 0; i < N; i += 2) {
    a[i] = 5 / b[i];
  }
}
```

CHAPTER 3 VECTOR EXTENSIONS IN CLANG-BASED COMPILERS

Listing 3-2. Command to compile.

```
clang --target=riscv64-unknown-linux -mcpu=sifive-x280 -c
test.c -O1 -Rpass=loop-vectorize -Rpass-missed=loop-vectorize
-Rpass-analysis=loop-vectorize
test.c:2:3: remark: loop not vectorized [-Rpass-missed=loop-
vectorize]
    2 |   for (int i = 0; i < N; i += 2) {
      |   ^
```

Listing 3-3. Original LLVM IR.

```
define void @foo(ptr noalias %a, ptr noalias %b, i32 %N) {
entry:
  %cmp6 = icmp sgt i32 %N, 0
  br i1 %cmp6, label %for.body.preheader, label %for.cond.cleanup

for.body.preheader:
  %0 = zext nneg i32 %N to i64
  br label %for.body

for.cond.cleanup:
  ret void

for.body:
  %indvars.iv = phi i64 [ 0, %for.body.preheader ],
  [ %indvars.iv.next, %for.body ]
  %arrayidx = getelementptr inbounds float, ptr %b,
  i64 %indvars.iv
  %1 = load float, ptr %arrayidx, align 4
  %div = fdiv float 5.000000e+00, %1
  %arrayidx2 = getelementptr inbounds float, ptr %a,
  i64 %indvars.iv
  store float %div, ptr %arrayidx2, align 4
```

CHAPTER 3 VECTOR EXTENSIONS IN CLANG-BASED COMPILERS

```
  %indvars.iv.next = add nuw nsw i64 %indvars.iv, 2
  %cmp = icmp ult i64 %indvars.iv.next, %0
  br i1 %cmp, label %for.body, label %for.cond.cleanup
}
```

Listing 3-4. *Original assembly.*

```
foo:                                            # @foo
        blez    a2, .LBB0_3
        slli    a2, a2, 2
        lui     a3, 264704
        addi    a2, a2, -4
        andi    a2, a2, -8
        add     a2, a2, a0
        fmv.w.x fa5, a3
        addi    a2, a2, 8
.LBB0_2:                                        # =>This Inner Loop
                                                Header: Depth=1
        flw     fa4, 0(a1)
        addi    a1, a1, 8
        fdiv.s  fa4, fa5, fa4
        fsw     fa4, 0(a0)
        addi    a0, a0, 8
        bne     a0, a2, .LBB0_2
.LBB0_3:
        ret
```

The loop in this example is not vectorized, since compilation mode -O1 (compile for size) suggests the optimizer to not vectorize the loop, since it increases the size of the resulting object file. But the directive allows to change this behavior as shown in Listing 3-5, Listing 3-6, Listing 3-7, and Listing 3-8.

CHAPTER 3 VECTOR EXTENSIONS IN CLANG-BASED COMPILERS

Listing 3-5. *Vectorizable source code example.*

```
void foo(float *restrict a, float *restrict b, int N) {
  #pragma clang loop vectorize(enable)
  for (int i = 0; i < N; i += 2) {
    a[i] = 5 / b[i];
  }
}
```

Listing 3-6. *Command to compile.*

```
clang --target=riscv64-unknown-linux -mcpu=sifive-x280 -c
test.c -O1 -Rpass=loop-vectorize -Rpass-missed=loop-vectorize
-Rpass-analysis=loop-vectorize
test.c:3:3: remark: the cost-model indicates that interleaving
is not beneficial and is explicitly disabled or interleave
count is set to 1 [-Rpass-analysis=loop-vectorize]
3 | for (int i = 0; i < N; i += 2) {
  | ^
test.c:3:3: remark: vectorized loop (vectorization width:
vscale x 4, interleaved count: 1) [-Rpass=loop-vectorize]
```

Listing 3-7. *Vectorized LLVM IR.*

```
define void @foo(ptr noalias %a, ptr noalias %b, i32 %N) {
entry:
  %cmp6 = icmp sgt i32 %N, 0
  br i1 %cmp6, label %for.body.preheader, label %for.cond.cleanup

for.body.preheader:
  %0 = zext nneg i32 %N to i64
  %1 = add nsw i64 %0, -1
  %2 = lshr i64 %1, 1
  %3 = tail call i64 @llvm.vscale.i64()
```

CHAPTER 3   VECTOR EXTENSIONS IN CLANG-BASED COMPILERS

```
  %4 = shl nuw nsw i64 %3, 2
  %min.iters.check.not.not = icmp ult i64 %2, %4
  br i1 %min.iters.check.not.not, label %for.body.preheader8,
  label %vector.ph

for.body.preheader8:
  %indvars.iv.ph = phi i64 [ 0, %for.body.preheader ],
  [ %ind.end, %vector.body ]
  br label %for.body

vector.ph:
  %5 = add nuw i64 %2, 1
  %6 = tail call i64 @llvm.vscale.i64()
  %7 = shl nuw nsw i64 %6, 2
  %8 = add nsw i64 %7, -1
  %n.mod.vf = and i64 %5, %8
  %9 = icmp eq i64 %n.mod.vf, 0
  %10 = select i1 %9, i64 %7, i64 %n.mod.vf
  %n.vec = sub i64 %5, %10
  %ind.end = shl i64 %n.vec, 1
  %11 = tail call i64 @llvm.vscale.i64()
  %12 = shl nuw nsw i64 %11, 2
  %13 = tail call <vscale x 4 x i64> @llvm.experimental.
  stepvector.nxv4i64()
  %14 = shl <vscale x 4 x i64> %13, shufflevector (<vscale x
  4 x i64> insertelement (<vscale x 4 x i64> poison,
  i64 1, i64 0), <vscale x 4 x i64> poison, <vscale x 4 x i32>
  zeroinitializer)
  %15 = tail call i64 @llvm.vscale.i64()
  %16 = shl nuw nsw i64 %15, 3
  %.splatinsert = insertelement <vscale x 4 x i64> poison,
  i64 %16, i64 0
```

```
  %.splat = shufflevector <vscale x 4 x i64> %.splatinsert,
    <vscale x 4 x i64> poison, <vscale x 4 x i32> zeroinitializer
  br label %vector.body

vector.body:
  %index = phi i64 [ 0, %vector.ph ], [ %index.next,
    %vector.body ]
  %vec.ind = phi <vscale x 4 x i64> [ %14, %vector.ph ],
    [ %vec.ind.next, %vector.body ]
  %.idx = shl i64 %index, 3
  %17 = getelementptr inbounds i8, ptr %b, i64 %.idx
  %wide.vec = load <vscale x 8 x float>, ptr %17, align 4
  %strided.vec = tail call { <vscale x 4 x float>, <vscale x 4
    x float> } @llvm.vector.deinterleave2.nxv8f32(<vscale x 8 x
    float> %wide.vec)
  %18 = extractvalue { <vscale x 4 x float>, <vscale x 4 x
    float> } %strided.vec, 0
  %19 = fdiv <vscale x 4 x float> shufflevector (<vscale x 4
    x float> insertelement (<vscale x 4 x float> poison, float
    5.000000e+00, i64 0), <vscale x 4 x float> poison, <vscale x
    4 x i32> zeroinitializer), %18
  %20 = getelementptr inbounds float, ptr %a, <vscale x
    4 x i64> %vec.ind
  tail call void @llvm.masked.scatter.nxv4f32.nxv4p0(<vscale x
    4 x float> %19, <vscale x 4 x ptr> %20, i32 4, <vscale x
    4 x i1> shufflevector (<vscale x 4 x i1> insertelement
    (<vscale x 4 x i1> poison, i1 true, i64 0), <vscale x 4 x i1>
    poison, <vscale x 4 x i32> zeroinitializer))
  %index.next = add nuw i64 %index, %12
  %vec.ind.next = add <vscale x 4 x i64> %vec.ind, %.splat
  %21 = icmp eq i64 %index.next, %n.vec
  br i1 %21, label %for.body.preheader8, label %vector.body
```

CHAPTER 3 VECTOR EXTENSIONS IN CLANG-BASED COMPILERS

```
for.cond.cleanup:
  ret void

for.body:
  %indvars.iv = phi i64 [ %indvars.iv.next, %for.body ],
  [ %indvars.iv.ph, %for.body.preheader8 ]
  %arrayidx = getelementptr inbounds float, ptr %b,
  i64 %indvars.iv
  %22 = load float, ptr %arrayidx, align 4
  %div = fdiv float 5.000000e+00, %22
  %arrayidx2 = getelementptr inbounds float, ptr %a,
  i64 %indvars.iv
  store float %div, ptr %arrayidx2, align 4
  %indvars.iv.next = add nuw nsw i64 %indvars.iv, 2
  %cmp = icmp ult i64 %indvars.iv.next, %0
  br i1 %cmp, label %for.body, label %for.cond.cleanup
}
```

Listing 3-8. Vectorized assembly.

```
foo:                                    # @foo
        blez    a2, .LBB0_7
        csrr    t0, vlenb
        addi    a3, a2, -1
        srli    a3, a3, 1
        srli    a6, t0, 1
        bgeu    a3, a6, .LBB0_3
        li      a3, 0
        j       .LBB0_5
.LBB0_3:
        addi    a3, a3, 1
        addi    a4, a6, -1
        and     a4, a4, a3
```

CHAPTER 3 VECTOR EXTENSIONS IN CLANG-BASED COMPILERS

```
        lui     a5, 264704
        slli    t0, t0, 2
        li      a7, 8
        mv      t2, a0
        bnez    a4, .LBB0_9
        mv      a4, a6
.LBB0_9:
        sub     t1, a3, a4
        fmv.w.x fa5, a5
        slli    a3, t1, 1
        mv      a5, a1
        vsetvli a4, zero, e32, m2, ta, ma
.LBB0_4:                                # =>This Inner Loop
                                        Header: Depth=1
        vlseg2e32.v     v8, (a5)
        add     a5, a5, t0
        sub     t1, t1, a6
        vfrdiv.vf       v8, v8, fa5
        vsse32.v        v8, (t2), a7
        add     t2, t2, t0
        bnez    t1, .LBB0_4
.LBB0_5:
        lui     a4, 264704
        sh2add  a0, a3, a0
        sh2add  a1, a3, a1
        fmv.w.x fa5, a4
.LBB0_6:                                # =>This Inner Loop
                                        Header: Depth=1
        flw     fa4, 0(a1)
        addi    a1, a1, 8
        addi    a3, a3, 2
```

```
        fdiv.s  fa4, fa5, fa4
        fsw     fa4, 0(a0)
        addi    a0, a0, 8
        bltu    a3, a2, .LBB0_6
.LBB0_7:
        ret
```

The compiler detects that the vectorization for the given loop is forced and vectorizes the loop, even if it is not profitable for the resulting size.

The vectorize_width hint provides fine-grained control over the vectorization process, allowing developers to specify both the vector width and the type of vectorization. This hint accepts two parameters:

- value: an optional positive integer specifying the desired vector width.

- fixed|scalable: an optional parameter determining the vectorization type.

The value parameter directly affects the number of elements processed in parallel. For instance, vectorize_width(4) instructs the compiler to attempt vectorization using 4-element vectors, as show in Listing 3-9, Listing 3-10, Listing 3-11, and Listing 3-12.

Listing 3-9. Vectorizable source code with vectorize_width specified example.

```
void foo(float *restrict a, float *restrict b, int N) {
  #pragma clang loop vectorize(enable) vectorize_width(4)
  for (int i = 0; i < N; i += 2) {
    a[i] = 5 / b[i];
  }
}
```

Listing 3-10. Command to compile.

```
clang --target=riscv64-unknown-linux -mcpu=sifive-x280 -c
test.c -O1 -Rpass=loop-vectorize -Rpass-missed=loop-vectorize
-Rpass-analysis=loop-vectorize
test.c:3:3: remark: Scalable vectorization is explicitly
disabled [-Rpass-analysis]
3 | for (int i = 0; i < N; i += 2) {
  | ^
test.c:3:3: remark: the cost-model indicates that interleaving
is beneficial but is explicitly disabled or interleave count is
set to 1 [-Rpass-analysis=loop-vectorize]
test.c:3:3: remark: vectorized loop (vectorization width: 4,
interleaved count: 1) [-Rpass=loop-vectorize]
```

Listing 3-11. Vectorized LLVM IR.

```
define i32 @foo(ptr noalias %a, ptr noalias %b, i32 %N) {
entry:
  %cmp6 = icmp sgt i32 %N, 0
  br i1 %cmp6, label %for.body.preheader, label %for.cond.
  cleanup # execute the loop only if N > 0

for.body.preheader:
  %0 = zext nneg i32 %N to i64
  %min.iters.check = icmp ult i32 %N, 9
  br i1 %min.iters.check, label %for.body.preheader8, label
  %vector.ph # execute vector loop only if N >= 8, otherwise
  execute scalar loop

for.body.preheader8:                              ; preds =
%vector.body, %for.body.preheader
  %indvars.iv.ph = phi i64 [ 0, %for.body.preheader ],
  [ %ind.end, %vector.body ]
```

CHAPTER 3   VECTOR EXTENSIONS IN CLANG-BASED COMPILERS

```
  br label %for.body

vector.ph:
  %1 = add nsw i64 %0, -1
  %2 = lshr i64 %1, 1
  %3 = add nuw i64 %2, 1
  %n.mod.vf = and i64 %3, 3
  %4 = icmp eq i64 %n.mod.vf, 0
  %5 = select i1 %4, i64 4, i64 %n.mod.vf
  %n.vec = sub i64 %3, %5
  %ind.end = shl i64 %n.vec, 1
  br label %vector.body

vector.body:
  %index = phi i64 [ 0, %vector.ph ], [ %index.next,
  %vector.body ]
  %vec.ind = phi <4 x i64> [ <i64 0, i64 2, i64 4, i64 6>,
  %vector.ph ], [ %vec.ind.next, %vector.body ]
  %.idx = shl i64 %index, 3
  %6 = getelementptr inbounds i8, ptr %b, i64 %.idx
  %wide.vec = load <8 x float>, ptr %6, align 4 # widened load
  of array b
  %strided.vec = shufflevector <8 x float> %wide.vec, <8 x
  float> poison, <4 x i32> <i32 0, i32 2, i32 4, i32 6> #
  selection of the required elements only
  %7 = fdiv <4 x float> <float 5.000000e+00, float
  5.000000e+00, float 5.000000e+00, float 5.000000e+00>,
  %strided.vec
  %8 = getelementptr inbounds float, ptr %a, <4 x i64> %vec.ind
  tail call void @llvm.masked.scatter.v4f32.v4p0(<4 x float>
  %7, <4 x ptr> %8, i32 4, <4 x i1> <i1 true, i1 true, i1 true,
  i1 true>)
```

```
  %index.next = add nuw i64 %index, 4
  %vec.ind.next = add <4 x i64> %vec.ind, <i64 8, i64 8,
  i64 8, i64 8>
  %9 = icmp eq i64 %index.next, %n.vec
  br i1 %9, label %for.body.preheader8, label %vector.body

for.cond.cleanup:
  ret i32 0

for.body:
  %indvars.iv = phi i64 [ %indvars.iv.next, %for.body ], [
  %indvars.iv.ph, %for.body.preheader8 ]
  %arrayidx = getelementptr inbounds float, ptr %b, i64
  %indvars.iv
  %10 = load float, ptr %arrayidx, align 4
  %div = fdiv float 5.000000e+00, %10
  %arrayidx2 = getelementptr inbounds float, ptr %a, i64
  %indvars.iv
  store float %div, ptr %arrayidx2, align 4
  %indvars.iv.next = add nuw nsw i64 %indvars.iv, 2
  %cmp = icmp ult i64 %indvars.iv.next, %0
  br i1 %cmp, label %for.body, label %for.cond.cleanup
}
```

Listing 3-12. Vectorized assembly.

```
foo:                                    # @foo
        blez    a2, .LBB0_7
        li      a6, 8
        bltu    a6, a2, .LBB0_3
        li      a3, 0
        j       .LBB0_5
.LBB0_3:
```

CHAPTER 3 VECTOR EXTENSIONS IN CLANG-BASED COMPILERS

```
        addi    a3, a2, -1
        li      a5, 4
        srli    a3, a3, 1
        lui     t0, 264704
        addi    a3, a3, 1
        vsetivli        zero, 4, e32, mf2, ta, ma
        andi    a4, a3, 3
        fmv.w.x fa5, t0
        beqz    a4, .LBB0_9
        mv      a5, a4
.LBB0_9:
        sub     a7, a3, a5
        mv      a4, a0
        slli    a3, a7, 1
        mv      a5, a1
.LBB0_4:                                # =>This Inner Loop Header: Depth=1
        vlseg2e32.v     v8, (a5)
        addi    a5, a5, 32
        addi    a7, a7, -4
        vfrdiv.vf       v8, v8, fa5
        vsse32.v        v8, (a4), a6
        addi    a4, a4, 32
        bnez    a7, .LBB0_4
.LBB0_5:
        lui     a4, 264704
        sh2add  a0, a3, a0
        sh2add  a1, a3, a1
        fmv.w.x fa5, a4
.LBB0_6:                                # =>This Inner Loop Header: Depth=1
```

CHAPTER 3   VECTOR EXTENSIONS IN CLANG-BASED COMPILERS

```
        flw     fa4, 0(a1)
        addi    a1, a1, 8
        addi    a3, a3, 2
        fdiv.s  fa4, fa5, fa4
        fsw     fa4, 0(a0)
        addi    a0, a0, 8
        bltu    a3, a2, .LBB0_6
.LBB0_7:
        ret
```

By default, the compiler uses fixed-length (VLS, Vector Length Specific) vectorization. This traditional method generates vector code for a specific, compile-time-known vector length. It offers predictable performance and is well-suited for architectures with fixed vector register sizes. Using special parameter 'scalable', developers can instruct the compiler to use scalable vectorization techniques instead (VLA, Vector Length Agnostic). This approach generates code that can adapt to different vector lengths at runtime, maximizing hardware utilization across varying implementations, as shown in Listing 3-13, Listing 3-14, Listing 3-15, and Listing 3-16.

Listing 3-13. Vectorizable source code with vectorize_width and scalable specified example.

```
void foo(float *restrict a, float *restrict b, int N) {
  #pragma clang loop vectorize(enable) vectorize_width(4, scalable)
  for (int i = 0; i < N; i += 2) {
    a[i] = 5 / b[i];
  }
}
```

CHAPTER 3 VECTOR EXTENSIONS IN CLANG-BASED COMPILERS

Listing 3-14. Command to compile.

```
clang --target=riscv64-unknown-linux -mcpu=sifive-x280 -c
test.c -O1 -Rpass=loop-vectorize -Rpass-missed=loop-vectorize
-Rpass-analysis=loop-vectorize
test.c:3:3: remark: the cost-model indicates that interleaving
is not beneficial and is explicitly disabled or interleave
count is set to 1 [-Rpass-analysis=loop-vectorize]
    3 |     for (int i = 0; i < N; i += 2) {
      |     ^
test.c:3:3: remark: vectorized loop (vectorization width:
vscale x 4, interleaved count: 1) [-Rpass=loop-vectorize]
```

Listing 3-15. Vectorized LLVM IR.

```
define i32 @foo(ptr noalias %a, ptr noalias %b, i32 %N) {
entry:
  %cmp6 = icmp sgt i32 %N, 0
  br i1 %cmp6, label %for.body.preheader, label %for.cond.
  cleanup   # execute the loop only if N > 0

for.body.preheader:
  %0 = zext nneg i32 %N to i64
  %1 = add nsw i64 %0, -1
  %2 = lshr i64 %1, 1
  %3 = tail call i64 @llvm.vscale.i64()
  %4 = shl nuw nsw i64 %3, 2
  %min.iters.check.not.not = icmp ult i64 %2, %4
  br i1 %min.iters.check.not.not, label %for.body.preheader8,
  label %vector.ph

for.body.preheader8:
  %indvars.iv.ph = phi i64 [ 0, %for.body.preheader ],
  [ %ind.end, %vector.body ]
```

```
  br label %for.body
vector.ph:
  %5 = add nuw i64 %2, 1
  %6 = tail call i64 @llvm.vscale.i64()
  %7 = shl nuw nsw i64 %6, 2
  %8 = add nsw i64 %7, -1
  %n.mod.vf = and i64 %5, %8
  %9 = icmp eq i64 %n.mod.vf, 0
  %10 = select i1 %9, i64 %7, i64 %n.mod.vf
  %n.vec = sub i64 %5, %10
  %ind.end = shl i64 %n.vec, 1
  %11 = tail call i64 @llvm.vscale.i64()
  %12 = shl nuw nsw i64 %11, 2
  %13 = tail call <vscale x 4 x i64> @llvm.experimental.stepvector.nxv4i64()
  %14 = shl <vscale x 4 x i64> %13, shufflevector (<vscale x 4 x i64> insertelement (<vscale x 4 x i64> poison, i64 1, i64 0), <vscale x 4 x i64> poison, <vscale x 4 x i32> zeroinitializer)
  %15 = tail call i64 @llvm.vscale.i64()
  %16 = shl nuw nsw i64 %15, 3
  %.splatinsert = insertelement <vscale x 4 x i64> poison, i64 %16, i64 0
  %.splat = shufflevector <vscale x 4 x i64> %.splatinsert, <vscale x 4 x i64> poison, <vscale x 4 x i32> zeroinitializer
  br label %vector.body
vector.body:
  %index = phi i64 [ 0, %vector.ph ], [ %index.next, %vector.body ]
```

```
%vec.ind = phi <vscale x 4 x i64> [ %14, %vector.ph ], [
%vec.ind.next, %vector.body ]
%.idx = shl i64 %index, 3
%17 = getelementptr inbounds i8, ptr %b, i64 %.idx
%wide.vec = load <vscale x 8 x float>, ptr %17, align 4
%strided.vec = tail call { <vscale x 4 x float>, <vscale x 4
x float> } @llvm.vector.deinterleave2.nxv8f32(<vscale x 8 x
float> %wide.vec)
%18 = extractvalue { <vscale x 4 x float>, <vscale x 4 x
float> } %strided.vec, 0
%19 = fdiv <vscale x 4 x float> shufflevector (<vscale x 4
x float> insertelement (<vscale x 4 x float> poison, float
5.000000e+00, i64 0), <vscale x 4 x float> poison, <vscale x
4 x i32> zeroinitializer), %18
%20 = getelementptr inbounds float, ptr %a, <vscale x 4 x
i64> %vec.ind
tail call void @llvm.masked.scatter.nxv4f32.nxv4p0(<vscale x
4 x float> %19, <vscale x 4 x ptr> %20, i32 4, <vscale x 4 x
i1> shufflevector (<vscale x 4 x i1> insertelement (<vscale
x 4 x i1> poison, i1 true, i64 0), <vscale x 4 x i1> poison,
<vscale x 4 x i32> zeroinitializer))
%index.next = add nuw i64 %index, %12
%vec.ind.next = add <vscale x 4 x i64> %vec.ind, %.splat
%21 = icmp eq i64 %index.next, %n.vec
br i1 %21, label %for.body.preheader8, label %vector.body

for.cond.cleanup:
  ret i32 0

for.body:
  %indvars.iv = phi i64 [ %indvars.iv.next, %for.body ], [
  %indvars.iv.ph, %for.body.preheader8 ]
```

CHAPTER 3   VECTOR EXTENSIONS IN CLANG-BASED COMPILERS

```
  %arrayidx = getelementptr inbounds float, ptr %b, i64
%indvars.iv
  %22 = load float, ptr %arrayidx, align 4
  %div = fdiv float 5.000000e+00, %22
  %arrayidx2 = getelementptr inbounds float, ptr %a, i64
%indvars.iv
  store float %div, ptr %arrayidx2, align 4
  %indvars.iv.next = add nuw nsw i64 %indvars.iv, 2
  %cmp = icmp ult i64 %indvars.iv.next, %0
  br i1 %cmp, label %for.body, label %for.cond.cleanup
}
```

Listing 3-16. Vectorized assembly.

```
foo:                                              # @foo
        blez    a2, .LBB0_7
        csrr    t0, vlenb
        addi    a3, a2, -1
        srli    a3, a3, 1
        srli    a6, t0, 1
        bgeu    a3, a6, .LBB0_3
        li      a3, 0
        j       .LBB0_5
.LBB0_3:
        addi    a3, a3, 1
        addi    a4, a6, -1
        and     a4, a4, a3
        lui     a5, 264704
        slli    t0, t0, 2
        li      a7, 8
        mv      t2, a0
        bnez    a4, .LBB0_9
```

```
            mv      a4, a6
.LBB0_9:
            sub     t1, a3, a4
            fmv.w.x fa5, a5
            slli    a3, t1, 1
            mv      a5, a1
            vsetvli a4, zero, e32, m2, ta, ma
.LBB0_4:                                    # =>This Inner Loop
Header: Depth=1
            vlseg2e32.v     v8, (a5)
            add     a5, a5, t0
            sub     t1, t1, a6
            vfrdiv.vf       v8, v8, fa5
            vsse32.v        v8, (t2), a7
            add     t2, t2, t0
            bnez    t1, .LBB0_4
.LBB0_5:
            lui     a4, 264704
            sh2add  a0, a3, a0
            sh2add  a1, a3, a1
            fmv.w.x fa5, a4
.LBB0_6:                                    # =>This Inner Loop
Header: Depth=1
            flw     fa4, 0(a1)
            addi    a1, a1, 8
            addi    a3, a3, 2
            fdiv.s  fa4, fa5, fa4
            fsw     fa4, 0(a0)
            addi    a0, a0, 8
            bltu    a3, a2, .LBB0_6
.LBB0_7:
            ret
```

Also, the user may specify this clause only with a 'scalable' parameter. This format provides a flexible approach to vector width selection, allowing the compiler to make informed decisions based on the target architecture's capabilities and constraints. By specifying 'scalable' only, the programmer delegates the choice of vector width to the compiler. This allows the compiler to consider

- The target processor's vector register size (VLEN)
- Available vector element widths (SEW)
- Optimal register group sizes (LMUL)
- Instruction set limitations and performance characteristics

Example is shown in Listing 3-17, Listing 3-18, Listing 3-19, and Listing 3-20.

Listing 3-17. Vectorizable source code with scalable specified example.

```
void foo(float *restrict a, float *restrict b, int N) {
  #pragma clang loop vectorize(enable) vectorize_width(scalable)
  for (int i = 0; i < N; i += 2) {
    a[i] = 5 / b[i];
  }
}
```

Listing 3-18. Command to compile.

```
clang --target=riscv64-unknown-linux -mcpu=sifive-x280 -c test.c -O1 -Rpass=loop-vectorize -Rpass-missed=loop-vectorize -Rpass-analysis=loop-vectorize
```

CHAPTER 3 VECTOR EXTENSIONS IN CLANG-BASED COMPILERS

test.c:3:3: remark: the cost-model indicates that interleaving is not beneficial and is explicitly disabled or interleave count is set to 1 [-Rpass-analysis=loop-vectorize]
    3 | for (int i = 0; i < N; i += 2) {
      | ^
test.c:3:3: remark: vectorized loop (vectorization width: vscale x 4, interleaved count: 1) [-Rpass=loop-vectorize]

Listing 3-19. Vectorized LLVM IR.

```
define i32 @foo(ptr noalias %a, ptr noalias %b, i32 %N) {
entry:
  %cmp6 = icmp sgt i32 %N, 0
  br i1 %cmp6, label %for.body.preheader, label %for.cond.
  cleanup   # execute the loop only if N > 0

for.body.preheader:
  %0 = zext nneg i32 %N to i64
  %1 = add nsw i64 %0, -1
  %2 = lshr i64 %1, 1
  %3 = tail call i64 @llvm.vscale.i64()
  %4 = shl nuw nsw i64 %3, 2
  %min.iters.check.not.not = icmp ult i64 %2, %4
  br i1 %min.iters.check.not.not, label %for.body.preheader8,
  label %vector.ph

for.body.preheader8:
  %indvars.iv.ph = phi i64 [ 0, %for.body.preheader ], [ %ind.
  end, %vector.body ]
  br label %for.body

vector.ph:
  %5 = add nuw i64 %2, 1
  %6 = tail call i64 @llvm.vscale.i64()
```

```
  %7 = shl nuw nsw i64 %6, 2
  %8 = add nsw i64 %7, -1
  %n.mod.vf = and i64 %5, %8
  %9 = icmp eq i64 %n.mod.vf, 0
  %10 = select i1 %9, i64 %7, i64 %n.mod.vf
  %n.vec = sub i64 %5, %10
  %ind.end = shl i64 %n.vec, 1
  %11 = tail call i64 @llvm.vscale.i64()
  %12 = shl nuw nsw i64 %11, 2
  %13 = tail call <vscale x 4 x i64> @llvm.experimental.
  stepvector.nxv4i64()
  %14 = shl <vscale x 4 x i64> %13, shufflevector (<vscale
  x 4 x i64> insertelement (<vscale x 4 x i64> poison, i64
  1, i64 0), <vscale x 4 x i64> poison, <vscale x 4 x i32>
  zeroinitializer)
  %15 = tail call i64 @llvm.vscale.i64()
  %16 = shl nuw nsw i64 %15, 3
  %.splatinsert = insertelement <vscale x 4 x i64> poison, i64
  %16, i64 0
  %.splat = shufflevector <vscale x 4 x i64> %.splatinsert,
  <vscale x 4 x i64> poison, <vscale x 4 x i32> zeroinitializer
  br label %vector.body

vector.body:
  %index = phi i64 [ 0, %vector.ph ], [ %index.next,
  %vector.body ]
  %vec.ind = phi <vscale x 4 x i64> [ %14, %vector.ph ],
  [ %vec.ind.next, %vector.body ]
  %.idx = shl i64 %index, 3
  %17 = getelementptr inbounds i8, ptr %b, i64 %.idx
  %wide.vec = load <vscale x 8 x float>, ptr %17, align 4
```

```
%strided.vec = tail call { <vscale x 4 x float>, <vscale x 4
x float> } @llvm.vector.deinterleave2.nxv8f32(<vscale x 8 x
float> %wide.vec)
%18 = extractvalue { <vscale x 4 x float>, <vscale x 4 x
float> } %strided.vec, 0
%19 = fdiv <vscale x 4 x float> shufflevector (<vscale x 4
x float> insertelement (<vscale x 4 x float> poison, float
5.000000e+00, i64 0), <vscale x 4 x float> poison, <vscale x
4 x i32> zeroinitializer), %18
%20 = getelementptr inbounds float, ptr %a, <vscale x 4 x
i64> %vec.ind
tail call void @llvm.masked.scatter.nxv4f32.nxv4p0(<vscale x
4 x float> %19, <vscale x 4 x ptr> %20, i32 4, <vscale x 4 x
i1> shufflevector (<vscale x 4 x i1> insertelement (<vscale
x 4 x i1> poison, i1 true, i64 0), <vscale x 4 x i1> poison,
<vscale x 4 x i32> zeroinitializer))
%index.next = add nuw i64 %index, %12
%vec.ind.next = add <vscale x 4 x i64> %vec.ind, %.splat
%21 = icmp eq i64 %index.next, %n.vec
br i1 %21, label %for.body.preheader8, label %vector.body

for.cond.cleanup:
  ret i32 0

for.body:
  %indvars.iv = phi i64 [ %indvars.iv.next, %for.body ], [
  %indvars.iv.ph, %for.body.preheader8 ]
  %arrayidx = getelementptr inbounds float, ptr %b, i64
  %indvars.iv
  %22 = load float, ptr %arrayidx, align 4
  %div = fdiv float 5.000000e+00, %22
```

```
  %arrayidx2 = getelementptr inbounds float, ptr %a, i64
  %indvars.iv
  store float %div, ptr %arrayidx2, align 4
  %indvars.iv.next = add nuw nsw i64 %indvars.iv, 2
  %cmp = icmp ult i64 %indvars.iv.next, %0
  br i1 %cmp, label %for.body, label %for.cond.cleanup
}
```

Listing 3-20. Vectorized assembly.

```
foo:                                    # @foo
        blez    a2, .LBB0_7
        csrr    t0, vlenb
        addi    a3, a2, -1
        srli    a3, a3, 1
        srli    a6, t0, 1
        bgeu    a3, a6, .LBB0_3
        li      a3, 0
        j       .LBB0_5
.LBB0_3:
        addi    a3, a3, 1
        addi    a4, a6, -1
        and     a4, a4, a3
        lui     a5, 264704
        slli    t0, t0, 2
        li      a7, 8
        mv      t2, a0
        bnez    a4, .LBB0_9
        mv      a4, a6
.LBB0_9:
        sub     t1, a3, a4
        fmv.w.x fa5, a5
```

CHAPTER 3 VECTOR EXTENSIONS IN CLANG-BASED COMPILERS

```
        slli    a3, t1, 1
        mv      a5, a1
        vsetvli a4, zero, e32, m2, ta, ma
.LBB0_4:                                # =>This Inner Loop
                                        Header: Depth=1
        vlseg2e32.v     v8, (a5)
        add     a5, a5, t0
        sub     t1, t1, a6
        vfrdiv.vf       v8, v8, fa5
        vsse32.v        v8, (t2), a7
        add     t2, t2, t0
        bnez    t1, .LBB0_4
.LBB0_5:
        lui     a4, 264704
        sh2add  a0, a3, a0
        sh2add  a1, a3, a1
        fmv.w.x fa5, a4
.LBB0_6:                                # =>This Inner Loop
                                        Header: Depth=1
        flw     fa4, 0(a1)
        addi    a1, a1, 8
        addi    a3, a3, 2
        fdiv.s  fa4, fa5, fa4
        fsw     fa4, 0(a0)
        addi    a0, a0, 8
        bltu    a3, a2, .LBB0_6
.LBB0_7:
        ret
```

To improve the vectorization for RVV, the programmer may use the clause 'vectorize_predicate(enable)'. This clause instructs the compiler to utilize vector predication when vectorizing the loops, which can be particularly beneficial for RVV's capabilities. RVV architecture provides robust support for predicated (or masked) vector operations. This feature allows selective execution of vector instructions based on a boolean mask, enabling efficient handling of conditional code within vectorized loops. By enabling predication, loops that might otherwise be challenging to vectorize due to complex control flow can now be effectively vectorized. This includes loops with conditional statements or irregular memory access patterns. For loops where the iteration count isn't a multiple of the vector length, predication allows more efficient processing of the remaining elements (the "loop tail") without passing the control to scalar code. Predication can often eliminate the need for scalar loop tail paths in vectorized code, reducing branch mispredictions, improving overall performance and reducing the size of the application.

RVV provides special mask register (v0) for predication. The vectorize_predicate(enable) clause encourages the compiler to utilize these hardware features effectively, as shown in Listing 3-21, Listing 3-22, Listing 3-23, and Listing 3-24.

Listing 3-21. Vectorizable source code with scalable specified and predication enabled.

```
void foo(float *restrict a, float *restrict b, int N) {
  #pragma clang loop vectorize(enable) vectorize_
  width(scalable) vectorize_predicate(enable)
  for (int i = 0; i < N; i += 2) {
    a[i] = 5 / b[i];
  }
}
```

CHAPTER 3 VECTOR EXTENSIONS IN CLANG-BASED COMPILERS

Listing 3-22. Command to compile.

```
clang --target=riscv64-unknown-linux -mcpu=sifive-x280 -c
test.c -O1 -Rpass=loop-vectorize -Rpass-missed=loop-vectorize
-Rpass-analysis=loop-vectorize
test.c:3:3: remark: the cost-model indicates that interleaving
is not beneficial and is explicitly disabled or interleave
count is set to 1 [-Rpass-analysis=loop-vectorize]
    3 |    for (int i = 0; i < N; i += 2) {
      |    ^
test.c:3:3: remark: vectorized loop (vectorization width:
vscale x 4, interleaved count: 1) [-Rpass=loop-vectorize]
```

Listing 3-23. Vectorized LLVM IR.

```
define i32 @foo(ptr noalias %a, ptr noalias %b, i32 %N) {
entry:
  %cmp6 = icmp sgt i32 %N, 0
  br i1 %cmp6, label %for.body.preheader, label %for.
  cond.cleanup

for.body.preheader:
  %0 = zext nneg i32 %N to i64
  %1 = add nsw i64 %0, -1
  %2 = lshr i64 %1, 1
  %3 = add nuw i64 %2, 1
  %4 = tail call i64 @llvm.vscale.i64()
  %5 = shl nuw nsw i64 %4, 2
  %n.rnd.up = add nuw i64 %2, %5
  %.not = sub nsw i64 0, %5
  %n.vec = and i64 %n.rnd.up, %.not
  %6 = tail call i64 @llvm.vscale.i64()
  %7 = shl nuw nsw i64 %6, 2
```

```
%8 = tail call <vscale x 4 x i64> @llvm.experimental.
stepvector.nxv4i64()
%9 = shl <vscale x 4 x i64> %8, shufflevector (<vscale x
4 x i64> insertelement (<vscale x 4 x i64> poison, i64
1, i64 0), <vscale x 4 x i64> poison, <vscale x 4 x i32>
zeroinitializer)
%10 = tail call i64 @llvm.vscale.i64()
%11 = shl nuw nsw i64 %10, 3
%.splatinsert = insertelement <vscale x 4 x i64> poison, i64
%11, i64 0
%.splat = shufflevector <vscale x 4 x i64> %.splatinsert,
<vscale x 4 x i64> poison, <vscale x 4 x i32> zeroinitializer
br label %vector.body

vector.body:
  %index = phi i64 [ 0, %for.body.preheader ], [ %index.next,
  %vector.body ]
  %vec.ind = phi <vscale x 4 x i64> [ %9, %for.body.preheader ],
  [ %vec.ind.next, %vector.body ]
  %active.lane.mask = tail call <vscale x 4 x i1> @llvm.get.
  active.lane.mask.nxv4i1.i64(i64 %index, i64 %3)
  %12 = getelementptr inbounds float, ptr %b, <vscale x 4 x
  i64> %vec.ind
  %wide.masked.gather = tail call <vscale x 4 x float> @
  llvm.masked.gather.nxv4f32.nxv4p0(<vscale x 4 x ptr> %12,
  i32 4, <vscale x 4 x i1> %active.lane.mask, <vscale x 4 x
  float> poison)
  %13 = fdiv <vscale x 4 x float> shufflevector (<vscale x 4
  x float> insertelement (<vscale x 4 x float> poison, float
  5.000000e+00, i64 0), <vscale x 4 x float> poison, <vscale x
  4 x i32> zeroinitializer), %wide.masked.gather
```

CHAPTER 3 VECTOR EXTENSIONS IN CLANG-BASED COMPILERS

```
  %14 = getelementptr inbounds float, ptr %a, <vscale x 4 x
  i64> %vec.ind
  tail call void @llvm.masked.scatter.nxv4f32.nxv4p0(<vscale x
  4 x float> %13, <vscale x 4 x ptr> %14, i32 4, <vscale x 4 x
  i1> %active.lane.mask)
  %index.next = add i64 %index, %7
  %vec.ind.next = add <vscale x 4 x i64> %vec.ind, %.splat
  %15 = icmp eq i64 %index.next, %n.vec
  br i1 %15, label %for.cond.cleanup, label %vector.body

for.cond.cleanup:
  ret i32 0
}
```

Listing 3-24. Vectorized assembly.

```
foo:                                            # @foo
        blez    a2, .LBB0_3
        csrr    t0, vlenb
        addi    a2, a2, -1
        srli    a2, a2, 1
        lui     t1, 264704
        li      a3, 0
        addi    a7, a2, 1
        srli    a6, t0, 1
        add     a4, a2, a6
        neg     a5, a6
        and     a5, a5, a4
        vsetvli a4, zero, e64, m4, ta, ma
        vid.v   v8
        slli    a2, t0, 2
        li      a4, 8
        fmv.w.x fa5, t1
```

```
.LBB0_2:                                # %vector.body
        vsetvli zero, zero, e64, m4, ta, ma
        vsaddu.vx       v12, v8, a3
        add     a3, a3, a6
        vmsltu.vx       v0, v12, a7
        vlse32.v        v12, (a1), a4, v0.t
        vsetvli zero, zero, e32, m2, ta, ma
        add     a1, a1, a2
        vfrdiv.vf       v12, v12, fa5
        vsse32.v        v12, (a0), a4, v0.t
        add     a0, a0, a2
        bne     a5, a3, .LBB0_2
.LBB0_3:                                # %for.cond.cleanup
        ret
```

The #pragma clang loop directive allows to control the vectorization for the RVV extension. Unfortunately, this pragma does not provide fine-grained control over RVV specific vector-length agnostic vectorization. The interface of this pragma does not allow to select LMUL and SEW explicitly, which are very specific to RVV, and only allows to try different combinations of the directive parameters. Also, the directive does not allow to get the best code, even with vectorize_predicate(enable) clause. It will emit some extra code, which may affect the performance.

The key limitations for RVV vectorization are as follows:

1. LMUL and SEW Control. The pragma lacks direct mechanisms to specify LMUL (register group multiplier) and SEW (selected element width), which are fundamental to RVV's operation. These parameters are very important for optimizing performance and resource utilization in RVV implementations.

2. Vector-Length Agnostic (VLA) Optimization. RVV's VLA paradigm supports code that adapts to different vector lengths at runtime. The current pragma structure doesn't provide fine-grained control over how it is implemented, potentially leading to suboptimal code generation.

3. Predication Inefficiencies. While the vectorize_predicate(enable) clause exists, it doesn't fully leverage RVV's sophisticated predication abilities. The resulting code may include unnecessary operations or fail to utilize RVV's mask instructions optimally.

4. Extra Code Generation. The pragma's current implementation may lead to the emission of additional, sometimes superfluous, code. This can impact both code size and runtime performance, especially in resource-constrained embedded systems.

It may cause extra implications for developers:

1. Performance Tuning Challenges. Achieving peak performance with RVV may require using manually written assembly code or intrinsics, bypassing the high-level pragma interface.

2. Portability vs. Optimization Trade-off. While the pragma offers a degree of portability, it may come at the cost of fully leveraging RVV's capabilities.

3. Increased Testing Burden. Developers may need to test multiple pragma configurations to find the best performance, as the optimal settings aren't directly specifiable.

CHAPTER 3 VECTOR EXTENSIONS IN CLANG-BASED COMPILERS

4. Potential for Suboptimal Vectorization. In some cases, the pragma-guided vectorization might be less efficient than scalar code, especially for complex control flows or when fine-grained predication would be beneficial.

To address these limitations, potential enhancements to the #pragma clang loop directive for RVV should include

1. Direct LMUL and SEW specification options.

2. Better control over VLA implementation strategies.

3. More tuned predication controls aligned with RVV's capabilities.

4. Options to minimize extra code generation for performance-critical sections.

It leads to the fact that currently developers working with RVV may still need to complement pragma usage with lower-level programming techniques, carefully balancing the trade-offs between code portability, maintainability, and optimal RVV utilization.

Compatibility with OpenMP

OpenMP (Open Multi-Processing) is an industry-standard API for shared-memory parallel programming in C, C++, and Fortran. It provides a powerful and flexible framework for developing multithreaded applications, enabling developers to harness the full potential of modern multicore processors.

The key components of OpenMP are

1. Compiler Directives. These are special pragma statements that instruct the compiler on how to parallelize specific sections of code, as shown in Listing 3-25.

CHAPTER 3   VECTOR EXTENSIONS IN CLANG-BASED COMPILERS

Listing 3-25. OpenMP code example.

```
#pragma omp parallel for
for (int i = 0; i < n; i++) {
    // Parallelized loop body
}
```

2. Runtime Library Routines. OpenMP provides a set of functions that can be called from within the program to control and query the parallel execution environment. Examples are as follows:

   a. omp_get_num_threads()—Returns the number of threads in the current team.

   b. omp_set_num_threads()—Sets the number of threads for subsequent parallel regions.

3. Environment Variables. These allow runtime control of parallel execution without modifying the source code. Key variables include the following:

   a. OMP_NUM_THREADS—Sets the default number of threads to use.

   b. OMP_SCHEDULE—Specifies how loop iterations are divided among threads.

OpenMP operates on a fork-join model for parallel execution. The program begins as a single threaded application with the only one active thread (the main thread). When a parallel region is encountered, the main thread 'forks' into a team of threads. At the end of the parallel region, these threads 'join' back into the main thread.

CHAPTER 3   VECTOR EXTENSIONS IN CLANG-BASED COMPILERS

This standard includes several advanced features:

1. Task-based Parallelism. OpenMP 3.0 introduced tasks, allowing more dynamic parallelism, as shown in Listing 3-26.

Listing 3-26. OpenMP task-based code example.

```
#pragma omp parallel
{
    #pragma omp single
    {
        #pragma omp task
        heavy_computation_1();
        #pragma omp task
        heavy_computation_2();
    }
}
```

2. Device Offloading. Recent versions of OpenMP support offloading computations to accelerators like GPUs/FPGAs etc., as shown in Listing 3-27.

Listing 3-27. OpenMP offloading code example.

```
#pragma omp target teams distribute parallel for
for (int i = 0; i < n; i++) {
    // Code to run on the accelerator
}
```

3. SIMD Vectorization. OpenMP 4.0 added support for vectorization directives (Listing 3-28).

Listing 3-28. OpenMP SIMD code example.

```
#pragma omp simd
for (int i = 0; i < n; i++) {
    c[i] = a[i] + b[i];
}
```

OpenMP has established itself as a cornerstone in shared-memory parallel programming, offering several compelling advantages for developers, allowing to optimize their applications for modern multicore architectures. OpenMP stands out as the de facto standard for high-performance computations and provides several important features:

- Portability across different hardware platforms and operating systems
- Consistent behavior across various compiler implementations
- A large community of users and experts for support and knowledge sharing

Major hardware and compiler vendors have implemented OpenMP support, including

- Intel (ICC)
- GNU (GCC)
- IBM (XL compilers)
- Microsoft (Visual Studio)
- Clang/LLVM

This broad support ensures optimized performance on various architectures. The OpenMP specification continues to evolve, incorporating cutting-edge parallel computing concepts.

CHAPTER 3 VECTOR EXTENSIONS IN CLANG-BASED COMPILERS

The Clang/LLVM compiler infrastructure provides robust support for OpenMP 5.2, offering developers a powerful toolkit for parallel programming on RISC-V architectures. This implementation supports most of OpenMP features, enabling efficient shared-memory parallelism for RISC-V-based systems.

Key OpenMP 5.2 features supported in Clang/LLVM for RISC-V are as follows:

1. Parallel Constructs. Full support for parallel regions, including nested parallelism.

2. Worksharing Directives. Efficient implementation of loop parallelization, sections, and single constructs, optimized for multicore configurations.

3. Synchronization Mechanisms. Robust support for barriers, critical sections, atomic operations, using RISC-V's atomic instruction set extensions where available.

4. Task-Based Parallelism. Advanced task constructs, including taskloop and task dependencies, allowing fine-grained parallelism on RISC-V processors.

5. Device Constructs. Basic support for offloading computations, though this may require additional configuration for specific RISC-V implementations.

While OpenMP offloading is supported, it may require fine-tuning for specific RISC-V hardware configurations:

1. Target Device Specification. Proper identification and utilization of available accelerators or specialized cores in heterogeneous RISC-V systems.

2. Compiler Flags. Use of appropriate flags to enable and optimize offloading, such as—fopenmp-targets=riscv64-unknown-linux-gnu.

One of the important features of the OpenMP support in clang is support for the OpenMP SIMD constructs. These directives enable vectorization support, potentially utilizing RISC-V Vector (RVV) extensions for enhanced performance.

The base directive for the SIMD support in OpenMP is omp simd construct (see Listing 3-29).

Listing 3-29. OpenMP SIMD directive format.

```
#pragma omp simd [clause[ [,] clause] ... ] new-line
for-loops

where clause is

if([simd :] scalar-expression)
safelen(length)
simdlen(length)
linear(list[ : linear-step])
aligned(list[ : alignment])
nontemporal(list)
private(list)
lastprivate([ lastprivate-modifier:] list)
reduction([ reduction-modifier,]reduction-identifier : list)
collapse(n)
order(concurrent)
```

To use OpenMP in Clang, developers must explicitly enable support via compiler flags. Clang offers two primary options for enabling OpenMP:

CHAPTER 3   VECTOR EXTENSIONS IN CLANG-BASED COMPILERS

1. Full OpenMP support with -fopenmp option. This flag activates support for all OpenMP features, excluding offloading capabilities. It enables

   - Thread-based parallelism
   - Task parallelism
   - SIMD vectorization
   - Synchronization constructs
   - Runtime library functions support

2. SIMD-only support with -fopenmp-simd. This option provides a lightweight alternative, focusing solely on SIMD (Single Instruction, Multiple Data) vectorization directives. It's ideal for scenarios where

   - Only vectorization support is needed
   - Thread-level parallelism is not required
   - Minimizing runtime dependencies is important

The basic example of using #pragma omp simd is shown in Listing 3-30, Listing 3-31, Listing 3-32, and Listing 3-33.

Listing 3-30. OpenMP SIMD example.

```
void foo(float * restrict a, float * restrict b, int N) {
  #pragma omp simd
  for (int i = 0; i < N; i += 2) { // i is linear with linear
  step 2, N is shared by default
    a[i] = 5 / b[i];                       // a and b are
                                           shared by default
  }
}
```

Listing 3-31. Compile command.

```
clang -fopenmp-simd --target=riscv64-unknown-linux
-mcpu=sifive-x280 -c test.c -O1 -Rpass=loop-vectorize -Rpass-
missed=loop-vectorize -Rpass-analysis=loop-vectorize
test.c:2:3: remark: the cost-model indicates that interleaving
is not beneficial and is explicitly disabled or interleave
count is set to 1 [-Rpass-analysis=loop-vectorize]
2 | #pragma omp simd
  | ^
test.c:2:3: remark: vectorized loop (vectorization width:
vscale x 4, interleaved count: 1) [-Rpass=loop-vectorize]
```

Listing 3-32. Vectorized LLVM IR.

```
define void @foo(ptr noalias %a, ptr noalias %b, i32 %N) {
entry:
  %or.cond = icmp sgt i32 %N, 0
  br i1 %or.cond, label %omp.inner.for.body.preheader, label
%simd.if.end

omp.inner.for.body.preheader:
  %sub = add nuw i32 %N, 1
  %div19 = lshr i32 %sub, 1
  %wide.trip.count = zext nneg i32 %div19 to i64
  %0 = tail call i64 @llvm.vscale.i64()
  %1 = shl nuw nsw i64 %0, 2
  %min.iters.check.not = icmp ult i64 %1, %wide.trip.count
  br i1 %min.iters.check.not, label %vector.ph, label %omp.
  inner.for.body.preheader23

vector.ph:
  %2 = tail call i64 @llvm.vscale.i64()
  %3 = shl nuw nsw i64 %2, 2
```

```
%4 = add nuw nsw i64 %3, 2147483647
%n.mod.vf = and i64 %4, %wide.trip.count
%5 = icmp eq i64 %n.mod.vf, 0
%6 = select i1 %5, i64 %3, i64 %n.mod.vf
%n.vec = sub nsw i64 %wide.trip.count, %6
%7 = tail call i64 @llvm.vscale.i64()
%8 = shl nuw nsw i64 %7, 2
%9 = tail call <vscale x 4 x i32> @llvm.experimental.
stepvector.nxv4i32()
%10 = tail call i32 @llvm.vscale.i32()
%11 = shl nuw nsw i32 %10, 2
%.splatinsert = insertelement <vscale x 4 x i32> poison, i32
%11, i64 0
%.splat = shufflevector <vscale x 4 x i32> %.splatinsert,
<vscale x 4 x i32> poison, <vscale x 4 x i32> zeroinitializer
br label %vector.body

vector.body:
  %index = phi i64 [ 0, %vector.ph ], [ %index.next,
  %vector.body ]
  %vec.ind = phi <vscale x 4 x i32> [ %9, %vector.ph ], [ %vec.
  ind.next, %vector.body ]
  %12 = shl <vscale x 4 x i32> %vec.ind, shufflevector (<vscale
  x 4 x i32> insertelement (<vscale x 4 x i32> poison, i32
  1, i64 0), <vscale x 4 x i32> poison, <vscale x 4 x i32>
  zeroinitializer)
  %13 = sext <vscale x 4 x i32> %12 to <vscale x 4 x i64>
  %14 = extractelement <vscale x 4 x i64> %13, i64 0
  %15 = getelementptr inbounds float, ptr %b, i64 %14
  %wide.vec = load <vscale x 8 x float>, ptr %15, align 4
```

```
%strided.vec = tail call { <vscale x 4 x float>, <vscale x 4
x float> } @llvm.vector.deinterleave2.nxv8f32(<vscale x 8 x
float> %wide.vec)
%16 = extractvalue { <vscale x 4 x float>, <vscale x 4 x
float> } %strided.vec, 0
%17 = fdiv <vscale x 4 x float> shufflevector (<vscale x 4
x float> insertelement (<vscale x 4 x float> poison, float
5.000000e+00, i64 0), <vscale x 4 x float> poison, <vscale x
4 x i32> zeroinitializer), %16
%18 = getelementptr inbounds float, ptr %a, <vscale x 4 x
i64> %13
tail call void @llvm.masked.scatter.nxv4f32.nxv4p0(<vscale x
4 x float> %17, <vscale x 4 x ptr> %18, i32 4, <vscale x 4 x
i1> shufflevector (<vscale x 4 x i1> insertelement (<vscale
x 4 x i1> poison, i1 true, i64 0), <vscale x 4 x i1> poison,
<vscale x 4 x i32> zeroinitializer))
%index.next = add nuw i64 %index, %8
%vec.ind.next = add <vscale x 4 x i32> %vec.ind, %.splat
%19 = icmp eq i64 %index.next, %n.vec
br i1 %19, label %omp.inner.for.body.preheader23, label
%vector.body

omp.inner.for.body.preheader23:
  %indvars.iv.ph = phi i64 [ 0, %omp.inner.for.body.preheader ],
  [ %n.vec, %vector.body ]
  br label %omp.inner.for.body

omp.inner.for.body:
  %indvars.iv = phi i64 [ %indvars.iv.next, %omp.inner.for.body ],
  [ %indvars.iv.ph, %omp.inner.for.body.preheader23 ]
  %indvars.iv.tr = trunc i64 %indvars.iv to i32
  %20 = shl i32 %indvars.iv.tr, 1
```

```
%idxprom = sext i32 %20 to i64
%arrayidx = getelementptr inbounds float, ptr %b, i64
%idxprom
%21 = load float, ptr %arrayidx, align 4
%div6 = fdiv float 5.000000e+00, %21
%arrayidx8 = getelementptr inbounds float, ptr %a, i64
%idxprom
store float %div6, ptr %arrayidx8, align 4
%indvars.iv.next = add nuw nsw i64 %indvars.iv, 1
%exitcond.not = icmp eq i64 %indvars.iv.next, %wide.
trip.count
br i1 %exitcond.not, label %simd.if.end, label %omp.inner.
for.body
simd.if.end:
  ret void
}
```

Listing 3-33. Vectorized assembly.

```
foo:                                    # @foo
        blez    a2, .LBB0_7
        csrr    a4, vlenb
        addi    a2, a2, 1
        srliw   a7, a2, 1
        srli    a4, a4, 1
        bgeu    a4, a7, .LBB0_4
        addi    a3, a4, -1
        lui     a6, 264704
        and     a3, a3, a7
        vsetvli a5, zero, e32, m2, ta, ma
        vid.v   v8
        fmv.w.x fa5, a6
```

CHAPTER 3   VECTOR EXTENSIONS IN CLANG-BASED COMPILERS

```
        bnez    a3, .LBB0_9
        mv      a3, a4
.LBB0_9:
        sub     a3, a7, a3
        mv      a5, a3
.LBB0_3:                                    # =>This Inner Loop
                                            Header: Depth=1
        vadd.vv v10, v8, v8
        vsetvli zero, zero, e64, m4, ta, ma
        sub     a5, a5, a4
        vsext.vf2       v12, v10
        vmv.x.s a2, v12
        vsetvli zero, zero, e32, m2, ta, ma
        sh2add  a2, a2, a1
        vlseg2e32.v     v16, (a2)
        vfrdiv.vf       v10, v16, fa5
        vsetvli zero, zero, e64, m4, ta, ma
        vsll.vi v12, v12, 2
        vsetvli zero, zero, e32, m2, ta, ma
        vsoxei64.v      v10, (a0), v12
        vadd.vx v8, v8, a4
        bnez    a5, .LBB0_3
        j       .LBB0_5
.LBB0_4:
        li      a3, 0
.LBB0_5:
        lui     a5, 264704
        slliw   a4, a3, 1
        sub     a2, a7, a3
        fmv.w.x fa5, a5
```

```
.LBB0_6:                                    # =>This Inner Loop
                                            Header: Depth=1
        sh2add  a3, a4, a1
        addi    a2, a2, -1
        flw     fa4, 0(a3)
        sh2add  a3, a4, a0
        addiw   a4, a4, 2
        fdiv.s  fa4, fa5, fa4
        fsw     fa4, 0(a3)
        bnez    a2, .LBB0_6
.LBB0_7:
        ret
```

Conditional vectorization is a powerful optimization technique that allows developers to selectively apply vector operations based on runtime conditions. This approach enables fine-grained control over vectorization, ensuring that it is used only when beneficial, thus optimizing performance across varying input sizes or hardware capabilities, as shown in Listing 3-34, Listing 3-35, Listing 3-36, and Listing 3-37.

Listing 3-34. OpenMP Conditional SIMD example.

```
void foo(float * restrict a, float * restrict b, int N) {
  #pragma omp simd if (N > 3)
  for (int i = 0; i < N; i += 2) {
    a[i] = 5 / b[i];
  }
}
```

Listing 3-35. Compile command.

```
clang -fopenmp-simd --target=riscv64-unknown-linux
-mcpu=sifive-x280 -c test.c -O1 -Rpass=loop-vectorize -Rpass-
missed=loop-vectorize -Rpass-analysis=loop-vectorize
test.c:2:3: remark: loop not vectorized: vectorization is
explicitly disabled [-Rpass-missed=loop-vectorize]
    2 |   #pragma omp simd if (N > 3)
      |   ^
test.c:2:3: remark: the cost-model indicates that interleaving
is not beneficial and is explicitly disabled or interleave
count is set to 1 [-Rpass-analysis=loop-vectorize]
test.c:2:3: remark: vectorized loop (vectorization width:
vscale x 4, interleaved count: 1) [-Rpass=loop-vectorize]
```

Listing 3-36. Vectorized LLVM IR.

```
define void @foo(ptr noalias %a, ptr noalias %b, i32 %N) {
entry:
  %sub = add i32 %N, 1
  %div45 = lshr i32 %sub, 1
  %cmp = icmp sgt i32 %N, 0
  br i1 %cmp, label %simd.if.then, label %simd.if.end

simd.if.then:
  %cmp4 = icmp sgt i32 %N, 3             ; If N > 3 - execute
                                         vector loop
  %cmp549.not = icmp ult i32 %sub, 2
  br i1 %cmp4, label %omp.inner.for.cond.preheader, label %omp.
  inner.for.cond11.preheader

omp.inner.for.cond11.preheader:
  br i1 %cmp549.not, label %simd.if.end, label %omp.inner.for.
  body15.preheader
```

```
omp.inner.for.body15.preheader:
  %wide.trip.count = zext nneg i32 %div45 to i64
  br label %omp.inner.for.body15

omp.inner.for.cond.preheader:
  br i1 %cmp549.not, label %simd.if.end, label %omp.inner.for.
  body.preheader

omp.inner.for.body.preheader:
  %wide.trip.count56 = zext nneg i32 %div45 to i64
  %0 = tail call i64 @llvm.vscale.i64()
  %1 = shl nuw nsw i64 %0, 2
  %min.iters.check.not = icmp ult i64 %1, %wide.trip.count56
  br i1 %min.iters.check.not, label %vector.ph, label %omp.
  inner.for.body.preheader59

vector.ph:
  %2 = tail call i64 @llvm.vscale.i64()
  %3 = shl nuw nsw i64 %2, 2
  %4 = add nuw nsw i64 %3, 2147483647
  %n.mod.vf = and i64 %4, %wide.trip.count56
  %5 = icmp eq i64 %n.mod.vf, 0
  %6 = select i1 %5, i64 %3, i64 %n.mod.vf
  %n.vec = sub nsw i64 %wide.trip.count56, %6
  %7 = tail call i64 @llvm.vscale.i64()
  %8 = shl nuw nsw i64 %7, 2
  %9 = tail call <vscale x 4 x i32> @llvm.experimental.
stepvector.nxv4i32()
  %10 = tail call i32 @llvm.vscale.i32()
  %11 = shl nuw nsw i32 %10, 2
  %.splatinsert = insertelement <vscale x 4 x i32> poison, i32
  %11, i64 0
```

```
  %.splat = shufflevector <vscale x 4 x i32> %.splatinsert,
  <vscale x 4 x i32> poison, <vscale x 4 x i32> zeroinitializer
  br label %vector.body

vector.body:
  %index = phi i64 [ 0, %vector.ph ], [ %index.next,
  %vector.body ]
  %vec.ind = phi <vscale x 4 x i32> [ %9, %vector.ph ], [ %vec.
  ind.next, %vector.body ]
  %12 = shl <vscale x 4 x i32> %vec.ind, shufflevector (<vscale
  x 4 x i32> insertelement (<vscale x 4 x i32> poison, i32
  1, i64 0), <vscale x 4 x i32> poison, <vscale x 4 x i32>
  zeroinitializer)
  %13 = sext <vscale x 4 x i32> %12 to <vscale x 4 x i64>
  %14 = extractelement <vscale x 4 x i64> %13, i64 0
  %15 = getelementptr inbounds float, ptr %b, i64 %14
  %wide.vec = load <vscale x 8 x float>, ptr %15, align 4
  %strided.vec = tail call { <vscale x 4 x float>, <vscale x 4
  x float> } @llvm.vector.deinterleave2.nxv8f32(<vscale x 8 x
  float> %wide.vec)
  %16 = extractvalue { <vscale x 4 x float>, <vscale x 4 x
  float> } %strided.vec, 0
  %17 = fdiv <vscale x 4 x float> shufflevector (<vscale x 4
  x float> insertelement (<vscale x 4 x float> poison, float
  5.000000e+00, i64 0), <vscale x 4 x float> poison, <vscale x
  4 x i32> zeroinitializer), %16
  %18 = getelementptr inbounds float, ptr %a, <vscale x 4 x
  i64> %13
  tail call void @llvm.masked.scatter.nxv4f32.nxv4p0(<vscale x
  4 x float> %17, <vscale x 4 x ptr> %18, i32 4, <vscale x 4 x
  i1> shufflevector (<vscale x 4 x i1> insertelement (<vscale
```

```
x 4 x i1> poison, i1 true, i64 0), <vscale x 4 x i1> poison,
<vscale x 4 x i32> zeroinitializer))
%index.next = add nuw i64 %index, %8
%vec.ind.next = add <vscale x 4 x i32> %vec.ind, %.splat
%19 = icmp eq i64 %index.next, %n.vec
br i1 %19, label %omp.inner.for.body.preheader59, label
%vector.body

omp.inner.for.body.preheader59:
  %indvars.iv53.ph = phi i64 [ 0, %omp.inner.for.body.preheader ],
  [ %n.vec, %vector.body ]
  br label %omp.inner.for.body

omp.inner.for.body:
  %indvars.iv53 = phi i64 [ %indvars.iv.next54, %omp.inner.for.
  body ], [ %indvars.iv53.ph, %omp.inner.for.body.preheader59 ]
  %indvars.iv53.tr = trunc i64 %indvars.iv53 to i32
  %20 = shl i32 %indvars.iv53.tr, 1
  %idxprom = sext i32 %20 to i64
  %arrayidx = getelementptr inbounds float, ptr %b, i64
  %idxprom
  %21 = load float, ptr %arrayidx, align 4
  %div7 = fdiv float 5.000000e+00, %21
  %arrayidx9 = getelementptr inbounds float, ptr %a, i64
  %idxprom
  store float %div7, ptr %arrayidx9, align 4
  %indvars.iv.next54 = add nuw nsw i64 %indvars.iv53, 1
  %exitcond57.not = icmp eq i64 %indvars.iv.next54, %wide.
  trip.count56
  br i1 %exitcond57.not, label %simd.if.end, label %omp.inner.
  for.body

omp.inner.for.body15:
```

CHAPTER 3 VECTOR EXTENSIONS IN CLANG-BASED COMPILERS

```
  %indvars.iv = phi i64 [ 0, %omp.inner.for.body15.preheader ],
[ %indvars.iv.next, %omp.inner.for.body15 ]
  %indvars.iv.tr = trunc i64 %indvars.iv to i32
  %22 = shl i32 %indvars.iv.tr, 1
  %idxprom18 = sext i32 %22 to i64
  %arrayidx19 = getelementptr inbounds float, ptr %b, i64
  %idxprom18
  %23 = load float, ptr %arrayidx19, align 4
  %div20 = fdiv float 5.000000e+00, %23
  %arrayidx22 = getelementptr inbounds float, ptr %a, i64
  %idxprom18
  store float %div20, ptr %arrayidx22, align 4
  %indvars.iv.next = add nuw nsw i64 %indvars.iv, 1
  %exitcond.not = icmp eq i64 %indvars.iv.next, %wide.
  trip.count
  br i1 %exitcond.not, label %simd.if.end, label %omp.inner.
  for.body15

simd.if.end:
  ret void
}
```

Listing 3-37. *Vectorized assembly.*

```
foo:                                    # @foo
        blez    a2, .LBB0_12
        addiw   a4, a2, 1
        li      a5, 3
        srliw   a3, a4, 1
        bge     a5, a2, .LBB0_6
        li      a2, 2
        bltu    a4, a2, .LBB0_12
        csrr    a4, vlenb
```

```
        srli    a4, a4, 1
        bgeu    a4, a3, .LBB0_9
        addi    a2, a4, -1
        lui     a6, 264704
        and     a2, a2, a3
        vsetvli a5, zero, e32, m2, ta, ma
        vid.v   v8
        fmv.w.x fa5, a6
        bnez    a2, .LBB0_14
        mv      a2, a4
.LBB0_14:
        sub     a7, a3, a2
        mv      a5, a7
.LBB0_5:                                 # =>This Inner Loop
                                         Header: Depth=1
        vadd.vv v10, v8, v8
        vsetvli zero, zero, e64, m4, ta, ma
        sub     a5, a5, a4
        vsext.vf2       v12, v10
        vmv.x.s a2, v12
        vsetvli zero, zero, e32, m2, ta, ma
        sh2add  a2, a2, a1
        vlseg2e32.v     v16, (a2)
        vfrdiv.vf       v10, v16, fa5
        vsetvli zero, zero, e64, m4, ta, ma
        vsll.vi v12, v12, 2
        vsetvli zero, zero, e32, m2, ta, ma
        vsoxei64.v      v10, (a0), v12
        vadd.vx v8, v8, a4
        bnez    a5, .LBB0_5
        j       .LBB0_10
```

```
.LBB0_6:
        li      a2, 2
        bltu    a4, a2, .LBB0_12
        lui     a4, 264704
        sh3add  a2, a3, a0
        fmv.w.x fa5, a4
.LBB0_8:                                        # =>This Inner Loop
                                                # Header: Depth=1
        flw     fa4, 0(a1)
        addi    a1, a1, 8
        fdiv.s  fa4, fa5, fa4
        fsw     fa4, 0(a0)
        addi    a0, a0, 8
        bne     a0, a2, .LBB0_8
        j       .LBB0_12
.LBB0_9:
        li      a7, 0
.LBB0_10:
        lui     a2, 264704
        slliw   a4, a7, 1
        sub     a3, a3, a7
        fmv.w.x fa5, a2
.LBB0_11:                                       # =>This Inner Loop
                                                # Header: Depth=1
        sh2add  a2, a4, a1
        addi    a3, a3, -1
        flw     fa4, 0(a2)
        sh2add  a2, a4, a0
        addiw   a4, a4, 2
        fdiv.s  fa4, fa5, fa4
        fsw     fa4, 0(a2)
```

```
        bnez    a3, .LBB0_11
.LBB0_12:
        ret
```

Unfortunately, current format of #pragma omp simd does not support explicit Vector Length Agnostic vectorization. The clauses simdlen/safelen allow to specify only vectorization factors for Vector Length Specific (fixed vector length) vectorization (see Listing 3-38, Listing 3-39, Listing 3-40, and Listing 3-41).

Listing 3-38. OpenMP SIMD VLS example.

```
void foo(float * restrict a, float * restrict b, int N) {
  #pragma omp simd simdlen(4)
  for (int i = 0; i < N; i += 2) {
    a[i] = 5 / b[i];
  }
}
```

Listing 3-39. Compile command.

```
clang -fopenmp-simd --target=riscv64-unknown-linux
-mcpu=sifive-x280 -c test.c -O1 -Rpass=loop-vectorize -Rpass-
missed=loop-vectorize -Rpass-analysis=loop-vectorize
test.c:2:3: remark: Scalable vectorization is explicitly
disabled [-Rpass-analysis]
    2 |   #pragma omp simd simdlen(4)
      |   ^
test.c:2:3: remark: the cost-model indicates that interleaving
is beneficial but is explicitly disabled or interleave count is
set to 1 [-Rpass-analysis=loop-vectorize]
test.c:2:3: remark: vectorized loop (vectorization width: 4,
interleaved count: 1) [-Rpass=loop-vectorize]
```

Listing 3-40. Vectorized LLVM IR.

```
define void @foo(ptr noalias %a, ptr noalias %b, i32 %N) {
entry:
  %or.cond = icmp sgt i32 %N, 0
  br i1 %or.cond, label %omp.inner.for.body.preheader, label
  %simd.if.end

omp.inner.for.body.preheader:
  %sub = add nuw i32 %N, 1
  %div19 = lshr i32 %sub, 1
  %wide.trip.count = zext nneg i32 %div19 to i64
  %min.iters.check = icmp ult i32 %N, 9
  br i1 %min.iters.check, label %omp.inner.for.body.
  preheader23, label %vector.ph

vector.ph:
  %n.mod.vf = and i64 %wide.trip.count, 3
  %0 = icmp eq i64 %n.mod.vf, 0
  %1 = select i1 %0, i64 4, i64 %n.mod.vf
  %n.vec = sub nsw i64 %wide.trip.count, %1
  br label %vector.body

vector.body:
  %index = phi i64 [ 0, %vector.ph ], [ %index.next,
  %vector.body ]
  %vec.ind = phi <4 x i32> [ <i32 0, i32 1, i32 2, i32 3>,
  %vector.ph ], [ %vec.ind.next, %vector.body ]
  %2 = shl <4 x i32> %vec.ind, <i32 1, i32 1, i32 1, i32 1>
  %3 = sext <4 x i32> %2 to <4 x i64>
  %4 = extractelement <4 x i64> %3, i64 0
  %5 = getelementptr inbounds float, ptr %b, i64 %4
  %wide.vec = load <8 x float>, ptr %5, align 4
```

```
%strided.vec = shufflevector <8 x float> %wide.vec, <8 x
float> poison, <4 x i32> <i32 0, i32 2, i32 4, i32 6>
%6 = fdiv <4 x float> <float 5.000000e+00, float
5.000000e+00, float 5.000000e+00, float 5.000000e+00>,
%strided.vec
%7 = getelementptr inbounds float, ptr %a, <4 x i64> %3
tail call void @llvm.masked.scatter.v4f32.v4p0(<4 x float>
%6, <4 x ptr> %7, i32 4, <4 x i1> <i1 true, i1 true, i1 true,
i1 true>)
%index.next = add nuw i64 %index, 4
%vec.ind.next = add <4 x i32> %vec.ind, <i32 4, i32 4, i32
4, i32 4>
%8 = icmp eq i64 %index.next, %n.vec
br i1 %8, label %omp.inner.for.body.preheader23, label
%vector.body

omp.inner.for.body.preheader23:
  %indvars.iv.ph = phi i64 [ 0, %omp.inner.for.body.preheader ],
  [ %n.vec, %vector.body ]
  br label %omp.inner.for.body

omp.inner.for.body:
  %indvars.iv = phi i64 [ %indvars.iv.next, %omp.inner.for.body ],
  [ %indvars.iv.ph, %omp.inner.for.body.preheader23 ]
  %indvars.iv.tr = trunc i64 %indvars.iv to i32
  %9 = shl i32 %indvars.iv.tr, 1
  %idxprom = sext i32 %9 to i64
  %arrayidx = getelementptr inbounds float, ptr %b, i64
  %idxprom
  %10 = load float, ptr %arrayidx, align 4
  %div6 = fdiv float 5.000000e+00, %10
```

```
  %arrayidx8 = getelementptr inbounds float, ptr %a, i64
  %idxprom
  store float %div6, ptr %arrayidx8, align 4
  %indvars.iv.next = add nuw nsw i64 %indvars.iv, 1
  %exitcond.not = icmp eq i64 %indvars.iv.next, %wide.
  trip.count
  br i1 %exitcond.not, label %simd.if.end, label %omp.inner.
  for.body
simd.if.end:
  ret void
}
```

Listing 3-41. Vectorized assembly.

```
foo:                                    # @foo
        blez    a2, .LBB0_7
        addi    a3, a2, 1
        li      a4, 9
        srliw   a3, a3, 1
        bgeu    a2, a4, .LBB0_3
        li      a2, 0
        j       .LBB0_5
.LBB0_3:
        andi    a2, a3, 3
        li      a4, 4
        vsetivli        zero, 4, e32, mf2, ta, ma
        vid.v   v8
        beqz    a2, .LBB0_9
        mv      a4, a2
.LBB0_9:
        sub     a2, a3, a4
        lui     a4, 264704
```

```
        fmv.w.x fa5, a4
        mv      a4, a2
.LBB0_4:                                    # =>This Inner Loop
                                            Header: Depth=1
        vadd.vv v9, v8, v8
        vsetvli zero, zero, e64, m1, ta, ma
        addi    a4, a4, -4
        vsext.vf2       v10, v9
        vmv.x.s a5, v10
        vsetvli zero, zero, e32, mf2, ta, ma
        sh2add  a5, a5, a1
        vlseg2e32.v     v11, (a5)
        vfrdiv.vf       v9, v11, fa5
        vsetvli zero, zero, e64, m1, ta, ma
        vsll.vi v10, v10, 2
        vsetvli zero, zero, e32, mf2, ta, ma
        vadd.vi v8, v8, 4
        vsoxei64.v      v9, (a0), v10
        bnez    a4, .LBB0_4
.LBB0_5:
        lui     a5, 264704
        slliw   a4, a2, 1
        sub     a3, a3, a2
        fmv.w.x fa5, a5
.LBB0_6:                                    # =>This Inner Loop
                                            Header: Depth=1
        sh2add  a2, a4, a1
        addi    a3, a3, -1
        flw     fa4, 0(a2)
        sh2add  a2, a4, a0
        addiw   a4, a4, 2
```

CHAPTER 3 VECTOR EXTENSIONS IN CLANG-BASED COMPILERS

```
        fdiv.s  fa4, fa5, fa4
        fsw     fa4, 0(a2)
        bnez    a3, .LBB0_6
.LBB0_7:
        ret
```

The OpenMP community is currently considering an extension to the existing 'simdlen' clause, aimed to provide more granular control over Vector Length Agnostic support, particularly those using the concepts of Selected Element Width (SEW) and Register Group Multiplier (LMUL) like RISC-V Vector (RVV) extension. The new format under consideration is shown in Listing 3-42.

Listing 3-42. Proposed format for VLA vectorization support in clause simdlen.

```
simdlen(scaled(<type>[, divider])) [: multiplier])
```

This proposed syntax offers several key advantages:

1. Explicit SEW specification. The <type> parameter allows developers to directly specify the Selected Element Width (see Listing 3-43).

Listing 3-43. SEW specification example.

```
#pragma omp simd simdlen(scaled(float))
```

This would indicate a SEW corresponding to the size of a float (typically 32 bits).

2. Flexible LMUL definition. The optional divider and multiplier parameters enable precise control over the LMUL value.

    a. Whole LMUL values can be specified using just the multiplier (see Listing 3-44).

CHAPTER 3 VECTOR EXTENSIONS IN CLANG-BASED COMPILERS

Listing 3-44. Whole LMUL example.

```
#pragma omp simd simdlen(scaled(int) : 2)
```

>   This would indicate an LMUL of 2 for SEW corresponding
>   to the size of int (typically 32 bits) operations.
>
>   b. Fractional LMUL values are achievable through the divider
>   parameter (see Listing 3-45).

Listing 3-45. Fractional LMUL example.

```
#pragma omp simd simdlen(scaled(double, 2) : 1)
```

>   This specifies an LMUL of 1/2 for SEW corresponding to
>   the size of a double (typically 64 bits) operation.
>
>   3. Architecture-Aware optimizations. This format
>   supports optimizations that align with the
>   underlying VLA architecture's capabilities,
>   potentially leading to more efficient code
>   generation.

The example of proposed format usage is shown in Listing 3-46, Listing 3-47, Listing 3-48, and Listing 3-49.

Listing 3-46. OpenMP SIMD VLA example.

```
void foo(float * restrict a, float * restrict b, int N) {
  #pragma omp simd simdlen(scaled(float):4) // SEW 32 (for
  float) and LMUL 4
  for (int i = 0; i < N; i += 2) {
    a[i] = 5 / b[i];
  }
}
```

CHAPTER 3   VECTOR EXTENSIONS IN CLANG-BASED COMPILERS

Listing 3-47. Compile command.

```
clang -fopenmp-simd --target=riscv64-unknown-linux
-mcpu=sifive-x280 -c test.c -O1 -Rpass=loop-vectorize -Rpass-
missed=loop-vectorize -Rpass-analysis=loop-vectorize
```

Listing 3-48. Vectorized LLVM IR.

```
define void @foo(ptr noalias %a, ptr noalias %b, i32 %N) {
entry:
  %cmp6 = icmp sgt i32 %N, 0
  br i1 %cmp6, label %for.body.preheader, label %for.
  cond.cleanup

for.body.preheader:
  %0 = zext nneg i32 %N to i64
  %1 = icmp ult i32 %N, 3
  br i1 %1, label %for.body.preheader9, label %vector.ph

for.body.preheader9:
  %indvars.iv.ph = phi i64 [ 0, %for.body.preheader ], [ %ind.
  end, %vector.body ]
  br label %for.body

vector.ph:
  %2 = add nsw i64 %0, -1
  %3 = lshr i64 %2, 1
  %ind.end = and i64 %2, -2
  br label %vector.body

vector.body:
  %evl.based.iv = phi i64 [ 0, %vector.ph ], [ %index.evl.next,
  %vector.body ]
  %4 = sub i64 %3, %evl.based.iv
```

```
%5 = tail call i32 @llvm.experimental.get.vector.length.
i64(i64 %4, i32 8, i1 true)
%offset.idx = shl i64 %evl.based.iv, 1
%6 = getelementptr inbounds float, ptr %b, i64 %offset.idx
%7 = shl nuw nsw i32 %5, 1
%wide.masked.load = tail call <vscale x 16 x float> @llvm.
vp.load.nxv16f32.p0(ptr align 4 %6, <vscale x 16 x i1>
shufflevector (<vscale x 16 x i1> insertelement (<vscale x
16 x i1> poison, i1 true, i64 0), <vscale x 16 x i1> poison,
<vscale x 16 x i32> zeroinitializer), i32 %7)
%deinterleaved.results = tail call { <vscale x 8 x float>,
<vscale x 8 x float> } @llvm.vector.deinterleave2.
nxv16f32(<vscale x 16 x float> %wide.masked.load)
%8 = extractvalue { <vscale x 8 x float>, <vscale x 8 x
float> } %deinterleaved.results, 0
%vp.op = tail call <vscale x 8 x float> @llvm.vp.fdiv.
nxv8f32(<vscale x 8 x float> shufflevector (<vscale x 8 x
float> insertelement (<vscale x 8 x float> poison, float
5.000000e+00, i64 0), <vscale x 8 x float> poison, <vscale x
8 x i32> zeroinitializer), <vscale x 8 x float> %8, <vscale
x 8 x i1> shufflevector (<vscale x 8 x i1> insertelement
(<vscale x 8 x i1> poison, i1 true, i64 0), <vscale x 8 x i1>
poison, <vscale x 8 x i32> zeroinitializer), i32 %5)
%9 = getelementptr inbounds float, ptr %a, i64 %offset.idx
tail call void @llvm.experimental.vp.strided.store.
nxv8f32.p0.i64(<vscale x 8 x float> %vp.op, ptr align 4
%9, i64 8, <vscale x 8 x i1> shufflevector (<vscale x 8
x i1> insertelement (<vscale x 8 x i1> poison, i1 true,
i64 0), <vscale x 8 x i1> poison, <vscale x 8 x i32>
zeroinitializer), i32 %5)
%10 = zext i32 %5 to i64
```

```
  %index.evl.next = add i64 %evl.based.iv, %10
  %11 = icmp eq i64 %index.evl.next, %3
  br i1 %11, label %for.body.preheader9, label %vector.body

for.cond.cleanup:
  ret void

for.body:
  %indvars.iv = phi i64 [ %indvars.iv.next, %for.body ], [
  %indvars.iv.ph, %for.body.preheader9 ]
  %arrayidx = getelementptr inbounds float, ptr %b, i64
%indvars.iv
  %12 = load float, ptr %arrayidx, align 4
  %div = fdiv float 5.000000e+00, %12
  %arrayidx2 = getelementptr inbounds float, ptr %a, i64
%indvars.iv
  store float %div, ptr %arrayidx2, align 4
  %indvars.iv.next = add nuw nsw i64 %indvars.iv, 2
  %cmp = icmp ult i64 %indvars.iv.next, %0
  br i1 %cmp, label %for.body, label %for.cond.cleanup
}
```

Listing 3-49. Vectorized assembly.

```
foo:                                    # @foo
    .cfi_startproc
# %bb.0:                                # %entry
    blez    a2, .LBB0_7
# %bb.1:                                # %for.body.preheader
    li      a3, 2
    bltu    a3, a2, .LBB0_3
# %bb.2:
    li      a3, 0
```

CHAPTER 3 VECTOR EXTENSIONS IN CLANG-BASED COMPILERS

```
    j     .LBB0_5
.LBB0_3:                                    # %vector.ph
.Lpcrel_hi0:
    auipc  a6, %pcrel_hi(.LCPI0_0)
    addi   a3, a2, -1
    li     a4, 0
    srli   a7, a3, 1
    andi   a3, a3, -2
    flw    fa5, %pcrel_lo(.Lpcrel_hi0)(a6)
    li     a6, 8
.LBB0_4:                                    # %vector.body
                                            # =>This Inner Loop
                                            Header: Depth=1

    sub a5, a7, a4
    vsetvli t0, a5, e32, m4, ta, ma
    sh3add  a5, a4, a1
    vlseg2e32.v v8, (a5)
    sh3add  a5, a4, a0
    add a4, a4, t0
    vfrdiv.vf   v8, v8, fa5
    vsse32.v    v8, (a5), a6
    bne a4, a7, .LBB0_4
.LBB0_5:                                    # %for.body.preheader9
    lui a4, 264704
    sh2add  a0, a3, a0
    sh2add  a1, a3, a1
    fmv.w.x fa5, a4
.LBB0_6:                                    # %for.body
                                            # =>This Inner Loop
                                            Header: Depth=1

    flw fa4, 0(a1)
```

```
    addi    a1, a1, 8
    addi    a3, a3, 2
    fdiv.s  fa4, fa5, fa4
    fsw fa4, 0(a0)
    addi    a0, a0, 8
    bltu    a3, a2, .LBB0_6
.LBB0_7:                            # %for.cond.cleanup
    ret
```

This proposed extension represents a significant step toward better support of VLA vectorization and RVV extension in OpenMP. As with any significant language extension, it will require careful consideration, testing, and refinement before potential inclusion in future OpenMP specifications.

Vector Function Application Binary Interface

A key feature necessary for full explicit and implicit vectorization support is called the Vector Function Application Binary Interface (VectorABI). This specification defines the application binary interface for vector functions that a compiler generates. It's essential for supporting specific syntax provided by OpenMP, which can create and use vectorized versions of functions. In C and C++, OpenMP uses a special pragma directive for this is shown in Listing 3-50.

Listing 3-50. OpenMP Declare SIMD directive format.

```
#pragma omp declare simd {<clauses>}
function declaration/definition
```

One of the main challenges with compiler autovectorization is handling function calls. Typically, compilers do a solid job of vectorizing built-in functions and intrinsics because these have well-known attributes

CHAPTER 3   VECTOR EXTENSIONS IN CLANG-BASED COMPILERS

and are generally free from dangerous side effects like uncontrolled memory access or unpredictable data dependencies. However, user-defined functions are a different story. These functions can introduce hidden dependencies, making it difficult for compilers to safely vectorize the code. Without additional information from the user, the compiler often fails to vectorize calls to such functions.

When a vectorized version of a user-defined function isn't available, compilers may "scalarize" the code instead. This means breaking down vector operations back into scalar ones, calling the scalar functions individually, and then gathering the results to re-create the vector. Unfortunately, this process can add significant overhead and, in many cases, result in worse performance than the original scalar code.

To address this issue, developers can give the compiler a hint that a function is safe for vectorization. This is where VectorABI comes in—it also allows for the creation and support of vectorized versions of popular math function libraries, commonly used across many codebases. Here are some notable examples:

- SLEEF (SIMD Library for Evaluating Elementary Functions): A high-performance library for math functions like sin, cos, and exp. It supports various platforms like SSE, AVX, AVX2, AVX-512, ARM NEON, and even RISC-V RVV (`https://github.com/shibatch/sleef`).

- Google Highway: A C++ library providing portable SIMD/vector intrinsics, with support for over 20 targets, including full RISC-V RVV support (`https://github.com/google/highway`).

- OpenBLAS: An optimized implementation of the Basic Linear Algebra Subprograms (BLAS). It includes tuning for the SiFive X280 and generic RISC-V cores with 128/256-bit vector registers. (`https://github.com/OpenMathLib/OpenBLAS`).

Many other open source libraries are also being updated to support the RISC-V RVV extension. Notable examples include

- Eigen: A widely used C++ library for linear algebra (https://gitlab.com/libeigen/eigen).
- GNU libm: The standard GNU math library (https://github.com/riscv-collab/riscv-gnu-toolchain).

By leveraging VectorABI alongside optimized libraries, developers can enhance performance and efficiency when working with vectorized code. A key aspect of this approach involves the use of specialized naming conventions—commonly referred to as "name mangling"—to differentiate the vectorized versions of functions. The recommended structure for name mangling in the context of vectorized functions is as follows as show in Listing 3-51.

Listing 3-51. VectorABI function name mangling format.

```
mangled-vector-name := "_ZGV" <isa> <mask> <len> <parameters>
"_" <func-name>
<isa> := "r" <lmul>
<lmul> := "1" | "2" | "4" | "8"   (LMUL in turn is 1, 2, 4, 8)
         | "h" | "q" | "e"        (LMUL in turn is 1/2,
                                   1/4, 1/8)
<mask> := "N"   (No mask, default for notinbranch clause)
        | "M"   (Mask, for inbranch clause)
<len> := SIMDLEN (VLS Mode, the number of elements processed
at a time)
        | "x"                (VLA Mode)
<parameters> := <parameter> { <parameter> }
<parameter> := <parameter_type> [ <alignment> ]
<parameter_type> := "v"
                  | "l" | "l" <number>
```

CHAPTER 3   VECTOR EXTENSIONS IN CLANG-BASED COMPILERS

```
                  | "R" | "R" <number>
                  | "L" | "L" <number>
                  | "U" | "U" <number>
                  | "ls" <pos>
                  | "Rs" <pos>
                  | "Ls" <pos>
                  | "Us" <pos>
                  | "u"
<number> := "n" <X>   // if linear step is negative
                  | <Y>
<pos> := <X>
<X> := integral number greater than or equal to 1
<Y> := integral number greater than or equal to 2
<alignment> := [ "a" <X> ]  // specified by aligned clause
<func-name> := the orignal name of the scalar function
```

All these attributes can be explicitly defined using pragmas. For instance, the parameter_type attribute specifies the nature of the parameters used in the vectorized function:

- v: vector parameter, default for no linear/uniform clause.

- u: uniform parameter. Uniform parameter has an invariant value for all concurrent invocations of the vectorized function: x'uniform(i)'.

- l|l<number>: linear parameter with optional <number> step compile time value. The value of such parameters changes linearly with the iteration space by the provided <number> step value: 'linear(i), linear(i:2)'.

- R|R<number>: linear parameter with optional <number> step compile time value, passed by reference: 'linear(ref(i):3)x'.

- L|L<number>: linear parameter with optional <number> step compile time value, explicitly passed by value: 'linear(val(i):2)'.

- U|U<number>: linear parameter with optional <number> step compile time value, passed by reference, but not keeping the original value upon exit from function (similar to const reference): 'linear(uval(i):2)'.

- ls<pos>: linear parameter with an invariant runtime step, passed in the parameter <pos>. The value of such parameter changes linearly with the iteration space by the provided <number> step value: 'linear(i:step) uniform(step)'.

- Rs<pos>: linear parameter with an invariant runtime step, passed in the parameter <pos>, passed by reference: 'linear(ref(i):val) uniform(val)'.

- Ls<pos>: linear parameter with an invariant runtime step, passed in the parameter <pos>, explicitly passed by value: 'linear(val(i):r) uniform(r)'.

- Us<pos>: linear parameter with an invariant runtime step, passed in the parameter <pos>, passed by reference, but not keeping the original value upon exit from function (similar to const reference): 'linear(uval(i):v) uniform(v)'

CHAPTER 3 VECTOR EXTENSIONS IN CLANG-BASED COMPILERS

The example in Listing 3-52 illustrates the fundamental principle behind function emission and the corresponding name mangling process.

Listing 3-52. OpenMP Declare SIMD exmple.

```
#pragma omp declare simd linear(i)
int foo(int i);
```

This will lead to the generation of functions, shown in Listing 3-53.

Listing 3-53. Generated versions of function.

```
// VLS Mode, VLEN=128
 vint32m1_t _ZGVr1N4l_foo(int i);   // LMUL=1
 vint32m2_t _ZGVr2N8l_foo(int i);   // LMUL=2
 vint32m4_t _ZGVr4N16l_foo(int i);  // LMUL=4
 vint32m8_t _ZGVr8N32l_foo(int i);  // LMUL=8
 vint32m1_t _ZGVr1M4l_foo(vbool32_t mask, int i);
// LMUL=1, masked version
 vint32m2_t _ZGVr2M8l_foo(vbool32_t mask, int i);
// LMUL=2, masked version
 vint32m4_t _ZGVr4M16l_foo(vbool32_t mask, int i);
// LMUL=4, masked version
 vint32m8_t _ZGVr8M32l_foo(vbool32_t mask, int i);
// LMUL=8, masked version
 // VLA Mode
 vint32m1_t _ZGVr1Nxvl_foo(int i);  // LMUL=1
 vint32m2_t _ZGVr2Nxvl_foo(int i);  // LMUL=2
 vint32m4_t _ZGVr4Nxvl_foo(int i);  // LMUL=4
 vint32m8_t _ZGVr8Nxvl_foo(int i);  // LMUL=8
vint32m1_t _ZGVr1Mxvl_foo(vbool32_t mask, int i);
// LMUL=1, masked version
```

```
vint32m2_t _ZGVr2Mxvl_foo(vbool32_t mask, int i);
// LMUL=2, masked version
vint32m4_t _ZGVr4Mxvl_foo(vbool32_t mask, int i);
// LMUL=4, masked version
vint32m8_t _ZGVr8Mxvl_foo(vbool32_t mask, int i);   // LMUL=8,
masked version
```

Clang and gcc compilers also provide 'vectorize' function attribute, which may be used to replace 'omp declare simd' directive in non-OpenMP code. This attribute is not so flexible as the pragma, but in many cases may help to vectorize the functions (see Listing 3-54).

Listing 3-54. vectorize function attribute exmple.

```
int foo(int i) __attribute((vectorize))
```

Unfortunately, this pragma and the attribute require extra support from the compiler on function vectorization. Currently LLVM does not provide support for this feature, but there is a plan to support it in the future.

SiFive Extension for Loop Vectorization

The SiFive clang-based toolchain introduces a specialized pragma directive tuned for the RISC-V Vector (RVV) extension, offering developers fine-grained control over loop vectorization. This pragma enables manual tuning of critical vectorization parameters, allowing the programmers to specify the Register Group Multiplier (LMUL) and Selected Element Width (SEW) (see Listing 3-55).

Listing 3-55. SiFive loop hint directive.

```
#pragma clang rvv lmul_sew(LMUL, SEW)
```

The pragma requires two parameters:

1. LMUL (Register Group Multiplier). Determines the number of vector registers grouped together for vector operations. Valid options are as follows:

   - Fractional: mf8/Mf8 (1/8), mf4/Mf4 (1/4), mf2/Mf2 (1/2)
   - Whole: m1/M1 (1), m2/M2 (2), m4/M4 (4), m8/M8 (8)

   The choice of LMUL affects the trade-off between the number of vector elements processed per instruction and the number of available vector registers.

2. SEW (Selected Element Width). Specifies the bit-width of individual vector elements. Valid options are

   - e8/E8 (8-bit)
   - e16/E16 (16-bit)
   - e32/E32 (32-bit)
   - e64/E64 (64-bit)

The code in Listing 3-56, Listing 3-57, Listing 3-58, and Listing 3-59 shows the example of using this pragma.

Listing 3-56. SiFive loop hint directive example.

```
void foo(float * restrict a, float * restrict b, int N) {
  #pragma clang rvv lmul_sew(m8, e32) // SEW 32 (for float)
  and LMUL 8
  for (int i = 0; i < N; i += 2) {
    a[i] = 5 / b[i];
  }
}
```

CHAPTER 3 VECTOR EXTENSIONS IN CLANG-BASED COMPILERS

Listing 3-57. Compile command.

```
clang --target=riscv64-unknown-linux -mcpu=sifive-x280 -c
test.c -O3 -Rpass=loop-vectorize -Rpass-missed=loop-vectorize
-Rpass-analysis=loop-vectorize
test.c:3:3: remark: the cost-model indicates that interleaving
is not beneficial and is explicitly disabled or interleave
count is set to 1 [-Rpass-analysis=loop-vectorize]
    3 |   for (int i = 0; i < N; i += 2) {
      |   ^
test.c:3:3: remark: vectorized loop ((lmul, type): (m8, i32))
[-Rpass=loop-vectorize]
```

Listing 3-58. Vectorized LLVM IR.

```
define void @foo(ptr noalias %a, ptr noalias %b, i32 %N) {
entry:
  %cmp6 = icmp sgt i32 %N, 0
  br i1 %cmp6, label %for.body.preheader, label %for.
  cond.cleanup

for.body.preheader:
  %0 = zext nneg i32 %N to i64
  %1 = icmp ult i32 %N, 3
  br i1 %1, label %for.body.preheader9, label %vector.ph

for.body.preheader9:
  %indvars.iv.ph = phi i64 [ 0, %for.body.preheader ], [ %ind.
  end, %vector.body ]
  br label %for.body

vector.ph:
  %2 = add nsw i64 %0, -1
  %3 = lshr i64 %2, 1
```

```
  %ind.end = and i64 %2, -2
  br label %vector.body

vector.body:
  %evl.based.iv = phi i64 [ 0, %vector.ph ], [ %index.evl.next,
  %vector.body ]
  %4 = sub i64 %3, %evl.based.iv
  %5 = tail call i32 @llvm.experimental.get.vector.length.
  i64(i64 %4, i32 16, i1 true)
  %offset.idx = shl i64 %evl.based.iv, 1
  %6 = getelementptr inbounds float, ptr %b, i64 %offset.idx
  %vp.strided.load = tail call <vscale x 16 x float> @llvm.
  experimental.vp.strided.load.nxv16f32.p0.i64(ptr align 4
  %6, i64 8, <vscale x 16 x i1> shufflevector (<vscale x 16
  x i1> insertelement (<vscale x 16 x i1> poison, i1 true,
  i64 0), <vscale x 16 x i1> poison, <vscale x 16 x i32>
  zeroinitializer), i32 %5)
  %vp.op = tail call <vscale x 16 x float> @llvm.vp.fdiv.
  nxv16f32(<vscale x 16 x float> shufflevector (<vscale x 16
  x float> insertelement (<vscale x 16 x float> poison, float
  5.000000e+00, i64 0), <vscale x 16 x float> poison, <vscale
  x 16 x i32> zeroinitializer), <vscale x 16 x float> %vp.
  strided.load, <vscale x 16 x i1> shufflevector (<vscale x
  16 x i1> insertelement (<vscale x 16 x i1> poison, i1 true,
  i64 0), <vscale x 16 x i1> poison, <vscale x 16 x i32>
  zeroinitializer), i32 %5)
  %7 = getelementptr inbounds float, ptr %a, i64 %offset.idx
  tail call void @llvm.experimental.vp.strided.store.
  nxv16f32.p0.i64(<vscale x 16 x float> %vp.op, ptr align 4
  %7, i64 8, <vscale x 16 x i1> shufflevector (<vscale x 16
  x i1> insertelement (<vscale x 16 x i1> poison, i1 true,
  i64 0), <vscale x 16 x i1> poison, <vscale x 16 x i32>
  zeroinitializer), i32 %5)
```

CHAPTER 3 VECTOR EXTENSIONS IN CLANG-BASED COMPILERS

```
  %8 = zext i32 %5 to i64
  %index.evl.next = add i64 %evl.based.iv, %8
  %9 = icmp eq i64 %index.evl.next, %3
  br i1 %9, label %for.body.preheader9, label %vector.body

for.cond.cleanup:
  ret void

for.body:
  %indvars.iv = phi i64 [ %indvars.iv.next, %for.body ], [ %indvars.iv.ph, %for.body.preheader9 ]
  %arrayidx = getelementptr inbounds float, ptr %b, i64 %indvars.iv
  %10 = load float, ptr %arrayidx, align 4
  %div = fdiv float 5.000000e+00, %10
  %arrayidx2 = getelementptr inbounds float, ptr %a, i64 %indvars.iv
  store float %div, ptr %arrayidx2, align 4
  %indvars.iv.next = add nuw nsw i64 %indvars.iv, 2
  %cmp = icmp ult i64 %indvars.iv.next, %0
  br i1 %cmp, label %for.body, label %for.cond.cleanup
}
```

Listing 3-59. Vectorized assembly.

```
foo:                                    # @foo
    .cfi_startproc
# %bb.0:                                # %entry
    blez    a2, .LBB0_7
# %bb.1:                                # %for.body.preheader
    li      a3, 2
    bltu    a3, a2, .LBB0_3
# %bb.2:
```

CHAPTER 3 VECTOR EXTENSIONS IN CLANG-BASED COMPILERS

```
    li   a3, 0
    j    .LBB0_5
.LBB0_3:                                  # %vector.ph
.Lpcrel_hi0:
    auipc   a7, %pcrel_hi(.LCPI0_0)
    addi    a3, a2, -1
    li   a4, 0
    srli    t0, a3, 1
    andi    a3, a3, -2
    li   a6, 8
    flw fa5, %pcrel_lo(.Lpcrel_hi0)(a7)
.LBB0_4:                                  # %vector.body
                                          # =>This Inner Loop
Header: Depth=1
    sub a5, t0, a4
    vsetvli a7, a5, e32, m8, ta, ma
    sh3add  a5, a4, a1
    vlse32.v    v8, (a5), a6
    sh3add  a5, a4, a0
    add a4, a4, a7
    vfrdiv.vf   v8, v8, fa5
    vsse32.v    v8, (a5), a6
    bne a4, t0, .LBB0_4
.LBB0_5:                                  # %for.body.preheader9
    lui a4, 264704
    sh2add  a0, a3, a0
    sh2add  a1, a3, a1
    fmv.w.x fa5, a4
.LBB0_6:                                  # %for.body
                                          # =>This Inner Loop
Header: Depth=1
```

```
    flw     fa4, 0(a1)
    addi    a1, a1, 8
    addi    a3, a3, 2
    fdiv.s  fa4, fa5, fa4
    fsw     fa4, 0(a0)
    addi    a0, a0, 8
    bltu    a3, a2, .LBB0_6
.LBB0_7:                                    # %for.cond.cleanup
    ret
```

In this example, the pragma specifies

- LMUL = 8 (m8): Using groups of 8 vector registers

- SEW = 32 bits (e32): Operating on 32-bit float elements

This format allows efficient processing of float arrays, potentially processing eight registers per vector instruction compared to the default configuration.

This pragma allows to carefully tune the program for the performance, considering performance implications:

1. Parallelism vs. Register Pressure. Higher LMUL increases parallelism but reduces the number of independent vector operations that can be in flight simultaneously due to register pressure. Lower LMUL values (fractional) allow more independent vector operations but process fewer elements per instruction.

2. Memory Access Efficiency. The combination of LMUL and SEW affects the efficiency of vector load and store operations, particularly in terms of memory alignment and utilization of memory bandwidth.

This extension allows to use best practices:

1. Profiling-Driven Tuning. Experiment with different LMUL and SEW combinations, using profiling tools to identify the most efficient configuration for your specific workload and target hardware.

2. Data Type Consideration. Align SEW with the natural size of the data types, used by the programmer, to avoid unnecessary type conversions or precision loss.

3. Algorithm Adaptation. Consider restructuring algorithms to take advantage of specific LMUL and SEW configurations, potentially unrolling loops or adjusting data layouts.

4. Portability Awareness. While this pragma offers powerful optimization capabilities, be mindful of portability. Consider creating conditional compilation blocks.

By leveraging this RVV-specific pragma, developers can achieve more precise control over the vectorization process, potentially unlocking significant performance improvements in RVV-enabled systems. However, it's significant to balance the use of such low-level optimizations with code readability and maintainability, reserving these techniques for performance-critical sections of the application.

CHAPTER 3   VECTOR EXTENSIONS IN CLANG-BASED COMPILERS

Common Recommendations for Successful Code Vectorization

Though current optimizing compilers support optimizations and autovectorization of the hot code, it is still very important to help the compiler as much as possible to get the best performance. In some cases, the compiler is just unable to make some important decision because of the source language rules and restrictions and limits its ability to do some transformation. Here are some basic recommendations on how to write a code for C/C++ (based on clang compiler) to allow better vectorization results.

Also, note that there is a RISC-V Optimization Guide document defined (https://riscv-optimization-guide.riseproject.dev/), which provides recommendations for software and toolchain developers for writing better code for RISC-V processors. This document was delivered by the members of the RISE (https://riseproject.dev/), a project focused on accelerating and improving the development of the Open Source software for RISC-V architecture, and includes recommendations from the leading members and developers of the RISC-V hardware and software.

Besides, there are common recommendations, which allow writing better code.

1. Try to use consecutive memory accesses where possible. Though RV supports segmented, strided and indexed memory accesses, consecutive memory accesses are still preferable in most cases, especially when compared to the cases with strided or indexed (irregular) memory accesses. For example, the cost of strided memory accesses is proportional to the number of memory operations implied, i.e., the number of vector elements. For

indexed operations, it may be even worse, because it requires building the vector address, having irregular accesses, which may cause stalls in the processor's pipelines.

This may include some code transformation, like AoS-to-SoA (array of structures to structure of arrays), memory layout flattening, which eliminates pointer indirection and irregular accesses, structure splitting, which may help for better emission of the segmented/strided accesses, etc.

2. Avoid pointer aliasing, where possible. This includes (but is not limited to) providing parameters hints, like restrict modifier in C (and nonstandard C ++ extension), which tells the compiler that, for the lifetime of the pointer, only it (or a value directly derived from it) will be used to access the object it points to. Without this hint, the compiler may need to generate extra checks for non-aliasing pointers, which may cause performance regressions.

3. Simplify control the flow; try to avoid early exits and other condition operations in the loops.

4. Avoid dependencies between iterations, which may prevent vectorization.

5. Try to write the loops with the known trip count. Try to avoid using class/structure members (both, fields and functions) as the loop trip count; instead, cache it in the local variable before the loop to make the compiler know that the trip count is a loop invariant and does not change during loop execution.

CHAPTER 3   VECTOR EXTENSIONS IN CLANG-BASED COMPILERS

6. Use vectorizable types, like float, double, int32_t, int, etc.; avoid mixing precision or non-standard bitwidths.

7. Mark the functions, used in the loop, as inline functions and/or use standard vector libraries, providing vector variants of the functions.

8. If the precision of the floating point operations is not so important, use -ffast-math and other float point related optimization options during compilation.

Summary

In this chapter, you learned

- How Clang extends C/C++ language to support RVV programming through attributes, built-in functions, and vector data types.

- How OpenMP integrates with LLVM/Clang for RISC-V, providing parallel constructs, worksharing, synchronization, tasks, and offloading, with support for SIMD vectorization that can leverage the RVV extension.

- That Clang supports both full OpenMP (-fopenmp) and SIMD-only (-fopenmp-simd) modes, enabling flexible use of OpenMP features depending on the application needs.

- How OpenMP SIMD directives enable loop vectorization, including conditional vectorization.

CHAPTER 3   VECTOR EXTENSIONS IN CLANG-BASED COMPILERS

- The proposed OpenMP extension to improve VLA support by explicitly controlling SEW (Selected Element Width) and LMUL (Length Multiplier), aligning with RVV's scalable model.

- The role of the Vector Function ABI (VectorABI) in supporting vectorized function calls, and how libraries like SLEEF, Google Highway, OpenBLAS, and Eigen provide optimized math and linear algebra functions for RVV.

- The use of pragma directives and function attributes (e.g., omp declare simd, vectorize) to guide function vectorization and avoid costly scalarization of function calls.

- The SiFive-specific pragma for loop vectorization, allowing explicit control over LMUL and SEW for performance tuning on RVV-enabled processors.

- Best practices for writing vectorization-friendly code in C/C.

CHAPTER 4

RISC-V RVV Specific LLVM-Based Optimizations

RISC-V Vector Extension Support in LLVM

The RISC-V Vector Extension (RVV) version 1.0 comes with some interesting challenges for compiler tools. LLVM tackles these challenges with some clever methods. The main idea behind LLVM's strategy is using scalable vector types. This concept was first created for ARM's Scalable Vector Extension (SVE), but it has been adapted successfully for RVV.

Scalable vector types in LLVM provide a flexible abstraction for representing vector registers with lengths that are unknown at compile-time. These types are denoted as <vscale x n x ty>, where 'vscale' is a runtime-constant multiplier, 'n' is a compile-time constant, and 'ty' represents the element type (`https://llvm.org/docs/LangRef.html#t-vector`). In the context of RVV, 'vscale x n' and 'ty' correspond to the LMUL (vector length multiplier) and SEW (selected element width), respectively—two key parameters in the RVV programming model.

The 'vscale' factor in LLVM's RVV implementation is defined as VLEN/64, where VLEN is the runtime-dependent vector length in bits. This definition implies a minimum supported VLEN of 64 bits, effectively precluding support for hypothetical 32-bit vector implementations. The constant RISCV::RVVBitsPerBlock sums up how 'vscale' and VLEN are connected.

LLVM's type system treats scalable vectors as first-class citizens. These types can be manipulated in ways like fixed-length vectors, with the crucial distinction that their exact size remains indeterminate until runtime. This property enables the creation of portable vector code that can conform to various hardware implementations with differing VLEN values.

LLVM enforces certain constraints on scalable vector types to ensure well-formed IR. The number of elements must be a positive integer, and zero-length vectors are prohibited.

The flexibility of scalable vector types allows LLVM to model the runtime-determined vector lengths implemented in the RVV architecture without compromising the ability to perform meaningful optimizations. This abstraction enables a wide range of vector operations to be represented and optimized in the IR, with the final mapping to specific RVV instructions occurring during the later stages of code generation. Table 4-1 provides the relations between SEW/LMULs and the scalable type encoding in LLVM IR.

Table 4-1. SEW/LMUL representation in LVM IR, <vscale x <factor> x <type>>.

SEW/ LMUL	1/8	1/4	½	1	2	4	8
i64	–	–	–	<v x 1 x i64>	<v x 2 x i64>	<v x 4 x i64>	<v x 8 x i64>
i32	–	–	<v x 1 x i32>	<v x 2 x i32>	<v x 4 x i32>	<v x 8 x i32>	<v x 16 x i32>
i16	–	<v x 1 x i16>	<v x 2 x i16>	<v x 4 x i16>	<v x 8 x i16>	<v x 16 x i16>	<v x 32 x i16>
i8	<v x 1 x i8>	<v x 2 x i8>	<v x 4 x i8>	<v x 8 x i8>	<v x 16 x i8>	<v x 32 x i8>	<v x 64 x i8>
double	–	–	–	<v x 1 x double>	<v x 2 x double>	<v x 4 x double>	<v x 8 x double>
float	–	–	<v x 1 x float>	<v x 2 x float>	<v x 4 x float>	<v x 8 x float>	<v x 16 x float>
half	–	<v x 1 x half>	<v x 2 x half>	<v x 4 x half>	<v x 8 x half>	<v x 16 x half>	<v x 32 x half>

In addition to data vectors, RVV introduces mask vectors, which are required for predicated execution and conditional operations. These mask vectors are physically implemented as densely packed bits within a vector register. LLVM represents these mask vectors using scalable vector types of i1 elements:

- <vscale x 1 x i1>
- <vscale x 2 x i1>

CHAPTER 4 RISC-V RVV SPECIFIC LLVM-BASED OPTIMIZATIONS

- <vscale x 4 x i1>
- <vscale x 8 x i1>
- <vscale x 16 x i1>
- <vscale x 32 x i1>
- <vscale x 64 x i1>

LLVM provides three primary mechanisms for representing vector instructions in its IR, each serving different purposes and offering varying levels of abstraction.

1. Standard Vector Instructions. These instructions operate with both scalable and fixed-length vector types, providing a general-purpose mechanism for vector operations within LLVM's existing instruction set, as shown in Listing 4-1.

Listing 4-1. Working with the scalable vector type using LLVM instructions.

```
%vmul = mul <vscale x 4 x i32> %va, %vb
%fva = load <4 x i32>, <4 x i32>* %fa, align 16
%fvmul = mul <4 x i32> %fva, %fvb
store <4 x i32> %fvmul, <4 x i32>* %fc, align 16
```

2. RISC-V vector intrinsics, which mirror the C intrinsics specification. The only valid types for this intrinsics are scalable vector types (shown in Listing 4-2).

Listing 4-2. *Working with the scalable vector type using RVV intrinsics.*

```
%vl = call i64 @llvm.vscale.i64()
%vl4 = mul i64 %vl, 4
%va = call <vscale x 4 x i32> @llvm.riscv.vle.nxv4i32.
i64(<vscale x 4 x i32> poison, i32* %a, i64 %vl4)
%vb = call <vscale x 4 x i32> @llvm.riscv.vle.nxv4i32.
i64(<vscale x 4 x i32> poison, i32* %b, i64 %vl4)
%vc = call <vscale x 4 x i32> @llvm.riscv.vmul.mask.nxv4i32.
nxv4i32.i64(
    <vscale x 4 x i32> poison,
    <vscale x 4 x i32> %va,
    <vscale x 4 x i32> %vb,
    <vscale x 4 x i1> %mask,
    i64 %vl4,
    i32 0)
call void @llvm.riscv.vse.nxv4i32.i64(<vscale x 4 x i32> %vadd,
i32* %c, i64 %vl4)
```

   3. Universal vector predication (VP) intrinsics
      (https://llvm.org/docs/LangRef.html#int-vp,
      Listing 4-3).

Listing 4-3. *Working with the scalable vector type using predicated intrinsics.*

```
%vscale = call i32 @llvm.vscale.i32()
%vl = mul i32 %vscale, 4
%va = call <vscale x 4 x i32> @llvm.vp.load.nxv4i32.p0i32(i32*
%a_ptr, <vscale x 4 x i1> %mask, i32 %vl)
%vb = call <vscale x 4 x i32> @llvm.vp.load.nxv4i32.p0i32(i32*
%b_ptr, <vscale x 4 x i1> %mask, i32 %vl)
```

```
%vd_mul = call <vscale x 4 x i32> @llvm.vp.mul.nxv4i32(<vscale
x 4 x i32> %va, <vscale x 4 x i32> %vb, <vscale x 4 x i1>
%mask, i32 %vl)
```

These target-agnostic intrinsics offer a higher level of abstraction, enabling vector operations to be expressed independently of the underlying hardware. Key features of VP intrinsics include

a) Support for both scalable and fixed-length vector types

b) Compatibility with middle-end optimization passes like the Loop vectorizer and SLP vectorizer

c) Absence of passthrough operands, with tail/mask undisturbed behavior emulated through a special predicated @llvm.vp.merge intrinsic

d) Efficient lowering to RVV instructions, with optimizations like merging vmerge operations into the underlying instruction's mask in RISC-V specific to the RISCVDAGToDAGISel pass

This comprehensive approach to vector instruction representation in LLVM supports code generation, optimization, and portability across different vector architectures, while still providing the specificity required for optimal RVV code generation.

Optimizations and Target-Specific Information

LLVM includes many target-independent optimizations out of the box, providing ready-to-use instrument for the RVV-ready compiler. These optimizations include

CHAPTER 4   RISC-V RVV SPECIFIC LLVM-BASED OPTIMIZATIONS

1. Instructions simplifications, combining and reassociation. These are fundamental optimization techniques implemented in LLVM to enhance code efficiency and performance.

   a. Instruction Simplification. This optimization allows replacing complex instructions or sequences of instructions with simpler, more efficient equivalents. The process involves analyzing instruction patterns and applying algebraic identities, constant folding, and other mathematical properties to reduce computational complexity. For example:

      i. Replacing multiplication by powers of two with left shifts: x * 8 becomes x << 3.

      ii. Simplifying arithmetic with identity elements: x + 0 becomes x.

      iii. Constant folding: 5 + 3 is computed at compile-time to 8.

   b. Instruction Combining. This technique focuses on merging multiple instructions into a single (or several), more efficient instruction(s). The InstCombine pass in LLVM is responsible for this optimization. It applies a wide range of peephole optimizations, including

      i. Arithmetic Combination: sequences of arithmetic operations can often be merged, e.g. (8-a)+3 can be merged into (8+3)-a or $a^2 + 2*a*b + b^2$ can be simplified into $(a+b)^2$.

      ii. Simplification of Logical Operations: complex logical expressions, such as a series of ANDs or ORs, can be combined into a more concise form.

CHAPTER 4 RISC-V RVV SPECIFIC LLVM-BASED OPTIMIZATIONS

   iii. Propagation and Merging: when multiple operations depend on the same value or can be simplified when combined, LLVM aggressively merges these operations. This not only reduces the instruction count but also improves data locality and cache efficiency.

  c. Reassociation. Involves reordering arithmetic operations to enable further optimizations. The primary goal is to group constants and create opportunities for constant folding and simplification. LLVM's Reassociate pass implements this optimization. Key aspects include

   i. Reordering commutative operations: $(a + 5) + 3$ becomes $a + (5 + 3)$, allowing constant folding.

   ii. Normalizing expressions: Ensuring similar terms are adjacent, e.g., $(a * b) * a$ becomes $(a * a) * b$.

   iii. Factoring out common subexpressions: $(a * c) + (b * c)$ can be transformed to $(a + b) * c$.

2. Loop invariant code motion (LICM). This transformation allows to improve program efficiency by identifying and relocating computations that yield identical results across all iterations of a loop to positions outside the loop body. By doing so, LICM reduces redundant calculations, potentially leading to significant code size reduction and performance improvements, especially for loops with high iteration counts. LICM begins with a comprehensive analysis to determine which instructions within a loop are invariant. An instruction is considered loop-invariant if

   a. It produces the same result in every iteration.

CHAPTER 4   RISC-V RVV SPECIFIC LLVM-BASED OPTIMIZATIONS

b. It has no side effects that could affect the loop's behavior.

c. All its operands are loop-invariant.

Once invariant instructions are identified, LICM attempts to move them out of the loop. It may perform hoisting or sinking of the invariant instructions. Doing the hoisting, the LLVM moves invariant instructions to the loop's preheader. If the instruction is only used after the loop, LICM can move it to a position following the loop exit (instruction sinking).

3. Loop Unrolling and Flattening. Loop unrolling is a pass that replicates the body of a loop multiple times, reducing the total number of iterations. This transformation can yield a range of performance benefits:

   a. Lower branch overhead. Fewer loop iterations mean fewer conditional jumps, potentially improving the accuracy of branch prediction.

   b. Increased instruction-level parallelism. Unrolling exposes more independent instructions, allowing for better utilization of superscalar processors.

   c. Improved cache utilization. Consecutive iterations may benefit from spatial locality, as data accessed in one iteration might already be in the cache for the next.

   Loop flattening, also known as loop collapsing, is a transformation that combines nested loops into a single loop. This technique is particularly useful for multidimensional arrays processing and can offer several advantages:

a. Reduced loop overhead. By combining multiple loops into one, the number of loop control instructions is decreased.

b. Improved vectorization opportunities. Flattened loops may be more sensitive to SIMD (Single Instruction, Multiple Data) vectorization, potentially leading to significant performance improvements on modern processors.

c. Enhanced cache utilization. Flattening can improve spatial locality by accessing elements in a more contiguous manner, potentially reducing cache misses.

d. Simplified loop analysis. A single flattened loop can be easier to analyze and optimize further compared to nested loops.

4. Load/stores analysis and optimizations. This is a whole set of different passes examining the program's memory access patterns, identifying redundant loads and stores, and determining potential aliasing relationships between memory references. Key components of load/store analysis and optimizations in LLVM include

    a. Alias Analysis. Alias analysis determines whether pointers may refer to the same memory location. LLVM implements several alias analysis algorithms, ranging from basic type-based analysis to more sophisticated context-sensitive interprocedural analysis. Accurate alias information is critical for enabling aggressive load/store optimizations, including vectorization.

b. Memory Dependence Analysis. This analysis identifies dependencies between memory operations, helping to determine which operations can be safely reordered or eliminated. LLVM's memory dependence analysis considers both data dependencies and potential side effects of intervening instructions.

c. Load Elimination. Allows to remove extra memory operations, if proved to be safe. Includes Common Subexpression Elimination (CSE), Load-after-store elimination, Load-after-load elimination, and others. These optimizations reduce memory usage and can significantly improve performance, especially in loop-heavy code.

d. Store Elimination. Like load elimination, LLVM attempts to remove unnecessary stores, like dead stores, store-to-load forwarding, merging of adjacent stores, etc. These optimizations not only reduce memory writes but can also simplify subsequent analysis and transformations.

e. Memory Access Reordering. The memory accesses can be reordered to improve locality and reduce stalls.

f. Scalar Replacement of Aggregates (SROA). This optimization breaks down aggregate data structures (like structs and arrays) into individual scalar values when possible. This can lead to better register allocation and enable further scalar optimizations.

g. Partial Redundancy Elimination (PRE). PRE identifies and eliminates partially redundant memory operations by adding some extra artificial computations to make fully redundant operations that can then be removed.

5. Data Alignment and Prefetching. Ensuring that data is aligned for vector operations and leveraging prefetching can significantly reduce memory access latencies. Data alignment refers to the way the data is arranged and accessed in memory. Proper alignment can significantly improve the performance due to the way the processors handle memory accesses. Prefetching is a technique used to reduce memory access latency by loading data into the cache before it is needed. LLVM's prefetching analysis allows to identify opportunities for inserting prefetch instructions to improve cache utilization.

6. Function inlining. This transformation tries to eliminate the overhead associated with function calls and provides the opportunities for further optimizations. In LLVM, function inlining is a sophisticated process that balances multiple factors to make informed decisions about when and how to inline functions. Key aspects of function inlining in LLVM include

   a. Inlining Heuristics. LLVM implements a set of heuristics to determine whether inlining a particular function call is beneficial. These heuristics consider factors such as

      i. Function size

      ii. Estimated performance gain

      iii. Potential code size increase

      iv. Register pressure

      v. Optimization level

The inliner uses a cost model to estimate the trade-offs between performance improvement and code size growth.

b. Inline Attributes. LLVM recognizes function attributes that provide hints to the inliner:

   i. 'always_inline': Suggests that the function should always be inlined if possible

   ii. 'noinline': Indicates that the function should never be inlined

   iii. 'inlinehint': Suggests that inlining is preferred but not mandatory

   These attributes can be specified in the source code or added by earlier optimization passes.

c. Threshold-Based Inlining. The inliner uses configurable thresholds to limit excessive inlining. These thresholds can be adjusted based on the optimization level or through compiler flags.

7. Loop strength reduction (LSR). Transforms expensive operations in loops into more efficient ones, improving the performance of the generated code. The primary goal of loop strength reduction is to minimize the number of complex arithmetic operations performed in each iteration of a loop, often by leveraging the loop's induction variables and algebraic properties of the computations involved. Key aspects of loop strength reduction in LLVM include

a. Induction Variable Analysis. LLVM's strength reduction pass begins by identifying and analyzing the induction variables in a loop.

b. Recurrence Detection. The optimizer detects recurrent expressions within the loop, focusing on those that can be efficiently rewritten in terms of the loop's induction variables.

c. Cost Model. LLVM uses cost model that estimates the relative expenses of different operations on the target architecture. This model guides the decision-making process for strength reduction opportunities.

d. Algebraic Simplification. Complex expressions are analyzed for potential algebraic simplifications that can lead to more efficient computations.

e. Addressing Mode Utilization. The strength reduction pass considers the target architecture's addressing modes, aiming to transform expressions into forms that can leverage efficient memory access patterns.

While compiler optimizations generally enhance code performance, certain early-stage transformations can affect significantly later optimization passes. This phenomenon is particularly notable in the interaction between instruction simplification passes and vectorization passes. For example, the effectiveness of SLP vectorization relies heavily on recognizing specific instruction patterns within the code, and this ability can be affected by the early optimization passes.

The passes, such as instruction simplification and combining, may alter these patterns in ways that, while locally beneficial, make them unrecognizable to the SLP vectorization pass. This transformation can occur as follows:

CHAPTER 4 RISC-V RVV SPECIFIC LLVM-BASED OPTIMIZATIONS

1. Pattern Disruption. Instruction combining might merge multiple simple operations into a single (simpler) instruction. While this reduces instruction count, it can hide the original sequence that could be recognizable previously by SLP vectorization.

2. Algebraic Simplifications. Algebraic transformations, while mathematically equivalent, may restructure expressions in ways that no longer align with the expected patterns for vectorization.

3. Strength Reduction. Replacing complex operations with simpler ones (e.g., multiplication with addition in loops) can eliminate vectorization opportunities that rely on specific arithmetic operations.

4. Common Subexpression Elimination (CSE). By removing redundant computations, CSE might break the symmetry between adjacent statements that SLP vectorization could have exploited.

To illustrate this, consider the code sequence shown in Listing 4-4.

Listing 4-4. Source code, affected by early optimizations.

```
a[i] = b[i] * 2 + 0;
a[i+1] = b[i+1] * 2 + 1;
```

This pattern is ready for SLP vectorization. However, early optimization transforms it to the code, shown in Listing 4-5.

Listing 4-5. The code after early optimizations.

```
a[i] = b[i] << 1;
a[i+1] = b[i+1] << 1 + 1;
```

While this transformation reduces multiplication to a potentially cheaper shift operation and removes extra addition, it disrupts the clear parallel structure that SLP vectorization could recognize and efficiently vectorize. So, it is important for the vectorizers to know about such transformations and properly recognize such patterns.

While these optimizations are not exclusively for RISC-V and its RVV extensions, they are tuned or have specific considerations for RISC-V targets. The RISC-V specific aspects are often implemented in the target-specific parts of these passes or in the RISC-V target information classes.

Many middle-level transformation passes, implemented in the LLVM compiler, require special information about features, supported by target hardware. This target-specific information is encapsulated within classes derived from TargetTransformInfo (TTI). The TTI plays a key role in LLVM's target support, offering cost modelling and transformation guidance to mid-level optimizers.

For the RISC-V Vector extension, the TTI is particularly significant. It steers vectorization decisions and other vector-related optimizations, ensuring that the compiler generates efficient code for RISC-V vector operations. The RISC-V-specific TTI implementation is found in the llvm/lib/Target/RISCV/RISCVTargetTransformInfo.h file. This class inherits from BasicTTIImplBase and provides RISC-V-specific implementations of various TTI functions. The TTI includes functions to estimate the cost of arithmetic, logic, reductions, and other vector instructions. These functions consider factors like the vector factor (VF), LMUL (vector register group size), and SEW (selected element width) to provide accurate cost estimates. The TTI also models the cost of vector memory operations. It considers alignment issues and the potential need for multiple operations when dealing with large vector sizes. Also, TTI implements various legality checks, which support optimization passes in their attempt to maintain correctness of the transformed optimized code.

CHAPTER 4 RISC-V RVV SPECIFIC LLVM-BASED OPTIMIZATIONS

RISC-V RVV Code Generation

The LLVM target-independent code generator is a modular framework that offers a collection of reusable components for converting LLVM IR into code specific to different targets. This framework supports both static compilation, which generates assembly, and JIT compilation, which creates binary machine code. The architecture of the code generator consists of six main components:

1. Target Description Interfaces. These interfaces, located in include/llvm/Target/, encapsulate key characteristics of different machines. They abstract details that are specific to individual targets, making it possible to develop portable algorithms for code generation. For support of the RISC-V Vector Extension, these interfaces would include descriptions of vector registers, the vector operations available, and constraints particular to vectors.

2. Code Representation Classes. Can be found in include/llvm/CodeGen/. These classes model the code generated for any target machine. They present mid-level concepts such as constant pool entries and jump tables. When dealing with RISC-V vectors, these classes would depict vector instructions, the allocation of vector registers, and optimizations specific to vectors.

3. MC Layer Classes. These classes represent assembly-level elements such as labels, sections, and instructions. They function at a lower level of abstraction than the Code Representation Classes, concentrating on the generation of object files. For the RISC-V Vector Extension, this layer would manage the encoding of vector instructions, and the creation of assembler directives related to vectors.

4. Target-Independent Algorithms. These algorithms, which are implemented in lib/CodeGen/, handle various aspects of native code generation, including register allocation, instruction scheduling, and stack frame representation. To support the RISC-V Vector Extension, they include register allocation strategies that are aware of vectors or scheduling algorithms that consider the latencies and throughput of vector instructions.

5. Target-Specific Implementations. Found in lib/Target/, these implementations bring the abstract target description interfaces for targets. They may include customized passes that are specific to the target, which help construct complete code generators. For the RISC-V Vector Extension, this would involve creating passes for vector-specific lowering, expanding intrinsics, and supporting auto-vectorization.

6. JIT Components. The target-independent JIT components, located in lib/ExecutionEngine/JIT, use the TargetJITInfo structure to manage target-specific challenges.

CHAPTER 4 RISC-V RVV SPECIFIC LLVM-BASED OPTIMIZATIONS

The code generator is designed to generate efficient, high-quality code for standard register-based processors. It is divided into seven main stages:

1. Instruction Selection. This stage maps LLVM IR to the target instructions. It is where the compiler determines how to represent LLVM operations using the target instruction set. The output is a Directed Acyclic Graph (DAG) of target instructions, using a combination of virtual registers (in SSA form) and physical registers (to accommodate target constraints and calling conventions). For the RISC-V Vector Extension, this required the addition of new SelectionDAG nodes for vector operations and the implementation of the logic needed to select the most efficient vector instructions for each LLVM vector operation.

   Another approach includes using the Global Instruction Selection pass (GlobalISel). GlobalISel is intended to be a replacement for SelectionDAG and FastISel, which tries to address three main problems:

   a. Performance. Classical SelectionDAG requires special intermediate representation, which adds to the compile-time cost. GlobalISel) instead operates directly on MIR (Machine IR), which is used as a machine-specific intermediate representation in LLVM.

   b. Modularity. GlobalISel tries to reuse the code as much as possible, reducing the size of the code base.

c. Better context awareness. SelectionDAG operates on separate basic block, thus losing some information about the context, while GlobalISel operates in the context of the whole function, allowing more global information to be used for better code emission.

2. Instruction scheduling. At this stage, the compiler takes the DAG of instructions and reorders them to execute in the optimal order. This results in a sequence of MachineInstrs. This stage is essential for vector operations, as effective scheduling can greatly affect performance due to latencies and throughput associated with vector instructions.

3. SSA-based Machine Code Optimizations. This optional stage performs optimizations on the SSA-form of the machine code.

4. Register Allocation. This stage involves mapping the infinite virtual registers to the actual physical registers of the target. For RISC-V vectors, this required managing the allocation of vector registers, which possess different characteristics compared to scalar registers. It also may generate spill code in this stage if there are not enough physical registers available.

5. Prolog/Epilog Insertion. After determining the required stack space (for spills and allocas), the compiler can insert the function's prolog and epilog. For vector code, this often includes saving and restoring vector registers while making any necessary adjustments to the stack to ensure proper alignment for vector operations.

CHAPTER 4   RISC-V RVV SPECIFIC LLVM-BASED OPTIMIZATIONS

6. Late Machine Code Optimizations. These are final adjustments that the compiler can apply to the "final" machine code. For vector code, it may reschedule the spill code to reduce its performance impact or apply target-specific peephole optimizations for vector instructions.

7. Code Emission. In this last stage, the compiler generates the actual machine code or assembly. For RISC-V vectors, this involved implementing the encoding of all new vector instructions and assembler directives.

Also, RISC-V Vector extension requires some extra support for code generation. One of the things, that requires special processing is support for fixed-length vectors. Fixed vectors should be expressed through a scalable vector idiom for RISC-V Vector extension. This requires special custom lowering for fixed vector length vectors. To do this correctly, fixed-length vectors are inserted into a special scalable "container" via insert_subvector nodes in the SelectionDAG. The type of the "container" value is chosen such that its minimum size may contain whole given fixed-length vector type (see getContainerForFixedLengthVector function in lib/Target/RISCV/RISCVISelLowering.cpp file). Then the requested operations are performed on the "container" node instead of the original fixed-length vector node. The nodes for the "containers" and some of the RVV instructions are defined in lib/Target/RISCV/RISCVInstrInfoVVLPatterns.td. These nodes (called VL nodes) have a special AVL operand, which is set to the size of the fixed-length vector explicitly. The result of the operations on the "containers" is then extracted via extract_subvector node and is written to the resulting fixed-length vector. Listing 4-6 and Listing 4-7 show the example of such transformations.

CHAPTER 4   RISC-V RVV SPECIFIC LLVM-BASED OPTIMIZATIONS

Listing 4-6. Original MIR code.

```
t2: v4i32 = mul t0, t1 # t0, t1 and t2 are 4 x vectors of i32
elements
```

Later optimization passes will remove these extra insert_/extract_ subvector nodes and only actual operations on the real VLA vectors will remain in the code.

Listing 4-7. Transformed MIR code.

```
t3: nxv2i32,ch = CopyFromReg t0, Register:nxv2i32 %0 # insert_
subvector for t0
t4: nxv2i32,ch = CopyFromReg t1, Register:nxv2i32 %1 # insert_
subvector for t1
t5: nxv2i1 = RISCVISD::VMSET_VL Constant:i64<4> # set VL to 4
t6: nxv2i32 = RISCVISD::MUL_VL t3, t4, undef:nxv2i32, t5,
Constant:i64<4> # mul on scalable vectors of 4 elements
t7: v4i32 = extract_subvector t6, Constant:i64<0>
```

Something similar happens also with the VP intrinsics. If they operate with the fixed vector length vectors, these vectors are inserted into scalable "containers" at first and the VP intrinsic is lowered to a special VL version of the RISC-V Vector node.

Current infrastructure does not allow to immediately emit the code with the correct vector length and vector type. To do it correctly, RISC-V backend defines the whole set of so-called pseudo instructions. These pseudo instructions are defined for each LMUL and include masked and unmasked versions. Listing 4-8 demonstrates how the backend handles it.

Listing 4-8. MIR pseudo instruction for MUL instruction.

```
%rd:vrm4 = PseudoVMUL_VV_M4_MASK %passthru:vrm4(tied-def 0),
%rs2:vrm4, %%rs1:vrm4, mask:$v0, %avl:gpr, sew:imm, policy:imm
```

Here it defines a pseudo MUL instruction for masked MUL instruction with LMUL 4. SEW and policy are passed as parameters and later will be used as the operands of the actual vsetvli instructions.

Also, some special tuning of the register allocated is required. For RISC-V target with RVV support, the register allocator is executed twice. At first, it tries to allocate the registers for the vector operations; then special RISCVInsertVSETVLI is called to optimize insertion and use of vsetvli instructions, and then the register allocator for the scalar operations is called. Such three-step approach is required because it vsetvli instructions creation may require the creation of a new virtual scalar register. But execution of RISCVInsertVSETVLI pass after vector register allocation phase reduces the number of constraints for the machine scheduler. This is important, as the scheduler cannot schedule instructions beyond vsetvli instructions, and it also enables the generation of additional vector pseudos instructions during spilling or constant rematerialization.

The vector register class defines four groups of virtual registers:

1. VR for registers v0, v1, etc., which is used when LMLUL<=1 or the mask register (v0) is required.

2. VRM2 for vectors with LMUL=2, i.e., v0, v2, etc. Register groups are encoded as v0m2, v2m2, etc.

3. VRM4 for vectors with LMUL=4, i.e., v0, v4, etc. Register groups are encoded as v0m4, v4m4, etc.

4. VRM8 for vectors with LMUL=8, i.e., v0, v8, etc. Register groups are encoded as v0m8, v8m8, etc.

RISCVInsertVSETVLI then tries to insert required vsetvli instructions, also performing some optimizations. It performs dataflow analysis and tries to emit as few vsetvli instructions as possible. It relies on VLOptimizer pass (implemented in lib/Target/RISCV/RISCVVLOptimizer.cpp), which

CHAPTER 4 RISC-V RVV SPECIFIC LLVM-BASED OPTIMIZATIONS

performs this analysis and reduces the total number of vsetvl instructions, which allows to improve the overall performance. Listing 4-9 and Listing 4-10 show how it works.

Listing 4-9. Original LLVM IR code.

```
%1 = load <4 x i32>, ptr %in, align 4
%2 = or <4 x i32> %1, <i32 9, i32 9, i32 9, i32 9>
store <4 x i32> %2, ptr %in, align 4
```

is lowered to something as follows.

Listing 4-10. Generated assembly

```
#without optimization of vset(i)vli
vsetivli zero, 4, e32, m1, ta, ma
vle32.v v9, (a0)
vsetivli zero, 4, e32, m1, ta, ma
vor.vi v8, v9, 9
vsetivli zero, 4, e32, m1, ta, ma
vse32.v v8, (a0)

#with optimization of vset(i)vli
vsetivli zero, 4, e32, m1, ta, ma
vle32.v v8, (a0)
vor.vi v8, v8, 9
vse32.v v8, (a0)
```

So, in general, the whole code generation process can be illustrated in Listing 4-11.

Listing 4-11. Code generation process from LLVM IR down to assembly.

```
%2 = or <4 x i32> %1, <i32 9, i32 9, i32 9, i32 9> # LLVM IR
...
t7: v4i32 = BUILD_VECTOR Constant:i32<9>, Constant:i32<9>,
Constant:i32<9>, Constant:i32<9>
t8: v4i32 = or t5, t7                 # SelectionDAG
...
t14: nxv2i32 = insert_subvector undef:nxv2i32, t5,
Constant:i64<0>
t7: v4i32 = BUILD_VECTOR Constant:i64<9>, Constant:i64<9>,
Constant:i64<9>, Constant:i64<9>
t15: nxv2i32 = insert_subvector undef:nxv2i32, t7,
Constant:i64<0>
t17: nxv2i1 = RISCVISD::VMSET_VL Constant:i64<4>
t18: nxv2i32 = RISCVISD::OR_VL t14, t15, undef:nxv2i32, t17,
Constant:i64<4>
t19: v4i32 = extract_subvector t18, Constant:i64<0>        #
Canonicalization of fixed-length vectors
...
t40: nxv2i32 = PseudoVOR_VI_M1 Register:nxv2i32 $noreg,
t41, TargetConstant:i64<9>, TargetConstant:i64<4>,
TargetConstant:i64<5>, TargetConstant:i64<1> # Instruction
Selection
...
dead $x0 = PseudoVSETIVLI 4, 208, implicit-def $vl, implicit-
def $vtype
```

CHAPTER 4   RISC-V RVV SPECIFIC LLVM-BASED OPTIMIZATIONS

```
$v8 = PseudoVOR_VI_M1 undef renamable $v8(tied-def 0), killed
renamable $v8, 9, 4, 5, 1, implicit $vl, implicit $vtype
#   RISCVInsertVSETVLI
...
vsetivli»-zero, 4, e32, m1, ta, ma
vor.vi»-v8, v8, 9      # code emission
```

Summary

In this chapter you learned

- How LLVM supports the RISC-V Vector Extension (RVV) 1.0 using scalable vector types.

- That scalable vectors are expressed as <vscale x n x ty>, where their size is determined at runtime, making them a natural fit for RVV's vector-length agnostic design.

- How LLVM represents mask vectors as scalable <vscale x n x i1> types, enabling predicated execution and conditional operations.

- That LLVM applies a wide range of target-independent optimizations that benefit RVV code.

- That TargetTransformInfo (TTI) plays a central role in guiding LLVM optimizations for RVV, modeling instruction costs, legality checks, and transformation constraints specific to RISC-V.

- The structure of LLVM's target-independent code generator, including target description interfaces, code representation classes, MC layer classes, target-independent algorithms, target-specific implementations, and JIT components.

CHAPTER 4   RISC-V RVV SPECIFIC LLVM-BASED OPTIMIZATIONS

- How the code generation pipeline works for RVV, how LLVM lowers fixed-length vectors into RVV's scalable model using "container" types, insert_subvector and extract_subvector transformations, and pseudo-instructions for SEW/LMUL variants.

- The special role of RISCVInsertVSETVLI and VLOptimizer passes in minimizing the number of vsetvli instructions through dataflow analysis, reducing overhead and improving performance.

CHAPTER 5

LLVM Loop Vectorizer

The Loop Vectorizer is a well-known optimization technique designed to enhance performance by transforming scalar code into vectorized form. This technique specifically targets loops, which are often the most time-consuming constructs in a program. By replacing scalar instructions with vector instructions, loop vectorization can significantly improve execution time.

The Loop Vectorizer relies on the loop detection infrastructure implemented in LLVM. The core item of the loop supporting infrastructure is LoopInfo. It provides an interface for enumerating all top-level loops (i.e., those not nested within other loops). From these top-level loops, you can traverse the tree of sub-loops. LoopInfo uses standard loop definitions and relies on specific terminology (see Figure 5-1):

(a) An Entering Block (or Loop Predecessor) is a non-loop node that has an edge leading into the loop, typically to the loop header. If there is only one entering block and its only edge is to the header, it is also called the loop's preheader. The preheader dominates the loop without being part of the loop.

(b) A Latch is a loop node that has an edge leading to the header.

(c) A Backedge is an edge from a latch to the header.

(d) An Exiting Edge is an edge from inside the loop to a node outside of the loop. The source block of such an edge is called an Exiting Block, and its target is an Exit Block.

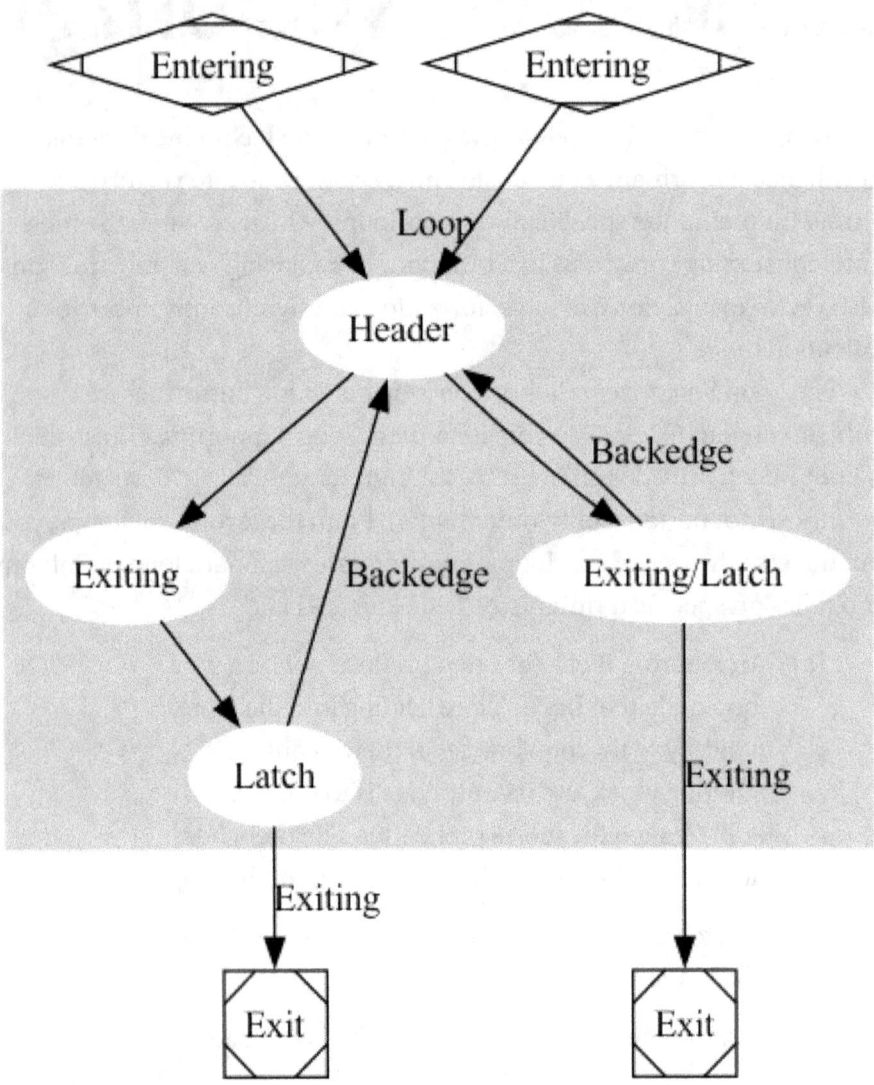

Figure 5-1. *Canonical loop form*

CHAPTER 5   LLVM LOOP VECTORIZER

The Loop Vectorizer adds the definition for a middle block, which serves as an exit block for the vectorized loop and a (pre)header for the scalar loop remainder. This middle block checks if all required iterations are covered by the vector version of the loop and executes the scalar remainder if necessary.

Listing 5-1. Loop vectorizer pass invocation.

```
$ opt -S -mtriple=riscv64-unknown-linux-gnu -mattr="+v"
--passes=loop-vectorize test.ll
```

Listing 5-2. Original code.

```
define void @foo(ptr noalias %a, ptr noalias %b, i64 %N) {
entry:
  br label %for.body

for.body:
  %iv = phi i64 [ 0, %entry ], [ %iv.next, %for.body ]
  %arrayidx = getelementptr inbounds i32, ptr %b, i64 %iv
  %0 = load i32, ptr %arrayidx, align 4
  %arrayidx4 = getelementptr inbounds i32, ptr %a, i64 %iv
  store i32 %0, ptr %arrayidx4, align 4
  %iv.next = add nuw nsw i64 %iv, 1
  %exitcond.not = icmp eq i64 %iv.next, %N
  br i1 %exitcond.not, label %for.cond.cleanup, label %for.body

for.cond.cleanup:
  ret void
}
```

Listing 5-3. Vectorized code.

```
define void @foo(ptr noalias nocapture writeonly %a, ptr
noalias nocapture readonly %b, i64 %N) {
```

CHAPTER 5   LLVM LOOP VECTORIZER

```llvm
entry:
  %0 = tail call i64 @llvm.vscale.i64()
  %1 = shl i64 %0, 2
  %min.iters.check = icmp ugt i64 %1, %N
  br i1 %min.iters.check, label %scalar.ph, label %vector.ph

vector.ph:                                        ; preds = %entry
  %n.mod.vf = urem i64 %N, %1
  %n.vec = sub i64 %N, %n.mod.vf
  br label %vector.body

vector.body:                    ; preds = %vector.body, %vector.ph
  %index = phi i64 [ 0, %vector.ph ], [ %index.next, %vector.body ]
  %2 = getelementptr inbounds i32, ptr %b, i64 %index
  %wide.load = load <vscale x 4 x i32>, ptr %2, align 4
  %3 = getelementptr inbounds i32, ptr %a, i64 %index
  store <vscale x 4 x i32> %wide.load, ptr %3, align 4
  %index.next = add nuw i64 %index, %1
  %4 = icmp eq i64 %index.next, %n.vec
  br i1 %4, label %middle.block, label %vector.body, !llvm.loop !0

middle.block:                                ; preds = %vector.body
  %cmp.n = icmp eq i64 %n.mod.vf, 0
  br i1 %cmp.n, label %for.cond.cleanup, label %scalar.ph

scalar.ph:                          ; preds = %middle.block, %entry
  %bc.resume.val = phi i64 [ %n.vec, %middle.block ], [ 0, %entry ]
  %5 = shl i64 %bc.resume.val, 2
  %scevgep = getelementptr i8, ptr %a, i64 %5
  %scevgep1 = getelementptr i8, ptr %b, i64 %5
```

```
  %6 = sub i64 %N, %bc.resume.val
  %7 = shl i64 %6, 2
  tail call void @llvm.memcpy.p0.p0.i64(ptr align 4 %scevgep,
  ptr align 4 %scevgep1, i64 %7, i1 false)
  br label %for.cond.cleanup

for.cond.cleanup:                  ; preds = %scalar.ph, %middle.block
  ret void
}
```

In Listing 5-1, Listing 5-2, and Listing 5-3, you can see the main blocks handled by the loop vectorizer. The entry block contains a TripCount check, which determines whether the vector loop should be executed or if the scalar version should run instead. The vector preheader (vector.ph) normalizes the number of vector loop iterations to the number of elements that can be handled in a single vector register. The vector body (vector.body) contains the vectorized version of the loop. The middle block (middle.block) checks if the remaining iterations must be executed by the scalar loop remainder, which contains the scalar code for these iterations.

Note that this example does not use RISC-V-specific code for code emission. Instead, it executes the vector body in the same manner as x86 or ARM-based processors, meaning it assumes the vector register length is constant across all loop iterations. It means, that this code must include a scalar loop remainder to handle cases where N rem VLMAX != 0. The assembly for this code is shown in Listing 5-4.

Listing 5-4. Assembly for vectorized code.

```
foo:                                # @foo
    .cfi_startproc
# %bb.0:                            # %entry
    csrr    a5, vlenb
    srli    a4, a5, 1
```

CHAPTER 5   LLVM LOOP VECTORIZER

```
        bgeu    a2, a4, .LBB0_2
# %bb.1:
        li      a3, 0
        j       .LBB0_5
.LBB0_2:                                        # %vector.ph
        neg     a3, a4
        and     a3, a2, a3
        slli    a5, a5, 1
        mv      a6, a1
        mv      a7, a0
        mv      t0, a3
.LBB0_3:                                        # %vector.body
                                                # =>This Inner Loop
Header: Depth=1
        vl2re32.v   v8, (a6)
        vs2r.v      v8, (a7)
        sub     t0, t0, a4
        add     a7, a7, a5
        add     a6, a6, a5
        bnez    t0, .LBB0_3
# %bb.4:                                        # %middle.block
        beq     a2, a3, .LBB0_7
.LBB0_5:                                        # %scalar.ph
        sub     a2, a2, a3
        slli    a3, a3, 2
        add     a0, a0, a3
        add     a1, a1, a3
.LBB0_6:                                        # %for.body
                                                # =>This Inner Loop
Header: Depth=1
        lw      a3, 0(a1)
        sw      a3, 0(a0)
```

174

```
        addi    a2, a2, -1
        addi    a0, a0, 4
        addi    a1, a1, 4
        bnez    a2, .LBB0_6
.LBB0_7:                                # %for.cond.cleanup
        ret
.Lfunc_end0:
```

In this assembly code

(a) The entry block checks if the total number of iterations (TripCount) is less than the vector length (VLMAX). If so, it jumps to the scalar loop.

(b) The vector.ph (label .LBB0_2) block prepares the number of iterations for the vectorized loop by aligning it to the nearest multiple of VLMAX.

(c) The vector.body (label .LBB0_3) block contains the vectorized loop instructions, which process VLMAX elements per iteration.

(d) The middle.block checks if there are any remaining iterations that need to be handled by the scalar loop.

(e) The scalar loop for.body (label .LBB0_6) processes these remaining iterations one by one.

(f) The end (label .LBB0_7) block marks the end of the loop.

This approach ensures that all iterations are processed correctly, using vector instructions when possible and falling back to scalar instructions for any remaining iterations.

CHAPTER 5 LLVM LOOP VECTORIZER

Instead, the loop vectorizer can generate vector code specific to the RISC-V target, leveraging its length agnostic vectorization feature. This approach allows the vectorizer to dynamically adjust the vector register length, optimizing performance without the need for a scalar loop remainder, as shown in Listing 5-5, Listing 5-6, and Listing 5-7.

Listing 5-5. Loop vectorizer pass invocation.

```
$ opt -S -mtriple=riscv64-unknown-linux-gnu -mattr="+v"
--passes=loop-vectorize test.ll -force-tail-folding-style=data-
with-evl -prefer-predicate-over-epilogue=predicate-dont-
vectorize
```

Listing 5-6. Vectorized code.

```
define void @foo(ptr noalias nocapture writeonly %a, ptr
noalias nocapture readonly %b, i64 %N) {
entry:
  br label %vector.body

vector.body:
; preds = %vector.body, %entry
  %index = phi i64 [ 0, %entry ], [ %index.evl.next,
%vector.body ]
  %0 = sub i64 %N, %index
  %1 = tail call i32 @llvm.experimental.get.vector.length.
  i64(i64 %0, i32 2, i1 true)
  %2 = getelementptr inbounds i32, ptr %b, i64 %index
  %vp.op.load = tail call <vscale x 2 x i32> @llvm.vp.load.
  nxv2i32.p0(ptr align 4 %2, <vscale x 2 x i1> shufflevector
  (<vscale x 2 x i1> insertelement (<vscale x 2 x i1> poison,
  i1 true, i64 0), <vscale x 2 x i1> poison, <vscale x 2 x i32>
  zeroinitializer), i32 %1)
```

```
%3 = getelementptr inbounds i32, ptr %a, i64 %index
tail call void @llvm.vp.store.nxv2i32.p0(<vscale x 2 x i32>
%vp.op.load, ptr align 4 %3, <vscale x 2 x i1> shufflevector
(<vscale x 2 x i1> insertelement (<vscale x 2 x i1> poison,
i1 true, i64 0), <vscale x 2 x i1> poison, <vscale x 2 x i32>
zeroinitializer), i32 %1)
%4 = zext i32 %1 to i64
%index.evl.next = add i64 %index, %4
%5 = icmp eq i64 %index.evl.next, %N
br i1 %5, label %for.cond.cleanup, label %vector.body,
!llvm.loop !0

for.cond.cleanup:                                 ; preds =
%vector.body
  ret void
}
```

Listing 5-7. Assembly for vectorized code.

```
foo:                                    # @foo
# %bb.0:                                 # %entry
        li      a3, 0
.LBB0_1:                                 # %vector.body
                                         # =>This Inner Loop
Header: Depth=1
        sub     a4, a2, a3
        vsetvli a4, a4, e8, mf4, ta, ma
        slli    a5, a3, 2
        add     a6, a1, a5
        vle32.v v8, (a6)
        add     a5, a0, a5
```

```
            add        a3, a3, a4
            vse32.v v8, (a5)
            bne        a3, a2, .LBB0_1
# %bb.2:                                    # %for.cond.cleanup
            ret
```

This example demonstrates RISC-V's Explicit Vector Length (EVL)-based vector length agnostic (VLA) vectorization support, dynamically adjusting vector lengths to maximize efficiency and minimize the need for scalar remainders. The EVL feature allows the vectorizer to handle loops more flexibly, ensuring that all iterations are processed optimally.

Design of the Loop Vectorizer

The LLVM Loop Vectorizer is based on VPlan representation to enhance loop vectorization. A VPlan is an explicit model that describes a loop for vectorization using specialized VPInstructions/VPRecipes instead of original LLVM IR instructions. These representations are then used for legalizing the vectorization by introducing recipes for reductions and interleaved groups, optimizing the plans by removing dead recipes, and incorporating Explicit Vector Length support and vectorization-factor specific optimizations.

VPlan is a high-level abstraction built on top of LLVM IR, which follows several key principles:

1. Nonmodification of Input IR. Building and manipulating VPlans should not alter the input IR. If vectorization is deemed unfeasible (e.g., not legal or not profitable), the original LLVM IR code remains as is. Only VPlans are modified and discarded if required.

2. Aligned Cost and Code Generation. Each VPlan must keep both cost estimation and final code generation in synchronization. This ensures that the estimated cost of the resulting vector code aligns with the actual emitted code.

3. Support for Advanced Constructs. VPlans should handle complex constructs like outer loop vectorization, SLP vectorization, function vectorization, and their combinations. They must accurately estimate and generate correct vector code for these constructs when they are more advantageous than simple inner loop vectorization.

4. Vectorization of Idioms. VPlans should support vectorizing of idioms such as interleaved groups (segmented loads/stores support), strided loads/stores, etc.

5. Multiple Vectorization Candidates. VPlans must accommodate different decisions regarding vectorization factors, unrolling factors, and approaches to vectorizing nested loops (e.g., outer vs. inner loop vectorization). They should be able to construct multiple candidates, discard nonviable ones, select the most performance-efficient plan, and generate vector code for the optimal candidate.

The whole process of the VPlan-based vectorization includes several stages:

1. Before vectorization, the Loop Vectorizer performs legality checks to ensure the loop can be safely vectorized.

2. Builds the initial VPlans, which represent the loop using VPInstructions/VPRecipes.

3. Legalizes the vectorization by introducing special recipes for reductions and interleaved groups.

4. Optimizes the VPlans by removing dead recipes and incorporating Explicit Vector Length support and other vectorization-specific optimizations.

5. Estimates the cost of the generated VPlans and selects the best one.

6. Emits the code for the best VPlan candidate, removing the original scalar loop, if possible.

The low-level design of the VPlan-based Loop Vectorizer includes several basic classes:

(a) LoopVectorizationPlanner serves as the central core for loop vectorization. It is responsible for constructing, optimizing, and managing VPlans (Vectorization Plans) for a given loop or loop nest. The planner can generate multiple VPlans, evaluate their efficiency, and ultimately select the most promising one for the code emission.

(b) VPRecipeBase is an abstract class representing a transformation recipe. Each recipe encapsulates the logic to convert one or more input LLVM IR instructions (ingredients) into a sequence of vectorized LLVM IR instructions. This abstraction provides modular and extensible vectorization strategies.

(c) VPValue is the class, describing def-use relations in VPlan. Being immediately instantiated represents constants or live-in values.

(d) VPUser models entities that consume VPValues as operands, establishing natural data dependencies.

(e) VPDef is a class to describe the entity that defines zero or more VPValues, used by the recipes to represent multiple defined VPValues.

(f) VPInstruction is a recipe, assigned a single opcode and optional flags, that represents single LLVM IR instruction with the given opcode or simple idiom, which does not require ingredients. Provides a direct mapping between scalar and vector operations.

(g) VPBlockBase is a pure virtual class and a building block of the VPlan, which models hierarchical control flow relations.

(h) VPBasicBlock is a subclass of VPBlockBase and represents a block of one or more recipes, resulting in the output LLVM IR basic block and its instructions.

(i) VPRegionBlock is a subclass of the VPBlockBase and models a graph, consisting of VPBasicBlocks and VPRegionBlocks for the purpose of effective reuse during output LLVM IR emission. Allows to model scalar and predicated instructions for multiple vectorization factors and unrolling factors.

It's important to note that while the current implementation focuses primarily on innermost loop vectorization, ongoing research and development efforts are exploring the vectorization of more complex loop structures. The modular design of the VPlan-based Loop Vectorizer lays the groundwork for these future improvements.

As we progress through this chapter, we will examine how these core classes interact to transform scalar loops into efficient vectorized code, unlocking the potential for significant performance improvements.

Legality Checks and Analysis

The preliminary loop vectorization analysis is a critical phase in the compilation process, which includes a series of complex checks to determine the feasibility of loop vectorization. This stage is essential for identifying loops that can benefit from vectorization while ensuring correctness and efficiency.

The analysis begins by verifying that the loop is in the Loop Simplify Form, a canonical representation characterized by a single preheader and a single backedge (LoopVectorizationLegality::canVectorizeLoopCFG). This simplified structure is the key loop form for subsequent analysis and transformation steps.

Next, the compiler assesses the loop's compatibility with IF-conversion, a technique that transforms control flow into data flow (LoopVectorizationLegality::canVectorizeWithIfConvert()). Loops qualifying for IF-conversion either consist of a single basic block or contain instructions that can be vectorized using predication or masking. Currently, predication support is limited to loads, stores, standard instruction operations, and intrinsics with masked vector variants, though future extensions may add user-defined functions annotated with OpenMP SIMD directives or similar constructs.

The analysis proceeds to evaluate individual instructions within the loop body. This step ensures that all instructions operate on vectorizable types and that PHI nodes are either part of reduction operations or can be safely IF-converted (see LoopVectorizationLegality::canVectorizeInstrs()).

A critical aspect of vectorization legality is the examination of memory access patterns and dependencies. The compiler scans memory operations to identify potentially nonvectorizable instructions, such as

(a) Complex memory instructions beyond simple loads and stores (atomic, volatile, etc.)

(b) Memory accesses with ambiguous aliasing

(c) Loop-carried dependencies that cannot be resolved through runtime checks

The LoopVectorizationLegality::canVectorizeMemory() function performs this complex analysis, determining whether memory operations can be safely vectorized or if runtime checks can eliminate potential dependencies.

By systematically evaluating these aspects, the preliminary analysis stage provides a base for subsequent vectorization transformations. It effectively filters out loops that are not suitable for vectorization while identifying promising candidates for further optimization. This approach ensures that the vectorization process focuses on loops where it can yield substantial performance improvements without compromising program correctness (see Listing 5-8).

Listing 5-8. Analysis for the vectorizable instructions.

```
for (BasicBlock *BB : all loop blocks) {
  for (Instruction &I : *BB) {
    if (is simple load or store (I)) {
      save access;
      collect strided accesses if enabled;
```

```
      continue;
    }
    if (non-vectorizable function call)
      return false;
    if (instruction may write to memory)
      return false;
  }
}
for (StoreInst *ST : collected stores) {
  collect addresses if users did not force vectorization;
}
for (LoadInst *LD : collected loads) {
  collect addresses if users did not force vectorization;
}
Go over all accesses and check if runtime checks required and
build sets of  dependency check candidates
if (Dep check is required and deps cannot be resolved with
runtime checks)
    return false;
return true;
```

In the context of loop vectorization, two primary categories of dependencies can prevent the safe transformation of a scalar loop into its vectorized version: data dependencies and control dependencies. Understanding these dependencies is important for implementing effective vectorization strategies and ensuring the correctness of the transformed code. Data dependencies appear when multiple iterations of a loop access the same memory locations. These dependencies can be classified into three main types: read-after-write (RAW), write-after-read (WAR), and write-after-write (WAW) conflicts.

1. Read-After-Write (RAW) Dependencies, also known as true dependencies, may occur when a loop iteration reads a value that was written by a previous iteration. In other words, the second instruction reads a value that the first instruction writes. This dependency enforces an ordering between the instructions: the read must not occur before the write is complete, or the program may read an incorrect (stale) value.

2. Write-After-Read (WAR) Dependencies, also called antidependencies, may happen when a loop iteration writes to a memory location that was read by a previous iteration. The key issue here is that the write must not happen before the read, or the program may read the wrong (new) value instead of the original one.

3. Write-After-Write (WAW) Dependencies, also called output dependencies, may occur when multiple iterations write to the same memory location. The key requirement is that the writes must occur in the original program order to preserve the correct final value.

Control dependencies arise from conditional statements within the loop that affect the execution path of subsequent iterations. Control dependencies don't involve conflicts over data like the data dependencies, but they constrain instruction ordering due to the program's logical control flow (see Listing 5-9 and Listing 5-10).

Listing 5-9. Examples of the dependencies

```
// read-after-write - true dependence - cannot be vectorized
for (int I = 1; I < N; ++I)
   Arr[I] = Arr[I-1] + I;

// write-after-read - anti dependence - can be safely
vectorized
for (int I = 0; I < N - 1; ++I)
   Arr[I] = Arr[I+1] + 6;

// write-after-write - output dependence - cannot be vectorized
directly, but can be vectorized after loop distribution
for (int I = 0; I < N - 1; ++I) {
   Arr[I] = I;
   Arr[I+1]=B[I] * 2;
}

// control dependence, can be vectorized with masking if Arr
and B do not alias
for (int I = 0; I < N; ++I) {
   if (Arr[I] == 0)
     Arr[I] = I;
   B[I] = Arr[I] * 3;
}
```

Listing 5-10. Compilation and the diagnostics

```
$ clang --target=riscv64-unknown-linux -mcpu=sifive-x280
-Rpass=loop-vectorize -Rpass-missed=loop-vectorize -Rpass-
analysis=loop-vectorize test.c -c -O3 -mllvm -force-tail-
folding-style=data-with-evl -mllvm -prefer-predicate-over-
epilogue=predicate-dont-vectorize -c
```

test.c:4:12: remark: loop not vectorized: unsafe dependent
memory operations in loop. Use #pragma clang loop
distribute(enable) to allow loop distribution to attempt to
isolate the offending operations into a separate loop
Backward loop carried data dependence. Memory location is
the same as accessed at test.c:4:14 [-Rpass-analysis=loop-
vectorize]
4 | Arr[I] = Arr[I - 1] + I;
| ^
test.c:3:3: remark: loop not vectorized [-Rpass-missed=loop-
vectorize]
3 | for (int I = 1; I < N; ++I)
| ^
test.c:7:3: remark: the cost-model indicates that interleaving
is not beneficial [-Rpass-analysis=loop-vectorize]
7 | for (int I = 0; I < N - 1; ++I)
| ^
test.c:7:3: remark: vectorized loop (vectorization width:
vscale x 4, interleaved count: 1) [-Rpass=loop-vectorize]
test.c:13:13: remark: loop not vectorized: unsafe dependent
memory operations in loop. Use #pragma clang loop
distribute(enable) to allow loop distribution to attempt to
isolate the offending operations into a separate loop
Backward loop carried data dependence. Memory location is
the same as accessed at test.c:12:5 [-Rpass-analysis=loop-
vectorize]
13 | Arr[I + 1] = B[I] * 2;
| ^
test.c:11:3: remark: loop not vectorized [-Rpass-missed=loop-
vectorize]
11 | for (int I = 0; I < N - 1; ++I) {

CHAPTER 5   LLVM LOOP VECTORIZER

```
  | ^
test.c:16:3: remark: the cost-model indicates that interleaving
is not beneficial [-Rpass-analysis=loop-vectorize]
16 | for (int I = 0; I < N; ++I) {
  | ^
test.c:16:3: remark: vectorized loop (vectorization width:
vscale x 4, interleaved count: 1) [-Rpass=loop-vectorize]
```

These dependencies represent significant challenges to loop vectorization:

(a) Data dependencies may require scalar operations or complex data shuffling, potentially negating the performance benefits of vectorization.

(b) Control dependencies might require predicated execution or mask operations, which can increase code complexity and potentially reduce vectorization efficiency. RISC-V Vector Extensions (RVV) allows to effectively express such operations, reducing the negative effect of the control dependencies.

(c) Some dependencies, particularly certain types of RAW dependencies, may completely prevent safe vectorization without substantial loop restructuring.

The LoopVectorizationLegality class functions as a sentinel, checking the code for potential vectorization hazards. It performs exhaustive analysis to identify aliasing risks, data dependencies, and control flow issues that could affect successful vectorization. Upon completion of this analysis, the class prepares the data for inserting runtime checks that should help to resolve these issues at the runtime at the cost of newly inserted scalar instructions, executed in the loop preheader. In the

CHAPTER 5 LLVM LOOP VECTORIZER

subsequent phase, the loop vectorizer uses the results of this preparatory work to implement a multiversioning strategy. This strategy is based on the emission of two variants of the loop:

(a) The original, unmodified loop

(b) An optimized (and vectorized) version that assumes nonaliasing memory accesses

This dual-loop structure enables dynamic selection between the safe, original implementation and the potentially faster, vectorized version based on runtime conditions. The system can thus adapt to different data patterns, maximizing performance while maintaining correctness. The examples of multiversioning are shown in Listing 5-11, Listing 5-12, and Listing 5-13.

Listing 5-11. Loop mutiversioning example.

```
// original loop
for (int I = 0; I < N; ++I) {
   if (Arr[I] == 0)
     Arr[I] = I;
   B[I] = Arr[I] * 3;
}

// mutiversioned loop
if (Arr and B do not alias (overlap)) {
  for (int I = 0; I < N; I+=VF) { // the vectorized version of
the loop
    Cmp = Arr[I:I+VF-1] == <0, .., 0>
    Store <I, I+1, ..., I+VF>, Arr[I:I+VF-1], Cmp // Masked
    store, only elements with mask set to true(1) will be
    written, with mask 0 remain unshanged
    B[I:I+VF-1] = Arr[I:I+VF-1] * <3, ..., 3>;
  }
```

```
} else {
  for (int I = 0; I < N; ++I) { // this version remains scalar
    if (Arr[I] == 0)
      Arr[I] = I;
    B[I] = Arr[I] * 3;
  }
}
```

Listing 5-12. LLVM IR code for loop multiversioning.

```
  %cmp16 = icmp sgt i32 %N, 0
  ; check if the loop has at least one iteration
  br i1 %cmp16, label %for.body.preheader, label %for.
  cond.cleanup

for.body.preheader:
; preds = %entry
; check for aliasing of Arr and B
  %wide.trip.count = zext nneg i32 %N to i64
  %0 = shl nuw nsw i64 %wide.trip.count, 2
  %scevgep = getelementptr i8, ptr %Arr, i64 %0         ; Arr + N
  %scevgep19 = getelementptr i8, ptr %B, i64 %0         ; B + N
  %bound0 = icmp ugt ptr %scevgep19, %Arr
  ; bound0 = B+N > Arr
  %bound1 = icmp ugt ptr %scevgep, %B
  ; bound1 = Arr + N > B
  %found.conflict = and i1 %bound0, %bound1
  ; aliasing = bound0 && bound1
  br i1 %found.conflict, label %for.body, label %vector.ph
  ; if (aliasing) goto scalar loop else goto vector loop

vector.ph:                                              ; preds =
%for.body.preheader                                     ; vector loop
```

```
  %1 = tail call <vscale x 8 x i32> @llvm.experimental.
  stepvector.nxv8i32()
  br label %vector.body

vector.body:                                      ; preds =
%vector.body, %vector.ph
  %evl.based.iv = phi i64 [ 0, %vector.ph ], [ %index.evl.next,
  %vector.body ]
  %vec.ind = phi <vscale x 8 x i32> [ %1, %vector.ph ], [ %vec.
  ind.next, %vector.body ]
  %2 = sub i64 %wide.trip.count, %evl.based.iv
  %3 = tail call i32 @llvm.experimental.get.vector.length.
  i64(i64 %2, i32 8, i1 true)
  %4 = getelementptr i32, ptr %Arr, i64 %evl.based.iv
  %vp.op.load = tail call <vscale x 8 x i32> @llvm.vp.load.
  nxv8i32.p0(ptr align 4 %4, <vscale x 8 x i1> shufflevector
  (<vscale x 8 x i1> insertelement (<vscale x 8 x i1> poison,
  i1 true, i64 0), <vscale x 8 x i1> poison, <vscale x 8 x i32>
  zeroinitializer), i32 %3)
  %vp.op.icmp = tail call <vscale x 8 x i1> @llvm.vp.icmp.
  nxv8i32(<vscale x 8 x i32> %vp.op.load, <vscale x 8 x
  i32> zeroinitializer, metadata !"eq", <vscale x 8 x i1>
  shufflevector (<vscale x 8 x i1> insertelement (<vscale x
  8 x i1> poison, i1 true, i64 0), <vscale x 8 x i1> poison,
  <vscale x 8 x i32> zeroinitializer), i32 %3)
  tail call void @llvm.vp.store.nxv8i32.p0(<vscale x 8 x
  i32> %vec.ind, ptr align 4 %4, <vscale x 8 x i1> %vp.
  op.icmp, i32 %3)
  %predphi = tail call <vscale x 8 x i32> @llvm.vp.select.
  nxv8i32(<vscale x 8 x i1> %vp.op.icmp, <vscale x 8 x i32>
  %vec.ind, <vscale x 8 x i32> %vp.op.load, i32 %3)
```

CHAPTER 5   LLVM LOOP VECTORIZER

```
  %vp.op = tail call <vscale x 8 x i32> @llvm.vp.mul.
  nxv8i32(<vscale x 8 x i32> %predphi, <vscale x 8 x i32>
  shufflevector (<vscale x 8 x i32> insertelement (<vscale x
  8 x i32> poison, i32 3, i64 0), <vscale x 8 x i32> poison,
  <vscale x 8 x i32> zeroinitializer), <vscale x 8 x i1>
  shufflevector (<vscale x 8 x i1> insertelement (<vscale x
  8 x i1> poison, i1 true, i64 0), <vscale x 8 x i1> poison,
  <vscale x 8 x i32> zeroinitializer), i32 %3)
  %5 = getelementptr inbounds i32, ptr %B, i64 %evl.based.iv
  tail call void @llvm.vp.store.nxv8i32.p0(<vscale x 8 x i32>
  %vp.op, ptr align 4 %5, <vscale x 8 x i1> shufflevector
  (<vscale x 8 x i1> insertelement (<vscale x 8 x i1> poison,
  i1 true, i64 0), <vscale x 8 x i1> poison, <vscale x 8 x i32>
  zeroinitializer), i32 %3)
  %6 = zext i32 %3 to i64
  %index.evl.next = add i64 %evl.based.iv, %6
  %.splatinsert20 = insertelement <vscale x 8 x i32> poison,
  i32 %3, i64 0
  %.splat21 = shufflevector <vscale x 8 x i32> %.splatinsert20,
  <vscale x 8 x i32> poison, <vscale x 8 x i32> zeroinitializer
  %vec.ind.next = tail call <vscale x 8 x i32> @llvm.vp.add.
  nxv8i32(<vscale x 8 x i32> %vec.ind, <vscale x 8 x i32>
  %.splat21, <vscale x 8 x i1> shufflevector (<vscale x 8
  x i1> insertelement (<vscale x 8 x i1> poison, i1 true,
  i64 0), <vscale x 8 x i1> poison, <vscale x 8 x i32>
  zeroinitializer), i32 %3)
  %7 = icmp eq i64 %index.evl.next, %wide.trip.count
  br i1 %7, label %for.cond.cleanup, label %vector.body

for.cond.cleanup:                                  ; preds =
%vector.body, %if.end, %entry
  ret void
```

```
for.body:                                        ; preds =
%for.body.preheader, %if.end                     ; scalar loop
  %indvars.iv = phi i64 [ %indvars.iv.next, %if.end ], [ 0,
%for.body.preheader ]
  %arrayidx = getelementptr inbounds i32, ptr %Arr, i64
%indvars.iv
  %8 = load i32, ptr %arrayidx, align 4
  %cmp1 = icmp eq i32 %8, 0
  br i1 %cmp1, label %if.then, label %if.end

if.then:
; preds = %for.body
  %9 = trunc i64 %indvars.iv to i32
  store i32 %9, ptr %arrayidx, align 4
  br label %if.end, !dbg !40

if.end:
; preds = %if.then, %for.body
  %10 = phi i32 [ %9, %if.then ], [ %8, %for.body ]
  %mul = mul nsw i32 %10, 3
  %arrayidx7 = getelementptr inbounds i32, ptr %B, i64
%indvars.iv
  store i32 %mul, ptr %arrayidx7, align 4
  %indvars.iv.next = add nuw nsw i64 %indvars.iv, 1
  %exitcond.not = icmp eq i64 %indvars.iv.next, %wide.
trip.count
  br i1 %exitcond.not, label %for.cond.cleanup, label %for.body
```

Listing 5-13. Assembly code for loop mutiversioning.

```
        blez    a2, .LBB0_9
# check if the loop has at least one iteration
# %bb.1:
```

CHAPTER 5   LLVM LOOP VECTORIZER

```
# %for.body.preheader
        sh2add  a3, a2, a1                      # B + N
        bgeu    a0, a3, .LBB0_7
# if (Arr >= B + N) goto vector loop
# %bb.2:                                        # %for.body.preheader
        sh2add  a3, a2, a0                      # Arr + N
        bgeu    a1, a3, .LBB0_7
# if (B >= Arr + N) goto vector loop
# %bb.3:                                        # %for.body.preheader24                              # scalar loop
        li      a3, 0
        j       .LBB0_5
.LBB0_4:                                        # %if.end
                                                #   in Loop: Header=BB0_5 Depth=1
        sh1add  a4, a4, a4
        addi    a0, a0, 4
        addi    a3, a3, 1
        sw      a4, 0(a1)
        addi    a1, a1, 4
        beq     a2, a3, .LBB0_9
.LBB0_5:                                        # %for.body
                                                # =>This Inner Loop Header: Depth=1
        lw      a4, 0(a0)
        bnez    a4, .LBB0_4
# %bb.6:                                        # %if.then
#   in Loop: Header=BB0_5 Depth=1
        mv      a4, a3
        sw      a3, 0(a0)
        j       .LBB0_4
```

CHAPTER 5 LLVM LOOP VECTORIZER

```
.LBB0_7:                # %vector.ph              # vector loop
        vsetvli a4, zero, e32, m4, ta, ma
        vid.v   v8                  # V8 = <0, 1, ..., VLMAX-1>
        li      a3, 0
        li      a6, 3
.LBB0_8:                                           # %vector.body
                             # =>This Inner Loop Header: Depth=1
        sh2add  a5, a3, a0
        sub     a4, a2, a3
        vsetvli a4, a4, e32, m4, ta, ma
        vle32.v v12, (a5)              # V12 = Arr[I:I+VF-1]
        vmseq.vi        v0, v12, 0     # V0 = V12 == 0
        vmerge.vvm      v12, v12, v8, v0
# V12 = (V0 ? V8 : V12) - do this instead of reloading of
Arr[I:I+VF-1] after next store
        vse32.v v8, (a5), v0.t
# store V8, Arr[I:I+VF-1], V0
        sh2add  a5, a3, a1
        add     a3, a3, a4
        vmul.vx v12, v12, a6           # V12 = V12 * <3, ..., 3>
        vadd.vx v8, v8, a4             # V8 = V8 + <I, ..., I>
        vse32.v v12, (a5)              # store V12, B[I:I+VF-1]
        bne     a3, a2, .LBB0_8
.LBB0_9:                                           # %for.cond.cleanup
        ret
```

The compiler then performs a thorough analysis of interleaved memory access patterns within the code. This process involves identifying and grouping related interleaved loads and stores into correlated units. These groups form the basis for efficient vectorization of interleaved accesses.

Vectorization of interleaved accesses is a key feature that significantly enhances performance of RISC-V RVV-enabled targets. By transforming multiple, strided memory operations into unified vector instructions (segmented memory operations in RVV), this optimization can dramatically reduce memory bandwidth requirements and improve instruction throughput. The compiler's ability to recognize and optimize these patterns is often critical in achieving peak performance, especially for algorithms that operate on noncontiguous data structures or perform strided data access (see Listing 5-14).

Listing 5-14. Interleaved memory accesses example.

```
for (int I = 0; I < N; I += 3) {
  R = RGB[I];
  G = RGB[I+1];
  B = RGB[I+2];
  R += C;
  G -= C;
  B *= C;
  RGB[I] = R;
  RGB[I + 1] = G;
  RGB[I + 2] = B;
}
```

In the given example, there are two groups of the interleaved loads and stores: the first group of the interleaved loads from RGB[I], RGB[I+1], and RGB[I+2] and the stores to the same addresses. While vectorization of noncontiguous memory accesses is feasible without explicit support for interleaved operations, the resulting code often suffers from suboptimal performance. The absence of dedicated interleaved load and store instructions typically leads to inefficient memory access patterns, increasing memory bandwidth usage and potentially introducing additional computational overhead.

CHAPTER 5   LLVM LOOP VECTORIZER

The interleaved accesses optimization is particularly valuable in scenarios such as

(a) Processing multichannel image data.

(b) Handling array-of-structs (AoS) to struct-of-arrays (SoA) conversions. By reorganizing data from an AoS format to SoA, the compiler can generate code that utilizes sequential vector loads and stores, which are generally more efficient than their strided or gather/scatter counterparts. For RVV, it allows effectively using segmented memory operations, specifically tuned for such scenarios.

(c) Optimizing scientific computing algorithms with complex data layouts.

The benefits of this approach include

(a) Improved cache utilization due to better spatial locality

(b) Reduced instruction count by eliminating shuffle operations

(c) Better vectorization factor

This optimization is particularly impactful in domains such as computer graphics, scientific simulations, and signal processing, where complex data structures are prevalent, and performance is critical.

For the given example, LLVM compiler can produce the following code with disabled interleaved memory accesses (InterleavedAccessInfo::analyzeInterleaving(), Listing 5-15, Listing 5-16, and Listing 5-17).

CHAPTER 5 LLVM LOOP VECTORIZER

Listing 5-15. Command to compile.

```
$ clang --target=riscv64-unknown-linux -mcpu=sifive-x280
-Rpass=loop-vectorize -Rpass-missed=loop-vectorize -Rpass-
analysis=loop-vectorize repro.c -c -O3 -mllvm -enable-
interleaved-mem-accesses=false
epro.c:22:1: remark: the cost-model indicates that interleaving
is not beneficial [-Rpass-analysis=loop-vectorize]
22 | for (int i = 0; i < N; i += 3) {
 | ^
repro.c:22:1: remark: vectorized loop ((lmul, type): (m4, i32))
[-Rpass=loop-vectorize]
```

Listing 5-16. LLVM IR vectorized code with strided memory accesses.

```
  %cmp34 = icmp sgt i32 %N, 0
  br i1 %cmp34, label %for.body.preheader, label %for.
  cond.cleanup

for.body.preheader:                               ; preds
= %entry
  %0 = zext nneg i32 %N to i64
  %1 = add nsw i64 %0, -1
  %2 = udiv i64 %1, 3
  %3 = add nuw nsw i64 %2, 1
  %broadcast.splatinsert = insertelement <vscale x 8 x i32>
  poison, i32 %C, i64 0
  %broadcast.splat = shufflevector <vscale x 8 x i32>
  %broadcast.splatinsert, <vscale x 8 x i32> poison, <vscale x
  8 x i32> zeroinitializer
  br label %vector.body
```

```
vector.body:
; preds = %vector.body, %for.body.preheader
  %evl.based.iv = phi i64 [ 0, %for.body.preheader ], [ %index.
  evl.next, %vector.body ]
  %offset.idx = mul i64 %evl.based.iv, 3
  %4 = sub i64 %3, %evl.based.iv
  %5 = tail call i32 @llvm.experimental.get.vector.length.
  i64(i64 %4, i32 8, i1 true)
  %6 = getelementptr inbounds i32, ptr %RGB, i64 %offset.idx
  %vp.strided.load = tail call <vscale x 8 x i32> @llvm.
  experimental.vp.strided.load.nxv8i32.p0.i64(ptr align 4
  %6, i64 12, <vscale x 8 x i1> shufflevector (<vscale x 8
  x i1> insertelement (<vscale x 8 x i1> poison, i1 true,
  i64 0), <vscale x 8 x i1> poison, <vscale x 8 x i32>
  zeroinitializer), i32 %5)
  %7 = getelementptr i8, ptr %6, i64 4
  %vp.strided.load37 = tail call <vscale x 8 x i32> @llvm.
  experimental.vp.strided.load.nxv8i32.p0.i64(ptr align 4
  %7, i64 12, <vscale x 8 x i1> shufflevector (<vscale x 8
  x i1> insertelement (<vscale x 8 x i1> poison, i1 true,
  i64 0), <vscale x 8 x i1> poison, <vscale x 8 x i32>
  zeroinitializer), i32 %5)
  %8 = getelementptr i8, ptr %6, i64 8
  %vp.strided.load38 = tail call <vscale x 8 x i32> @llvm.
  experimental.vp.strided.load.nxv8i32.p0.i64(ptr align 4
  %8, i64 12, <vscale x 8 x i1> shufflevector (<vscale x 8
  x i1> insertelement (<vscale x 8 x i1> poison, i1 true,
  i64 0), <vscale x 8 x i1> poison, <vscale x 8 x i32>
  zeroinitializer), i32 %5)
```

CHAPTER 5   LLVM LOOP VECTORIZER

```
%vp.op = tail call <vscale x 8 x i32> @llvm.vp.add.
nxv8i32(<vscale x 8 x i32> %vp.strided.load, <vscale x 8
x i32> %broadcast.splat, <vscale x 8 x i1> shufflevector
(<vscale x 8 x i1> insertelement (<vscale x 8 x i1> poison,
i1 true, i64 0), <vscale x 8 x i1> poison, <vscale x 8 x i32>
zeroinitializer), i32 %5)
%vp.op39 = tail call <vscale x 8 x i32> @llvm.vp.sub.
nxv8i32(<vscale x 8 x i32> %vp.strided.load37, <vscale x 8
x i32> %broadcast.splat, <vscale x 8 x i1> shufflevector
(<vscale x 8 x i1> insertelement (<vscale x 8 x i1> poison,
i1 true, i64 0), <vscale x 8 x i1> poison, <vscale x 8 x i32>
zeroinitializer), i32 %5)
%vp.op40 = tail call <vscale x 8 x i32> @llvm.vp.mul.
nxv8i32(<vscale x 8 x i32> %vp.strided.load38, <vscale x 8
x i32> %broadcast.splat, <vscale x 8 x i1> shufflevector
(<vscale x 8 x i1> insertelement (<vscale x 8 x i1> poison,
i1 true, i64 0), <vscale x 8 x i1> poison, <vscale x 8 x i32>
zeroinitializer), i32 %5)
tail call void @llvm.experimental.vp.strided.store.
nxv8i32.p0.i64(<vscale x 8 x i32> %vp.op, ptr align 4
%6, i64 12, <vscale x 8 x i1> shufflevector (<vscale x 8
x i1> insertelement (<vscale x 8 x i1> poison, i1 true,
i64 0), <vscale x 8 x i1> poison, <vscale x 8 x i32>
zeroinitializer), i32 %5)
tail call void @llvm.experimental.vp.strided.store.
nxv8i32.p0.i64(<vscale x 8 x i32> %vp.op39, ptr align 4
%7, i64 12, <vscale x 8 x i1> shufflevector (<vscale x 8
x i1> insertelement (<vscale x 8 x i1> poison, i1 true,
i64 0), <vscale x 8 x i1> poison, <vscale x 8 x i32>
zeroinitializer), i32 %5)
```

```
  tail call void @llvm.experimental.vp.strided.store.
  nxv8i32.p0.i64(<vscale x 8 x i32> %vp.op40, ptr align 4
  %8, i64 12, <vscale x 8 x i1> shufflevector (<vscale x 8
  x i1> insertelement (<vscale x 8 x i1> poison, i1 true,
  i64 0), <vscale x 8 x i1> poison, <vscale x 8 x i32>
  zeroinitializer), i32 %5)
  %9 = zext i32 %5 to i64
  %index.evl.next = add i64 %evl.based.iv, %9
  %10 = icmp eq i64 %index.evl.next, %3
  br i1 %10, label %for.cond.cleanup, label %vector.body

for.cond.cleanup:
; preds = %vector.body, %entry
  ret void
}
```

Listing 5-17. Assembly vectorized code with strided accesses.

```
        blez    a2, .LBB0_3
# %bb.1:                                # %for.body.preheader
        lui     a1, 699051
        addi    a2, a2, -1
        addiw   a1, a1, -1365
        li      a0, 0
        slli    a5, a1, 32
        li      t0, 12
        add     a1, a1, a5
        mulhu   a1, a2, a1
        srli    a1, a1, 1
        addi    a6, a1, 1
.LBB0_2:                                # %vector.body
                                        # =>This Inner Loop
                                        Header: Depth=1
```

CHAPTER 5   LLVM LOOP VECTORIZER

```
        sh1add   a5, a0, a0
        sub      a1, a6, a0
        sh2add   a5, a5, a4
        vsetvli  a7, a1, e32, m4, ta, ma
        addi     a1, a5, 4
        addi     a2, a5, 8
        vlse32.v         v8, (a5), t0
# strided load RGB[I, I+VF, I+2*VF, ...]
        add      a0, a0, a7
        vlse32.v         v12, (a1), t0
# strided load RGB[I+1, I+1+VF, I+1+2*VF, ...]
        vadd.vx  v8, v8, a3
        vlse32.v         v16, (a2), t0
# strided load RGB[I+2, I+2+VF, I+2+2*VF, ...]
        vsse32.v         v8, (a5), t0
# strided store RGB[I, I+VF, I+2*VF, ...]
        vsub.vx  v8, v12, a3
        vsse32.v         v8, (a1), t0
# strided store RGB[I+1, I+1+VF, I+1+2*VF, ...]
        vmul.vx  v8, v16, a3
        vsse32.v         v8, (a2), t0
# strided store RGB[I+1, I+1+VF, I+1+2*VF, ...]
        bne      a0, a6, .LBB0_2
.LBB0_3:
# %for.cond.cleanup
        ret
```

The naive vectorization approach for this code pattern requires the use of six strided memory operations: three strided loads followed by three strided stores. However, when compiled with support for interleaved accesses, the optimizer can employ more efficient memory access patterns.

CHAPTER 5 LLVM LOOP VECTORIZER

By using interleaved load and store support in the Loop Vectorizer, the compiler can generate code that utilizes segmented RVV memory operations. These specialized instructions are designed to handle noncontiguous data access patterns more efficiently than their strided counterparts. The resulting assembly is not only more compact but also provides significantly improved performance (See Listing 5-18, Listing 5-19, and Listing 5-20).

Benchmarks indicate that this optimization can yield substantial speedups:

(a) Performance improvements typically range from 50% to 80% faster execution times.

(b) The exact gains vary based on factors such as specific hardware architecture, cache behavior, and data set size.

Listing 5-18. Command to compile.

```
$ clang --target=riscv64-unknown-linux -mcpu=sifive-x280
-Rpass=loop-vectorize -Rpass-missed=loop-vectorize -Rpass-
analysis=loop-vectorize repro.c -c -O3
repro.c:22:1: remark: the cost-model indicates that
interleaving is not beneficial [-Rpass-analysis=loop-vectorize]
   22 | for (int i = 0; i < N; i += 3) {
      | ^
repro.c:22:1: remark: vectorized loop ((lmul, type): (m2, i32))
[-Rpass=loop-vectorize]
```

Listing 5-19. LLVM IR vectorized code with interleaved accesses.

```
%cmp34 = icmp sgt i32 %N, 0
br i1 %cmp34, label %for.body.preheader, label %for.
cond.cleanup
```

CHAPTER 5   LLVM LOOP VECTORIZER

```
for.body.preheader:
; preds = %entry
  %0 = zext nneg i32 %N to i64
  %1 = add nsw i64 %0, -1
  %2 = udiv i64 %1, 3
  %3 = add nuw nsw i64 %2, 1
  %broadcast.splatinsert = insertelement <vscale x 4 x i32>
  poison, i32 %C, i64 0
  %broadcast.splat = shufflevector <vscale x 4 x i32>
  %broadcast.splatinsert, <vscale x 4 x i32> poison, <vscale x
  4 x i32> zeroinitializer
  br label %vector.body

vector.body:                                      ; preds =
%vector.body, %for.body.preheader
  %evl.based.iv = phi i64 [ 0, %for.body.preheader ], [ %index.
  evl.next, %vector.body ]
  %offset.idx = mul i64 %evl.based.iv, 3
  %4 = sub i64 %3, %evl.based.iv
  %5 = tail call i32 @llvm.experimental.get.vector.length.
  i64(i64 %4, i32 4, i1 true)
  %6 = getelementptr inbounds i32, ptr %RGB, i64 %offset.idx
  %7 = mul i32 %5, 3
  %wide.masked.load = tail call <vscale x 12 x i32> @llvm.
  vp.load.nxv12i32.p0(ptr align 4 %6, <vscale x 12 x i1>
  shufflevector (<vscale x 12 x i1> insertelement (<vscale x
  12 x i1> poison, i1 true, i64 0), <vscale x 12 x i1> poison,
  <vscale x 12 x i32> zeroinitializer), i32 %7)
  %deinterleaved.results = tail call { <vscale x 4 x i32>,
  <vscale x 4 x i32>, <vscale x 4 x i32> } @llvm.experimental.
  vector.deinterleave3.nxv12i32(<vscale x 12 x i32> %wide.
  masked.load)
```

```
%8 = extractvalue { <vscale x 4 x i32>, <vscale x 4 x i32>,
<vscale x 4 x i32> } %deinterleaved.results, 0
%9 = extractvalue { <vscale x 4 x i32>, <vscale x 4 x i32>,
<vscale x 4 x i32> } %deinterleaved.results, 1
%10 = extractvalue { <vscale x 4 x i32>, <vscale x 4 x i32>,
<vscale x 4 x i32> } %deinterleaved.results, 2
%vp.op = tail call <vscale x 4 x i32> @llvm.vp.add.
nxv4i32(<vscale x 4 x i32> %8, <vscale x 4 x i32> %broadcast.
splat, <vscale x 4 x i1> shufflevector (<vscale x 4 x
i1> insertelement (<vscale x 4 x i1> poison, i1 true,
i64 0), <vscale x 4 x i1> poison, <vscale x 4 x i32>
zeroinitializer), i32 %5)
%vp.op37 = tail call <vscale x 4 x i32> @llvm.vp.sub.
nxv4i32(<vscale x 4 x i32> %9, <vscale x 4 x i32> %broadcast.
splat, <vscale x 4 x i1> shufflevector (<vscale x 4 x
i1> insertelement (<vscale x 4 x i1> poison, i1 true,
i64 0), <vscale x 4 x i1> poison, <vscale x 4 x i32>
zeroinitializer), i32 %5)
%vp.op38 = tail call <vscale x 4 x i32> @llvm.vp.mul.
nxv4i32(<vscale x 4 x i32> %10, <vscale x 4 x i32>
%broadcast.splat, <vscale x 4 x i1> shufflevector (<vscale
x 4 x i1> insertelement (<vscale x 4 x i1> poison, i1
true, i64 0), <vscale x 4 x i1> poison, <vscale x 4 x i32>
zeroinitializer), i32 %5)
%interleaved.vec = tail call <vscale x 12 x i32> @llvm.
experimental.vector.interleave3.nxv12i32(<vscale x 4 x i32>
%vp.op, <vscale x 4 x i32> %vp.op37, <vscale x 4 x i32>
%vp.op38)
%11 = mul i32 %5, 3
```

CHAPTER 5 LLVM LOOP VECTORIZER

```
  tail call void @llvm.vp.store.nxv12i32.p0(<vscale x 12 x
  i32> %interleaved.vec, ptr align 4 %6, <vscale x 12 x i1>
  shufflevector (<vscale x 12 x i1> insertelement (<vscale x
  12 x i1> poison, i1 true, i64 0), <vscale x 12 x i1> poison,
  <vscale x 12 x i32> zeroinitializer), i32 %11)
  %12 = zext i32 %5 to i64
  %index.evl.next = add i64 %evl.based.iv, %12
  %13 = icmp eq i64 %index.evl.next, %3
  br i1 %13, label %for.cond.cleanup, label %vector.body

for.cond.cleanup:                                  ; preds =
%vector.body, %entry
  ret void
```

Listing 5-20. Assembly vectorized code with interleaved accesses.

```
        blez    a2, .LBB0_3
# %bb.1:                                    # %for.body.preheader
        lui     a1, 699051
        addi    a2, a2, -1
        addiw   a5, a1, -1365
        li      a0, 0
        slli    a1, a5, 32
        zext.w  a6, a5
        add     a1, a1, a5
        mulhu   a1, a2, a1
        srli    a1, a1, 1
        addi    a7, a1, 1
.LBB0_2:                                    # %vector.body
                                            # =>This Inner Loop
Header: Depth=1
        sub     a5, a7, a0
        sh1add  a1, a0, a0
```

```
        vsetvli a5, a5, e8, mf2, ta, ma
        sh2add  a1, a1, a4
        sh1add  a2, a5, a5
        add     a0, a0, a5
        mul     a2, a2, a6
        srli    a2, a2, 33
        vsetvli zero, a2, e32, m2, ta, ma
        vlseg3e32.v     v8, (a1)
# unit strided segmented load of 3 vector registers of 32 bit
elements. Segments saved in V8, V10, V12
        vsetvli zero, a5, e32, m2, ta, ma
        vmul.vx v12, v12, a3
        vadd.vx v8, v8, a3
        vsub.vx v10, v10, a3
        vsetvli zero, a2, e32, m2, ta, ma
        vsseg3e32.v     v8, (a1)
# unit strided segmented store of 3 vector registers of 32 bit
elements. Segments saved in V8, V10, V12
        bne     a0, a7, .LBB0_2
.LBB0_3:                                # %for.cond.cleanup
        ret
```

Loop Vectorization Planner

The next phase involves the compiler's attempt to formulate a vectorization strategy and construct initial Vector Plans (VPlans), if feasible. This process begins with a comprehensive analysis to determine potential vectorization and unroll factors, followed by the selection of an optimal approach for handling loop remainders.

CHAPTER 5 LLVM LOOP VECTORIZER

The compiler's behavior can be fine-tuned through LLVM options. For instance, using '-prefer-predicate-over-epilogue=scalar-epilogue' instead of '-prefer-predicate-over-epilogue=predicate-else-scalar-epilogue|predicate-dont-vectorize', which instructs the compiler to avoid tail folding. In this scenario, the compiler calculates both fixed and scalable vector factors that the loop can support, based on safe aliasing distances and the target architecture's capabilities.

Fixed vectorization factors are primarily employed for architectures lacking scalable vectorization support, such as x86 platforms with SSE and AVX extensions, or ARM systems with NEON. For these targets, fixed factors are the sole option. In contrast, architectures like RISC-V with RVV Extension or ARM SVE support both fixed and runtime-determined scalable vectorization. In these cases, the compiler evaluates both fixed and scalable factors, ultimately selecting the most efficient approach.

It's important to note that even with scalable vectorization, a scalar loop remainder (or "tail") typically exists, if the tail folding is not enabled (or not supported by the hardware). Effective management of this remainder is a critical aspect of loop vectorization. This necessity arises from the fact that the total iteration count often isn't an exact multiple of the vector width, thus requiring separate processing for the final iterations (see Listing 5-21).

Listing 5-21. Loop with the runtime defined trip count

```
for (int I = 0; I < N; ++I) {
  Arr[I] = B[I];
}

// Being vectorized with vectorization factor 4
int I = 0;
for (; I < (N / 4) * 4; I+=4) {
  Arr[I:I+3] =B[I:I+3];
}
```

```
// What if N%4 != 0? Need to process last elements separately,
in the loop remainder
for (; I < N; ++I) { // scalar loop remainder, executes
0-2 times
  Arr[I] = B[I];
}
```

The utilization of a vectorized main loop followed by a scalar remainder is a common and effective strategy for handling loops where the iteration count isn't perfectly divisible by the vector width. However, this isn't the only viable approach to ensure correct processing of all loop iterations.

An alternative approach involves a vectorized main loop coupled with a vectorized remainder. This approach offers potential performance benefits but comes with specific hardware requirements:

(a) Hardware support for masked vector operations

(b) Efficient implementation of predicated instructions

The key feature for this strategy is the availability of masked (or predicated) vector operations. It allows the processor to selectively apply vector instructions to a subset of lanes based on a mask, effectively "turning off" unused lanes in the final iteration.

Architectures supporting this approach include

(a) AVX-512 on recent x86 processors

(b) ARM's SVE (Scalable Vector Extension)

(c) RISC-V's vector extension

When targeting these architectures, the compiler can generate code that processes all iterations using vector instructions, adjusting the mask for the final, partial vector operation (see Listing 5-22).

Listing 5-22. Loop with the runtime defined trip count, masked remainder.

```
// Vectorized with vectorization factor 4
int I = 0;
for (; I < (N / 4) * 4; I+=4) {
  Arr[I:I+3] =B[I:I+3];
}
// Vector loop remainder with masking
for (; I < N; I += 4) { // scalar loop remainder, executes 0-3 times
  WidenI = <I, I+1, I+2, I+3>
  Cmp = WidenI < <N, N, N, N> // If have just 1 iteration, Cmp will have <T, F, F, F>, if 2 iterations - <T,T,F,F>, etc.
  Res = load Arr[I:I+3], Cmp // Masked load, only elements with T in mask are loaded
  store Res, B[I:I+3], Cmp; // Masked store, only elements with T in mask are stored
}
```

Hardware support for masked vector operations enables a sophisticated optimization technique known as loop tail folding. This strategy allows full loop vectorization without the need for a separate scalar remainder loop, streamlining code execution and potentially boosting performance.

Loop tail folding leverages predicated execution to handle the final, potentially partial, vector operation within the main vectorized loop. By dynamically adjusting a vector mask, the processor can selectively enable or disable individual lanes of vector operations, effectively "folding" the loop tail into the primary vector loop (see Listing 5-23).

Listing 5-23. Loop with the runtime defined trip count, folded tail.

```
// Vectorized with vectorization factor 4
for (int I = 0; I < ((N + 3) / 4) * 4; I+=4) { // Need to
adjust the trip count, since I has increment 4
  WidenI = <I, I+1, I+2, I+3>
  Cmp = WidenI < <N, N, N, N> // Mask
  Res = load Arr[I:I+3], Cmp // Masked load, only elements with
  T in mask are loaded
  store Res, B[I:I+3], Cmp; // Masked store, only elements
  with T in mask are stored
}
```

Key benefits of loop tail folding include

(a) Reduced code size and complexity

(b) Improved instruction cache utilization

(c) Simplified loop control flow

While loop tail folding offers significant advantages, it's important to consider its implementation costs. This approach typically incurs a small overhead in the form of two additional instructions per iteration: one to widen the loop counter and another for mask comparison. Furthermore, its efficiency depends on the target architecture's support for high-performance masked operations.

However, the RISC-V Vector Extension introduces a more elegant solution to this problem. This architecture allows dynamic adjustment of the vector length within the loop, potentially eliminating the need for explicit masking at all. In the context of the LLVM compiler, this optimization strategy is referred to as "tail folding with predicated EVL (Explicit Vector Length) instructions."

CHAPTER 5   LLVM LOOP VECTORIZER

The EVL-based approach offers several key benefits:

(a) Reduced instruction overhead compared to traditional masking

(b) Simplified control flow within the vectorized loop

(c) Potential for improved performance due to the elimination of mask management

This technique leverages the RISC-V Vector Extension's ability to set the vector length register (vl) to any value up to the maximum vector length (VLMAX) supported by the hardware. By adjusting the EVL on each iteration based on the remaining elements to be processed, the hardware naturally handles partial vector operations without requiring explicit masks (see Listing 5-24).

Listing 5-24. Loop with the runtime defined trip count, folded tail, no mask.

```
// Vectorized with vectorization factor 4
for (int I = 0; I < N;) {
   int VF = get_vector_length(N-I); // translated to vsetvli
   instruction for RISC-V
   Arr[I:I+VF-1] =B[I:I+VF-1];
   I += VF;
}
```

The RISC-V Vector Extension's approach to vectorization introduces a paradigm shift in how we handle loop vectorization. By allowing a fully variable vectorization factor within the range of (1, VLMAX/SEW] (where VLMAX is the maximum vector length and SEW is the Selected Element Width, determined by the size of the array elements), this architecture offers wide flexibility in vector processing. This dynamic vectorization strategy yields several key advantages:

CHAPTER 5 LLVM LOOP VECTORIZER

(a) Elimination of loop remainder. The compiler no longer needs to generate separate code paths for handling partial vector operations at the end of the loop.

(b) Avoidance of explicit masking. Unlike traditional tail folding techniques, there's no need to calculate or apply vector masks for the final iterations.

(c) Preservation of original loop structure. The loop's iteration count remains unmodified, reducing the instruction overhead typically associated with vectorization.

Considering these capabilities, the compiler's vectorization strategy changes. It now focuses on determining the maximum legal fixed or scalable vector factor that aligns with the chosen tail folding approach. This determination considers various factors such as data dependencies, memory access patterns, and the specific capabilities of the target RISC-V implementation.

The resulting code is often more streamlined and potentially more efficient, as it eliminates several sources of overhead typically associated with vectorized loops. However, the actual performance impact can vary based on the specific loop characteristics and the hardware implementation of the RISC-V Vector Extension.

So, the compiler tries to get maximum possible legal fixed/scalable vector factor based on the tail folding strategy (see Listing 5-25).

Listing 5-25. Logic for vector factor selection.

```
MaxSafeVectorWidthInBits is the number of elements (from
consecutive iterations) that are safe to operate on
simultaneously, multiplied by the size of the element in bits.
unsigned MaxSafeElements = MaxSafeVectorWidthInBits / WidestType;
```

CHAPTER 5   LLVM LOOP VECTORIZER

```
MaxSafeFixedVF = ElementCount::getFixed(MaxSafeElements);
MaxSafeScalableVF = ElementCount::getScalable(MaxSafeElements /
TTI.getMaxVScale());
MaxSafeFixedVF = min(MaxSafeFixedVF, best vector factor with
the register size and register pressure)
MaxSafeScalableVF = min(MaxSafeScalableVF, best vector factor
with the register size and register pressure)
```

The compiler then constructs a comprehensive list of potential vectorization factor candidates. This list typically spans from 2 to MaxSafeFixedVF for fixed-width vectors, and from <vscale x 2> to <vscale x MaxSafeScalableVF> for scalable vectors. These upper bounds are determined based on various factors, including hardware constraints, data dependencies, and memory access patterns. For each candidate vectorization factor, the compiler performs a detailed analysis of the loop body. This analysis involves instruction classification and it performs the following actions(see Listing 5-26):

(a) Identifies instructions that must remain scalar.

(b) Determines which operations can be safely vectorized.

(c) Recognizes uniform operations (and potentially can be hoisted out of the vector loop). The operation is uniform if it is represented with a single scalar value in the vectorized loop corresponding to each iteration. For example, pointer operands of consecutive, strided, or interleaved memory accesses can be considered uniform. Each uniform operation is scalar, but not each scalar value is uniform.

Listing 5-26. Algorithm for instruction classification.

```
for (unsigned VF : VFs) {
  if (isa<LoadInst, StoreInst>(I)) {
    if (TTI reports in can be vectorized)
      mark as vectorized for VF;
    if (part of interleavr group and good cost)
      mark as interleaved for VF;
    if (TTI reports in will be gathered/scatter and good cost)
      mark as gather/scatter for VF;
    if (TTI reports in will be scalairzed)
      mark as scalarize for VF;
  }
  if (isa<CallInst>(I)) {
    if (TTI allows vectoriztion with possible masking,
    vectorized params, etc.)
      mask as vectorized for the given VF;
  }
}
```

Following the comprehensive analysis of potential vectorization factors, the loop vectorizer proceeds to the following phase of Vector Plan (VPlan) construction. This process is encapsulated within the LoopVectorizationPlanner::buildVPlansWithVPRecipes() member function.

For each viable vectorization factor identified in the previous stage, the vectorizer attempts to construct a detailed VPlan. These VPlans serve as blueprints for the vectorized loop, outlining the sequence of Vector Plan Recipes (VPRecipes) necessary to implement the vectorization strategy (see Listing 5-27).

Listing 5-27. Algorithm of VPlan building and transformation.

```
for (unsigned VF : VFs) {
  VPlan Plan = tryToBuildVPlanWithVPRecipes(VF);
  if (Plan is not scalar)
    PlanTransforms::runPass(VPlanTransforms::truncateToMinimalB
    itwidths, Plan); // try to perform minbitwidth analysis for
    used recipies
  VPlanTransforms::optimize(Plan); // Remove redundant, dead
  recipies, simplify canonical loop IV recipes, merge blocks
  if (CM.foldTailWithEVL() && Plan is not
  scalar)              // If enabled tail folding with
  predicateinstructions
    PlanTransforms::runPass(VPlanTransforms::addExplicitVecto
    rLength, Plan); // Transform VPlan and its recipes to use
    this vectorization plan
}

VPlan LoopVectorizationPlanner::tryToBuildVPlanWithVPRec
ipes(VF) {
  Build initial loop CFG;
  Add the necessary canonical IV and branch recipes required to
  control the loop.
  for (each basic block) {
    VPBB = new VPBasicBlock();
    for (each instruction in block) {
      VPRecipeBase *Recipe = RecipeBuilder.
      tryToCreateWidenRecipe(I, VF);
      VPBB->appendRecipe(Recipe);
    }
  }
}
```

The initial Vector Plans (VPlans) generated during this stage serve as the foundation for all subsequent transformations, estimations, and optimizations in the vectorization process. These VPlans encapsulate the core structure and strategy for vectorizing the loop, providing a robust framework for further refinement.

As the compiler progresses through its optimization pipeline, it continually refines and transforms these VPlans. This iterative process may involve

(a) Cost model refinements

(b) Instruction selection optimizations

(c) Register pressure analysis and mitigation

(d) Memory access pattern optimizations

(e) Control flow transformations

For developers and compiler engineers seeking to gain insight into the VPlan generation process, the LLVM compiler provides a debugging mechanism. By building the compiler with assertions enabled and utilizing the -debug-only=loop-vectorize command-line option, the developers can obtain a textual representation of the generated VPlans. This debug output offers valuable information about

(a) The structure of vectorized operations

(b) Data flow within the vectorized loop

(c) Decisions made during the VPlan construction process

Analyzing this output can be very useful in understanding the compiler's decision-making process and identifying opportunities for further optimization or diagnosing unexpected vectorization behaviors (see Listing 5-28, Listing 5-29, and Listing 5-30).

CHAPTER 5 LLVM LOOP VECTORIZER

Listing 5-28. Original loop (LLVM IR).

```
%cmp34 = icmp sgt i32 %N, 0
br i1 %cmp34, label %for.body.preheader, label %for.
cond.cleanup

for.body.preheader:                                    ; preds
= %entry
  %0 = zext nneg i32 %N to i64
  br label %for.body

for.body:
; preds = %for.body.preheader, %for.body
  %indvars.iv = phi i64 [ 0, %for.body.preheader ],
  [ %indvars.iv.next, %for.body ]
  %arrayidx = getelementptr inbounds i32, ptr %RGB, i64
  %indvars.iv
  %1 = load i32, ptr %arrayidx, align 4
  %arrayidx2 = getelementptr i8, ptr %arrayidx, i64 4
  %2 = load i32, ptr %arrayidx2, align 4
  %arrayidx6 = getelementptr i8, ptr %arrayidx, i64 8
  %3 = load i32, ptr %arrayidx6, align 4
  %add7 = add nsw i32 %1, %C
  %sub = sub nsw i32 %2, %C
  %mul = mul nsw i32 %3, %C
  store i32 %add7, ptr %arrayidx, align 4
  store i32 %sub, ptr %arrayidx2, align 4
  store i32 %mul, ptr %arrayidx6, align 4
  %indvars.iv.next = add nuw nsw i64 %indvars.iv, 3
  %cmp = icmp ult i64 %indvars.iv.next, %0
  br i1 %cmp, label %for.body, label %for.cond.cleanup
```

```
for.cond.cleanup:                                      ; preds =
%for.body, %entry
  ret void
```

Listing 5-29. Compile command.

```
$ opt -S -mtriple=riscv64-unknown-linux-gnu -mcpu=sifive-x280
--passes=loop-vectorize -debug-only=loop-vectorize test.ll
```

Listing 5-30. Initial VPlan for loop.

```
VPlan 'Initial VPlan for VF={2,4,8,16,32},UF>=1' {
Live-in vp<%0> = VF * UF
; Canonical step
Live-in vp<%1> = vector-trip-count
; Vector trip count value
vp<%2> = original trip-count
; Original trip count value

ph:
  EMIT vp<%2> = EXPAND SCEV (1 + ((-1 + (zext i32 %N to
  i64))<nsw> /u 3))<nuw><nsw>
No successors

vector.ph:
Successor(s): vector loop

<x1> vector loop: {
  vector.body:
    EMIT vp<%3> = CANONICAL-INDUCTION ir<0>, vp<%6>
    ; VPCanonicalIVPHIRecipe, canonical induction recipe,
    initial value is ir<0>=0, next value is vp<%6>
    vp<%4>   = DERIVED-IV ir<0> + vp<%3> * ir<3>
    ; VPDerivedIVRecipe, recipe for converting the input value
    vp<%3>, producing 0 + vp<%3> * 3
```

CHAPTER 5   LLVM LOOP VECTORIZER

```
    vp<%5> = SCALAR-STEPS vp<%4>, ir<3>
    ; VPScalarIVStepsRecipe, recipe for handling phi nodes of
    scalar integer induction
    CLONE ir<%arrayidx> = getelementptr inbounds ir<%RGB>,
    vp<%5> ; VPReplicateRecipe, uniform recipe, which
    replicates original getelelemtnptr instruction %arrayidx
    INTERLEAVE-GROUP with factor 3 at %1, ir<%arrayidx>
    ; VPInterleaveRecipe, recipe for transforming an interleave
    group of loads %1-%3
      ir<%1> = load from index 0
      ir<%2> = load from index 1
      ir<%3> = load from index 2
    CLONE ir<%arrayidx6> = getelementptr inbounds
ir<%arrayidx>, ir<8> ; VPReplicateRecipe, uniform recipe, which
replicates original getelelemtnptr instruction %arrayidx6
    WIDEN ir<%add7> = add nsw ir<%1>, ir<%C>
; VPWidenRecipe, recipe for widened add
    WIDEN ir<%sub> = sub nsw ir<%2>, ir<%C>
; VPWidenRecipe, recipe for widened sub
    WIDEN ir<%mul> = mul nsw ir<%3>, ir<%C>
    ; VPWidenRecipe, recipe for widened mul
    INTERLEAVE-GROUP with factor 3 at <badref>,
    ir<%arrayidx6>       ; VPInterleaveRecipe, recipe for
    transforming an interleave group of stores
      store ir<%add7> to index 0
      store ir<%sub> to index 1
      store ir<%mul> to index 2
    EMIT vp<%6> = add nuw vp<%3>, vp<%0>
    ; VPInstruction, increments canonical induction value with
    the step vp<%0>
```

CHAPTER 5   LLVM LOOP VECTORIZER

```
    EMIT branch-on-count vp<%6>, vp<%1>
    ; VPInstruction, models backedge
  No successors
}
```

For a more visual and structured representation of the Vector Plan (VPlan), LLVM provides the option to generate output in DOT format. This feature significantly enhances the ability to analyze and understand the vectorization strategy implemented by the compiler. To enable this functionality, you can use the compiler option -vplan-print-in-dot-format (see Figure 5-2).

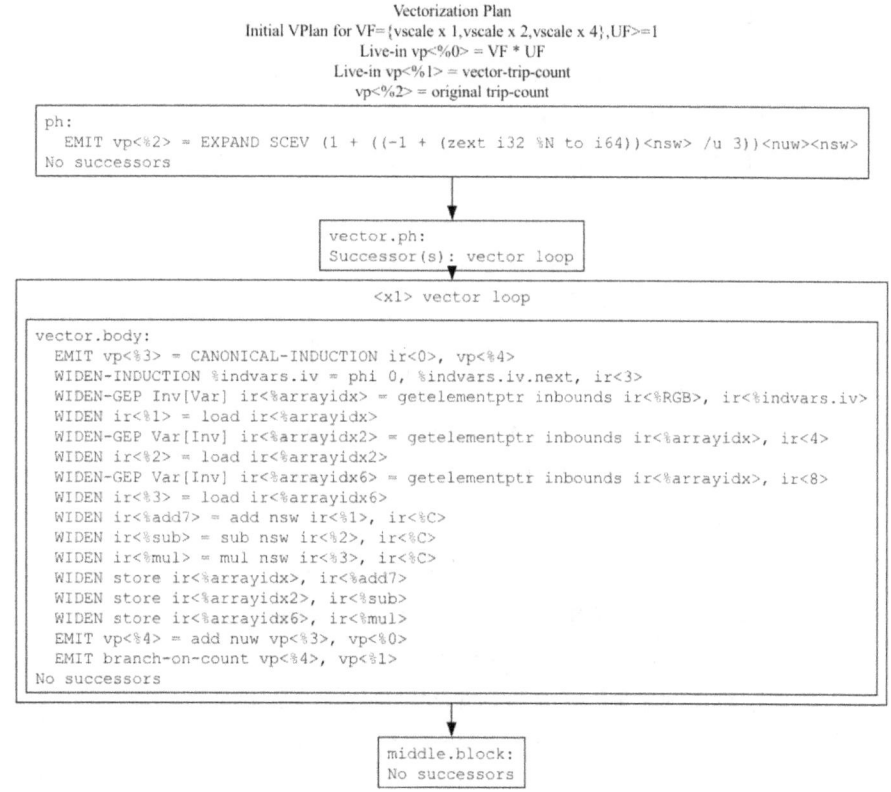

Figure 5-2. *VPlan visual representation*

The loop vectorizer's initial planning phase constructs only canonical Vector Plans (VPlans) that do not inherently account for the RISC-V Vector Length Agnostic (VLA) Explicit Vector Length (EVL) capabilities. To adapt these VPlans for EVL-based vectorization, a subsequent transformation step is necessary.

This transformation is performed by the VPlanTransforms::addExplicit VectorLength() function. Its primary responsibilities include

1. Introducing VPEVLBasedIVPHIRecipe. This recipe represents the induction variable (IV) that's dynamically adjusted based on the explicit vector length.

2. Augmenting existing VPlans. The function integrates new EVL-based recipes into each VPlan, ensuring compatibility with RISC-V's dynamic vector length capabilities.

3. Replacing canonical IV uses. All uses of the VPCanonicalIVPHIRecipe (except for the canonical IV increment) are substituted with the newly introduced VPEVLBasedIVPHIRecipe. This substitution allows for dynamic adjustment of vector operations based on the explicit vector length.

4. Preserving iteration counting. The original VPCanonicalIVPHIRecipe is retained solely for the purpose of tracking overall loop iterations. This separation of concerns allows for efficient vectorization while maintaining canonical (countable) loop form.

CHAPTER 5   LLVM LOOP VECTORIZER

5. Disables the unrolling. In most cases, EVL-based vectorization just suffers from the loop unrolling, so currently it is just explicitly disabled. Also, loop unrolling can be considered in terms of LMUL concept, which can represent hardware-based approach to the loop unrolling.

This transformation effectively closes the gap between the initial, architecture-agnostic VPlans and the specialized requirements of RISC-V's VLA capabilities (see Listing 5-31, Listing 5-32, and Listing 5-33).

Listing 5-31. Transformation from initial Vplan to EVL-based VPlan

```
// This logic is still under development, subject to change
auto *EVLPhi = new VPEVLBasedIVPHIRecipe(CanonicalIVPHI-
>getStartValue());
EVLPhi->insertAfter(CanonicalIVPHI);
// Compute original TC - IV as the AVL (application vector
length).
VPValue *AVL = Builder.createNaryOp(
  Instruction::Sub, {Plan.getTripCount(), EVLPhi},
DebugLoc(), "avl");
if (safe store-to-load forwarding distance exists) {
  AVL = min(safe store-to-load forwarding distance exists, AVL)
}
auto *VPEVL = Builder.createNaryOp(VPInstruction::ExplicitVecto
rLength, AVL, DebugLoc());
auto *NextEVLIV = Builder.createOverflowingOp(Instruction::Add,
{VPEVL, EVLPhi}, {CanonicalIVIncrement->hasNoUnsignedWrap(),
CanonicalIVIncrement->hasNoSignedWrap()}, CanonicalIVIncrement-
>getDebugLoc(), "index.evl.next");
EVLPhi->addOperand(NextEVLIV);
```

CHAPTER 5 LLVM LOOP VECTORIZER

```
for (each recipe) {
  replace with EVL-based recipe replacing mask WideCanonicalIV
  <= backedge-taken-count by all-true masks.
}

disable unrolling; // EVL-based vectorizer does not need to
unroll loops.
```

Listing 5-32. Compile command.

```
$ opt -S -mtriple=riscv64-unknown-linux-gnu -mcpu=sifive-x280
--passes=loop-vectorize -debug-only=loop-vectorize -force-
tail-folding-style=data-with-evl -prefer-predicate-over-
epilogue=predicate-dont-vectorize test.ll
```

Listing 5-33. EVL-based VPlan for loop.

```
VPlan 'Initial VPlan for VF={vscale x 1,vscale x 2,vscale x
4},UF={1}' {
Live-in vp<%0> = VF * UF
Live-in vp<%1> = vector-trip-count
vp<%3> = original trip-count

ph:
  EMIT vp<%3> = EXPAND SCEV (1 + ((-1 + (zext i32 %N to
  i64))<nsw> /u 3))<nuw><nsw>
No successors

vector.ph:
Successor(s): vector loop

<x1> vector loop: {
  vector.body:
    EMIT vp<%4> = CANONICAL-INDUCTION ir<0>, vp<%9>
```

```
    EXPLICIT-VECTOR-LENGTH-BASED-IV-PHI vp<%5> = phi ir<0>, vp<%8>
    ; VPEVLBasedIVPHIRecipe, recipe for generating the phi node
    for the current index of elements, adjusted in accordance
    with EVL value, initial value is ir<0>=0, next value
    is vp<%8>
    WIDEN-INDUCTION %indvars.iv = phi 0, %indvars.
    iv.next, ir<3>
    EMIT vp<%6> = EXPLICIT-VECTOR-LENGTH vp<%5>, vp<%3>
    ; VPInstruction::ExplicitVectorLength, calculates EVL based
    on operands, results in @llvm.experimental.get.vector.
    length(vp<%3> - vp<%5>)
    WIDEN-GEP Inv[Var] ir<%arrayidx> = getelementptr inbounds
    ir<%RGB>, ir<%indvars.iv>
    WIDEN ir<%1> = vp.load ir<%arrayidx>, vp<%6>
    WIDEN-GEP Var[Inv] ir<%arrayidx2> = getelementptr inbounds
    ir<%arrayidx>, ir<4>
    WIDEN ir<%2> = vp.load ir<%arrayidx2>, vp<%6>
    WIDEN-GEP Var[Inv] ir<%arrayidx6> = getelementptr inbounds
    ir<%arrayidx>, ir<8>
    WIDEN ir<%3> = vp.load ir<%arrayidx6>, vp<%6>
    WIDEN ir<%add7> = add nsw ir<%1>, ir<%C>
    WIDEN ir<%sub> = sub nsw ir<%2>, ir<%C>
    WIDEN ir<%mul> = mul nsw ir<%3>, ir<%C>
    WIDEN vp.store ir<%arrayidx>, ir<%add7>, vp<%6>
    WIDEN vp.store ir<%arrayidx2>, ir<%sub>, vp<%6>
    WIDEN vp.store ir<%arrayidx6>, ir<%mul>, vp<%6>
    SCALAR-CAST vp<%7> = zext vp<%6> to i64
; VPScalarCastRecipe, scalar cast recipe, casts vp<%6> to i64
    EMIT vp<%8> = add vp<%7>, vp<%5>
; VPInstruction, increments EVL-based canonical induction value
with the step vp<%7>
```

```
    EMIT vp<%9> = add vp<%4>, vp<%0>
    EMIT branch-on-count vp<%9>, vp<%1>
  No successors
}
```

In the next phase, the LoopVectorizationPlanner attempts to identify the optimal VPlan with the most suitable vectorization factor (refer to LoopVectorizationPlanner::selectVectorizationFactor()). This involves estimating the cost of both the original scalar loop and the potential vectorized loop (see LoopVectorizationCostModel::expectedCost()). The process iterates over all instructions, requesting reciprocal throughput estimates for both the current (scalar) and future (vector) versions of each instruction from the TargetTransformInterface.

Reciprocal throughput is a form of instruction cost measurement. Traditionally, instruction cost analysis involves counting the total number of instructions and summing their cycle costs. However, modern hardware requires a more nuanced approach, considering both dependency chain latency and reciprocal throughput. Instruction latency indicates the number of clock cycles needed to execute an instruction and obtain a result, crucial for data dependency chains.

Reciprocal throughput, the inverse of an instruction's maximum throughput, measures the number of instructions per cycle, expressed in cycles per instruction. This metric indicates how many instructions the vector unit (or vectorizer) can schedule for execution.

The LoopVectorizationPlanner calculates the sum of reciprocal throughputs for each instruction. It then compares the costs of the original scalar loop with all potential VPlans, assessing whether the per-lane cost of vectorized instructions is more efficient than that of the scalar loop. For loops with a known trip count, the cost is estimated as SumOfRThroughputs * ((TripCount + VectorizationFactor - 1) / VectorizationFactor). For loops vectorized with a scalar remainder, the cost is SumOfRThroughputs * (TripCount / VectorizationFactor) + ScalarSumOfRThroughputs * (TripCount % VectorizationFactor). For unknown trip counts, the planner compares SumOfRTthroughput <= VectorizationFactor * ScalarSumOfRThroughput.

Once the LoopVectorizationPlanner successfully constructs the VPlans and selects the best VPlan and vectorization factor, the loop vectorizer initiates the vectorization process.

Loop Vectorization Generation

For innermost loop vectorization, the loop vectorizer utilizes the InnerLoopVectorizer class. This class facilitates the construction of an initial empty vectorized loop graph, or skeleton (see InnerLoopVectorize r::createVectorizedLoopSkeleton()). It modifies the original preheader to incorporate necessary runtime checks (such as memory aliasing checks and iteration count validations), and generates the vector preheader, the main vectorized loop graph, and a middle block (which may be optimized out later). Additionally, it rectifies the structure of the vectorized code post-vectorization (refer to InnerLoopVectorizer::fixVectorizedLoop()) and performs other related tasks, including runtime check emission (which is slated to be part of the VPlan in the future), trip count adjustments, and more (see Figure 5-3).

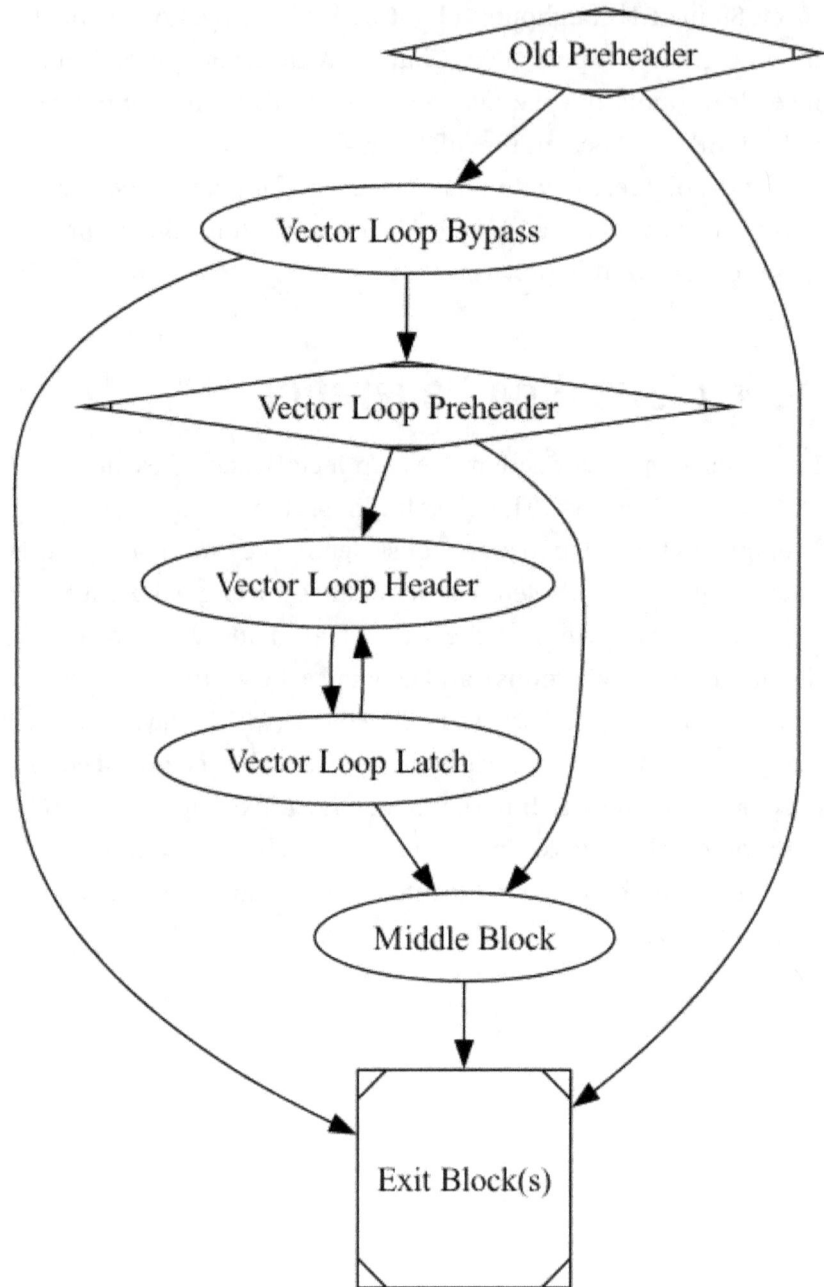

Figure 5-3. *Vectorized loop control flow graph*

CHAPTER 5　LLVM LOOP VECTORIZER

The LoopVectorizationPlanner is also responsible for vector code emission (see LoopVectorizationPlanner::executePlan()) for the optimal VPlan/vectorization factor. It sets up the necessary infrastructure and utilizes VPlan to handle the vector code emission process (refer to VPlan::prepareToExecute() and VPlan::execute(), see Listing 5-34).

Listing 5-34. Vector code emission for the best VPlan.

```
LoopVectorizationPlanner::executePlan() {
  Generate SCEV-dependent code into the preheader, including
  TripCount, before making any changes to the CFG;
  Generate vectorized loop skeleton (InnerLoopVectorizer::creat
  eVectorizedLoopSkeleton());
  Prepapre noaliasing metadata if the runtime checks for non-
  aliasing were generated;

  BestVPlan.prepareToExecute();
  BestVPlan.execute();

  Restore loop hints;
  Fix the vectorized code: take care of header phi`s, live-outs,
  predication, updating analyses (InnerLoopVectorizer::
  fixVectorizedLoop());
}

VPlan::prepareToExecute() {
  Check if the backedge taken count is needed, and if so
build it;
  Model vector trip count;
  Model iteration step;
}

VPlan::execute() {
  Initialize CFG state;
  for (VPBlockBase *Block : Vector loop preheader)
```

```
    Block->execute();
  for (VPRecipeBase &R : Header->phis()) {
    Emit correct incoming values for for canonical IV, first-
    order recurrences and reduction phis.
  }
}
```

The execute() member function of the VPBlockBase class generates the corresponding basic block in LLVM IR. It then iterates over all recipes defined in the current block, invoking their respective execute() functions. This process emits the final LLVM IR for each specific VPInstruction/VPRecipe, completing the loop vectorization process.

The Loop Vectorizer in LLVM, particularly tuned for the RISC-V Vector (RVV) extension, represents a significant advancement in optimizing loop performance. By leveraging vectorization, we can exploit data-level parallelism, greatly enhancing the execution efficiency of loops on RVV-enabled architectures. The Loop Vectorizer in LLVM still continues to adapt to RVV-specific requirements, integrating new optimizations and features. In summary, mastering the Loop Vectorizer in LLVM for the RVV extension is essential for developing high-performance applications.

Summary

In this chapter you learned

- That the LLVM Loop Vectorizer transforms scalar loops into vectorized form to exploit data-level parallelism and improve performance.

- The structure of loops in LLVM's loop analysis framework, including preheaders, latches, backedges, exit blocks, and middle blocks for handling scalar remainders.

CHAPTER 5   LLVM LOOP VECTORIZER

- How traditional vectorization generates loops assuming a fixed vector length, requiring scalar remainder handling, while RISC-V's Explicit Vector Length (EVL) enables vector-length agnostic (VLA) vectorization without scalar remainders.

- The role of VPlan, LLVM's high-level representation of loops for vectorization, which introduces VPInstructions and VPRecipes to model transformations without altering the original IR.

- The stages of VPlan-based vectorization: legality checks, plan construction, legalization (e.g., reductions, interleaved groups), optimization, cost modeling, and final code emission.

- The key VPlan classes: LoopVectorizationPlanner, VPRecipeBase, VPValue, VPUser, VPDef, VPInstruction, VPBasicBlock, VPRegionBlock, and their roles in representing vectorization strategies.

- The legality analysis phase, which ensures a loop can be safely vectorized by checking control flow, instruction compatibility, memory dependencies (RAW, WAR, WAW), and opportunities for IF-conversion and predication.

- How LLVM applies multiversioning, generating both scalar and vectorized loop variants with runtime checks to ensure correctness and maximize performance.

- The optimization of interleaved memory accesses, transforming strided operations into efficient segmented memory instructions in RVV.
- The role of tail handling strategies: scalar remainders, masked vectorized remainders, loop tail folding with predication, and EVL-based folding in RVV.

CHAPTER 6

LLVM SLP Vectorizer

Superword-Level Parallelism (SLP) vectorization is an advanced optimization technique designed to exploit parallelism in straight-line code segments. This approach focuses on identifying and combining independent, compatible scalar instructions into their vector equivalents, potentially yielding significant performance improvements.

The SLP vectorizer operates by constructing a vectorization graph through def-use data analysis. This graph represents the relationships and dependencies between scalar instructions, serving as a blueprint for potential vectorization opportunities. By analyzing this graph, the vectorizer can determine which instruction sequences are amenable to vectorization and how they can be efficiently combined.

Key objectives of SLP vectorization include

(a) Utilization of vector instructions. Leveraging SIMD and vector capabilities of modern processors.

(b) Expansion of register utilization. Exploiting vector registers to increase the effective number of used registers (along with the general purpose registers).

(c) Reduction of instruction count. Combining multiple scalar operations into single vector operations reduces the total number of instructions and improves throughput.

CHAPTER 6　LLVM SLP VECTORIZER

SLP vectorization has been implemented in various compiler frameworks, including GCC (GNU Compiler Collection), LLVM (Low-Level Virtual Machine), and numerous proprietary and open source LLVM-based compilers.

While the fundamental principles of SLP vectorization are consistent across implementations, this discussion will focus on the design and functionality specific to LLVM-based compilers.

The LLVM implementation of SLP vectorization is notable for its

(a) Integration with the broader LLVM optimization pipeline

(b) Target-specific customization capabilities

(c) Interaction with other vectorization passes, such as loop vectorization (this is currently work in progress)

By analyzing code at the basic block level, the SLP vectorizer can identify vectorization opportunities that might be missed by loop-centric approaches, complementing other optimization techniques in the compiler's arsenal (see Listing 6-1, Listing 6-2, and Listing 6-3).

Listing 6-1. Compile command.

```
$ opt -S -mtriple=riscv64-unknown-linux-gnu -mcpu=sifive-x280
--passes=slp-vectorizer test.ll
```

Listing 6-2. Original and vectorized LLVM IR.

```
target triple = "riscv64-unknown-linux-gnu"
@c = global [12 x i64] zeroinitializer
define i16 @test() {
entry:
  %0 = load i64, ptr @c, align 8
```

```
  %conv = trunc i64 %0 to i32
  %conv3 = and i32 %conv, 65535
  %conv4 = xor i32 %conv3, 65535
  %1 = load i64, ptr getelementptr inbounds ([12 x i64], ptr
  @c, i64 0, i64 3), align 8
  %conv.1 = trunc i64 %1 to i32
  %conv3.1 = and i32 %conv.1, 65535
  %conv4.1 = xor i32 %conv3.1, 65535
  %.conv4.1 = tail call i32 @llvm.umax.i32(i32 %conv4,
  i32 %conv4.1)
  %2 = load i64, ptr getelementptr inbounds ([12 x i64],
  ptr @c, i64 0, i64 6), align 8
  %conv.2 = trunc i64 %2 to i32
  %conv3.2 = and i32 %conv.2, 65535
  %conv4.2 = xor i32 %conv3.2, 65535
  %.conv4.2 = tail call i32 @llvm.umax.i32(i32 %.conv4.1,
  i32 %conv4.2)
  %3 = load i64, ptr getelementptr inbounds ([12 x i64],
  ptr @c, i64 0, i64 9), align 8
  %conv.3 = trunc i64 %3 to i32
  %conv3.3 = and i32 %conv.3, 65535
  %conv4.3 = xor i32 %conv3.3, 65535
  %.conv4.3 = tail call i32 @llvm.umax.i32(i32 %.conv4.2,
  i32 %conv4.3)
  %t = trunc i32 %.conv4.3 to i16
  ret i16 %t
}
define i16 @test() {
  %0 = call <4 x i64> @llvm.experimental.vp.strided.load.v4i64.
  p0.i64(ptr align 8 @c, i64 24, <4 x i1> <i1 true, i1 true, i1
  true, i1 true>, i32 4)
```

```
%1 = trunc <4 x i64> %0 to <4 x i16>
%2 = xor <4 x i16> %1, <i16 -1, i16 -1, i16 -1, i16 -1>
%3 = call i16 @llvm.vector.reduce.umax.v4i16(<4 x i16> %2)
%4 = zext i16 %3 to i32
%t = trunc i32 %4 to i16
ret i16 %t
}
```

Listing 6-3. Generated assembly for vector code.

```
lui a0, %hi(c)                              # Load higher
part of address @c to a0
addi a0, a0, %lo(c)
# Load lower part of address @c to a0
li a1, 24
# Store stride 24 to a1
vsetivli zero, 4, e32, m1, ta, ma
# Operate initially on the vector of 4 x i32
vlse64.v v8, (a0), a1
# Strided load of 4 i64 elements from address (a0) with
stride in a1
vnsrl.wi v10, v8, 0                         # Truncate 4 x
i64 in v8 to 4 x i32 and store the result in v10
# RISC-V does not support immediate truncation from 4 x i64 to
4 x i16, so truncate to 4 x i32 at first
vsetvli zero, zero, e16, mf2, ta, ma    # Operate on the
4 x i16 vector
vnsrl.wi v8, v10, 0                         # Truncate
4 x i32 in v10 to 4 x i16 and store the result in v8
vnot.v v8, v8
# xor v8, -1
```

```
vredmaxu.vs v8, v8, v8
# Vector unsigned max reduction of 4 x i16 stored in v8
vmv.x.s a0, v8                              # Move single
i16 from first element in v8 to a0
ret
```

This example effectively demonstrates the advanced capabilities of the LLVM compiler's SLP vectorizer. Let's break down the key features demonstrated:

(a) Strided Load Recognition. The compiler demonstrates the ability to identify and generate efficient strided load operations. This is important for handling noncontiguous memory access patterns, which are common in many algorithms.

(b) Vector Reductions. The SLP vectorizer successfully recognizes reduction patterns and transforms them into vector reduction operations. This can significantly improve performance for operations like sum, max, or min across an array.

(c) Enhanced Bitwidth Analysis. The compiler implements sophisticated bitwidth analysis to optimize the use of vector lanes and minimize unnecessary data movement or extension operations.

(d) Cost-Aware Optimization. The SLP vectorizer intelligently excludes the cost of the final scalar sign-/zero-extension (sext/zext) operations when evaluating the overall cost of vectorization. This approach allows more aggressive vectorization in cases where post-vectorization scalar operations can be efficiently handled by subsequent optimization passes.

(e) Interaction with Other Optimization Passes. While the example points out a suboptimal sext/zext/trunc sequence at the end of the vectorized code, it's worth noting that this is expected to be addressed by the InstructionCombiner optimization pass. This highlights the importance of considering the entire optimization pipeline when evaluating vectorization decisions.

The ability of the SLP vectorizer to recognize and optimize these patterns demonstrates its sophistication and potential for improving code performance. By leveraging these capabilities, developers can write more idiomatic scalar code and rely on the compiler to effectively vectorize it.

It's important to note that while the SLP vectorizer is powerful, its effectiveness can vary depending on the specific code structure and target architecture. Developers working on performance-critical applications may still benefit from understanding these optimizations to write code that is more amenable to effective vectorization.

Design of SLP Vectorizer

The SLP vectorizer in LLVM implements a bottom-up greedy approach, striking a balance between optimization quality and compilation efficiency. This design choice reflects the pragmatic considerations inherent in compiler development, where improvement in code performance must be weighed against increases in compilation time.

The vectorizer's structure can be broken down into several key phases:

(a) Analysis Phase. This initial stage involves scanning the code to identify potential vectorization candidates. It leverages LLVM's rich intermediate representation (IR) to gather information about instruction patterns, data dependencies, and memory access characteristics.

(b) SLP Tree Building and Legality Checking. The vectorizer constructs a tree representation of the code, capturing the relationships between instructions. Concurrently, it performs legality checks to ensure that potential vectorization transformations preserve program semantics and adhere to architectural constraints.

(c) Transformation Phase. Based on the SLP tree, the vectorizer determines which instruction groups can be more effectively combined into vector operations and transforms initial tree appropriately. This phase involves complex decision-making processes to optimize for both performance and code size.

(d) Cost Estimation Phase. The vectorizer employs a sophisticated cost model to evaluate the potential benefits of each vectorization opportunity. This model considers factors such as reciprocal throughput and register pressure, based on the target-specific architectural features.

(e) Vector Code Emission Phase. Finally, the vectorizer generates LLVM IR for the selected vector operations, replacing the original scalar code, where beneficial.

The SLP vectorizer is implemented as SLPVectorizerPass within the LLVM framework, integrating seamlessly with other optimization passes. This modular design allows easy maintenance and extensibility, enabling ongoing improvements to the vectorization process.

While more exhaustive analysis techniques could potentially result in better vectorization in some cases, the current approach offers a practical compromise. It achieves significant performance improvements for a wide range of code patterns without excessively impacting compilation times, which is very important for large-scale software development.

CHAPTER 6   LLVM SLP VECTORIZER

Analysis Phase

The initial phase of SLP vectorization in LLVM identifies potential root nodes for the SLP tree. This preliminary analysis is pivotal in determining the scope and effectiveness of the subsequent vectorization process. Currently, the vectorizer focuses on a limited set of instruction types as potential tree roots, reflecting a targeted approach to identifying vectorization opportunities.

The process of root node identification is primarily implemented in the SLPVectorizerPass::collectSeedInstructions method. This method scans the intermediate representation (IR) to locate instructions that serve as promising starting points for SLP tree construction. Currently, two main categories of instructions are considered as seed instructions:

(a) Store Instructions. Store operations often represent the terminal points of computation chains and can indicate opportunities for backward propagation for the vectorization. Starting from stores, the vectorizer can potentially identify sequences of computations that feed into these stores, which might be suitable for the vectorization.

(b) GetElementPtr (GEP) Instructions. GEP instructions, which are used for complex address calculations in LLVM IR, can signal potential for vectorizing memory access patterns. They often indicate structured data access that might benefit from vector operations.

The focus on these specific instruction types as seed candidates reflects a pragmatic approach to vectorization:

(a) Stores and GEPs often represent natural boundaries in computation and memory access patterns.

CHAPTER 6   LLVM SLP VECTORIZER

(b) Starting from these points allows the vectorizer to work backwards, identifying independent chains of computation that can be combined.

(c) This approach helps in managing the complexity of the analysis, as it provides clear entry points for tree construction.

Need to mention that while this approach is effective for many common code patterns, it may not capture all potential vectorization opportunities. The limited set of seed instruction types is a design choice that balances thoroughness with compilation efficiency (see Listing 6-4).

Listing 6-4. Seed candidates analysis.

```
for each Instruction I in BasicBlock:
    if I is a simple StoreInst with a vectorizable value type:
        Append I to Stores[base pointer of I]
    else if I is a single indexed (non-constant) GEP with a vectorizable index type:
        Append I to GEPs[base pointer of I]
```

The SLP vectorizer's approach to store sequences, implemented in SLPVectorizerPass::vectorizeStoreChains, focuses currently on a specific and common pattern: consecutive stores with a stride of 1. This targeted approach reflects a balance between optimization potential and implementation complexity.

Key aspects of this store vectorization process include

1. Consecutive Store Identification. The vectorizer scans for sequences of store instructions that operate on adjacent memory locations. This contiguous memory access pattern is a corner stone for efficient vector store operations.

2. Stride Analysis. Currently, the vectorizer only supports stores with a stride of 1, meaning each store operation accesses the immediately following memory location relative to the previous store. This restriction simplifies the analysis and ensures compatibility with most hardware vector store instructions.

3. Chain Formation. Once identified, these consecutive stores are grouped into chains. The length of these chains is typically determined by the vector data width supported by the target architecture.

4. Alignment Considerations. The vectorizer considers memory alignment requirements, as vector store operations often have stricter alignment constraints than scalar stores.

5. Value Operand Analysis. Beyond just the store instructions themselves, the vectorizer examines the values being stored. If these values are computed by operations that can also be vectorized, it may extend the vectorization opportunity up the def-use chain.

6. Legal Check. Before proceeding with vectorization, the compiler performs legality checks to ensure that combining the stores into a vector operation doesn't violate any program semantics or introduce incorrect behavior.

The focus on consecutive stores with stride 1 is pragmatic for several reasons:

(a) It covers a large percentage of common use cases in real-world code.

CHAPTER 6   LLVM SLP VECTORIZER

(b) It aligns well with the capabilities of most vector instruction sets.

(c) It simplifies the analysis and transformation process, helping to keep compilation times reasonable. However, this approach does leave room for future enhancements:

(d) Support for non-unit strides could expand vectorization opportunities.

(e) Handling of more complex memory access patterns could benefit certain algorithms.

The basic algorithm for this analysis is shown in Listing 6-5.

Listing 6-5. Store instructions analysis.

```
sort(stores) using the types of the stored values
group stores by the instructions opcodes
group stores with constant values

while stored values looks promising to be vectorized:
    sort(stores slice by pointers)
    find consecutive stores

    for each consecutive stores slice:
        MaxVF = max(power_of_2_floor(slice.size()), store_
        maximum_vf(value_type))
        MinVF = max(2, store_minimum_vf(value_type))

        for VF = MaxVF downto MinVF (dividing VF by 2 each
        iteration):
            Cnt = 0
            while Cnt < slice.size():
                subslice = slice.slice(Cnt, VF)
```

```
            try_to_vectorize(subslice)

        if subslice vectorized:
            mark values in subslice as vectorized
            Cnt += VF
        else:
            Cnt += 1

    if looks promising to try larger vector factors:
        VF = 2 * largest previous vector factor
        continue to the next iteration of the outer
        while loop
```

The SLP vectorizer implements complex algorithm to identify and transform chain sequences within the code. This process, implemented in the SLPVectorizerPass::vectorizeChainsInBlock method, targets two primary categories of instruction sequences:

1. Reduction patterns. These involve operations that combine multiple values into a single result, such as sum, product calculation, or finding minimum/maximum values.

2. Homogeneous instruction sequences. These consist of a series of similar operations that can be efficiently combined into vector instructions.

To do this, the vectorizer performs several steps:

1. The vectorizer begins by gathering PHI nodes from the current basic block. These nodes are then sorted and grouped based on two primary criteria: a) Instruction opcodes and b) Constant values associated with the PHIs. The sorted PHI nodes are analyzed for compatibility. Compatibility factors include

(a) Similar types

(b) Matching incoming basic blocks

(c) Related computations in their incoming values

The vectorizer identifies "slices" of PHI nodes that are most compatible with each other. A slice represents a group of PHI nodes that can potentially be combined into a vector PHI with the most effective SLP tree. For each identified slice, starting with the most promising (typically the largest compatible group), the vectorizer attempts to combine the PHIs into a vector operation. This process is repeated for all identified slices, prioritizing larger, more compatible groups first. After processing the slices, the vectorizer makes a final pass to attempt vectorization of any remaining, nonvectorized PHI nodes.

The significance of this approach lies in its ability to handle control flow convergence points effectively. By vectorizing compatible PHI nodes, the compiler can maintain vectorized computation across basic block boundaries, potentially leading to more comprehensive vectorization of the entire function. This process is particularly beneficial for

(a) Loops with complex control flow

(b) Algorithms involving conditional computations

(c) Code patterns resulting from high-level language constructs like switch statements or nested if-else blocks (see Listing 6-6).

Listing 6-6. PHI nodes analysis.

```
sort(PHIs from the current block)
group PHIs by the instructions opcodes
group PHIs with constant values

for each slice of PHIs with the most compatible values:
    try_to_vectorize(slice)

try_to_vectorize(all remaining non-vectorized PHIs)
```

2. The SLP vectorizer tries to identify potential roots for reduction trees, focusing on instructions with specific characteristics. This process is important for uncovering vectorization opportunities that might not be immediately obvious.
   Key Characteristics of Potential Reduction Tree Roots:

   (a) No Users: Instructions that are not used by any other instructions in the current scope.

   (b) Void Return Type: Operations that do not produce a value but rather have side effects.

   Common examples of such instructions are return instructions (rets), store operations, and void function calls. These instructions are considered potential roots of reduction trees for several reasons:

   (a) Terminal Operations. They often represent the end point of a computation chain, making them ideal starting points for backward analysis.

   (b) Side Effect Isolation. Void-type instructions typically encapsulate side effects, which is critical for maintaining program semantics during vectorization.

(c) Reduction Pattern Identification. Starting from these instructions allows the vectorizer to trace back through the IR, potentially uncovering reduction patterns that can be vectorized (see Listing 6-7).

Listing 6-7. Reduction roots analysis.

```
if the instruction I has no uses and (the type is void or I is
a call instruction):
    if (I is a store instruction and store reduction
vectorization is enabled) or (I is not a store instruction):
        try_to_vectorize_reduction(the operand values of
instruction I)
```

3. In addition to the instructions analyzed earlier, PHI nodes are also considered as potential roots of reduction trees (see Listing 6-8).

Listing 6-8. Reduction roots analysis for PHI nodes.

```
if PHINode exists and PHINode has exactly 2 incoming values:
    try_to_vectorize_reduction(incoming values of PHINode)
```

4. Comparison instructions (cmp) and insertvalue/insertelement instructions are collected for the later analysis.

5. SLP vectorizer tries to vectorize reductions, rooted by the scalar operands of the insertelement and/or insertvalue instructions, and tries to optimize gathers/buildvectors/buildvalues by vectorizing these sequences, where possible (Listing 6-9).

Listing 6-9. Reduction roots analysis for insertelement/insertvalue.

```
# Process insertelement instructions for reduction
vectorization
for each insertelement in insertelement_instructions:
    if insertelement is not vectorized:
        operand = get_operand(insertelement)
        try_to_vectorize_reduction(operand)

# Process insertelement instructions for buildvector/buildvalue
vectorization
for each insertelement in insertelement_instructions:
    if insertelement is not vectorized and is_buildvector_or_
    buildvalue_root(insertelement):
        try_to_vectorize_buildvector_sequence(insertelement)
```

In the context of vectorization, gathers, buildvectors, and buildvalues are fundamental vectorization operations that involve constructing vectors/aggregate values from individual elements. To optimize these operations effectively, it is essential to understand the structure and characteristics of the underlying instruction sequences.

A gather, buildvector, or buildvalue sequence consists of series of dependent insertelement/insertvalue instructions. Each insertelement/insertvalue instruction takes the result of the previous insertelement/insertvalue instruction or another vector/aggregate value as its base and inserts a new value (in the case of buildvector/buildvalue) or a load instruction (in the case of gathers) at a specific index.

The key characteristics of a gather, buildvector, or buildvalue sequence are as follows:

(a) Dependency Chain. Each insertelement (or insertvalue for buildvalue sequence) instruction depends on the result of the previous insertelement (insertvalue) instruction or another vector value. This creates a chain of dependencies, where the output of one insertelement (insertvalue) becomes the input of the next.

(b) Single User. If an insertelement (insertvalue) instruction has only a single user (i.e., it is used as an operand by only one other instruction), it is part of the gather/buildvector (buildvalue) sequence. This property helps to identify the instructions that are exclusively involved in constructing the vector.

(c) Root Instruction. The initial instruction or value that serves as the starting point of the sequence is considered the root of the gather/buildvector(buildvalue) sequence. This root can be a non-insertelement (non-insertvalue for buildvalue) instruction or an insertelement (insertvalue) instruction with multiple users. The root represents the base vector or the first element (root) of the sequence.

By identifying the root instruction and the chain of dependent insertelement instructions, we can analyze the entire sequence as a whole and apply appropriate optimizations.

The root instruction plays a significant role in determining the vectorization strategy. If the root is a non-insertelement instruction or an insertelement instruction with multiple users, it indicates that the sequence is not a standalone buildvector or buildvalue operation. In such cases, the vectorization approach may involve combining the sequence with other vector operations (through the insertsubvector/shuffle instructions) or applying more advanced techniques.

On the other hand, if the root is an insertelement instruction with a single user, it signifies the beginning of a dedicated buildvector or buildvalue sequence. In this scenario, the entire sequence can be analyzed and vectorized as a unit, potentially leading to more efficient code generation (see Listing 6-10).

Listing 6-10. Buildvector sequences.

```
define i32 @test(ptr %p, ptr %p1, ptr %p2, i32 %v0,
%i32 %v1) {
...
  %0 = load i32, %p, align 4
  %1 = load i32, %p1, align 4
  %2 = load i32, %p2, align 4
  %ins1 = insertelement <4 x i32> poison, i32 %0, 0    ;
  result is <4 x i32> <i32 %0, i32 poison, i32 poison,
  i32 poison>
  %ins2 = insertelement <4 x i32> %ins1, i32 %1, 1     ;
  result is <4 x i32> <i32 %0, i32 %1, i32 poison, i32 poison>
  %ins3 = insertelement <4 x i32> %ins2, i32 %2, 2     ;
  result is <4 x i32> <i32 %0, i32 %1, i32 %2, i32 poison>
  %ins4 = insertelement <4 x i32> %ins2, i32 %v0, 3    ;
  result is <4 x i32> <i32 %0, i32 poison, i32 poison, i32 %v0>
  %ins5 = insertelement <4 x i32> %ins4, i32 %v1, 1    ;
  result is <4 x i32> <i32 %0, i32 poison, i32 %v1, i32 %v0>
...
}
```

In the given example above, there are two gather sequences and one buildvector sequence.

(a) First Gather Sequence:

- The first gather sequence consists of only the single %ins1 instruction.
- This instruction inserts a load value (%0) into the vector at index 0, forming a gather sequence.
- The root of this gather sequence is the <4 x i32> poison value, which serves as the initial vector.

(b) Second Gather Sequence:

- The second gather sequence starts with the %ins2 instruction as its root.
- The %ins2 instruction is not part of the first gather sequence because it has two users: %ins3 and %ins4.
- The gather sequence includes only the %ins3 instruction, which inserts the load value %2 into the vector at index 2.

(c) BuildVector Sequence:

- The buildvector sequence consists of the %ins4 and %ins5 instructions.
- These instructions insert scalar values (%v1 and %v0) into different lanes of the vector.
- The root of the buildvector sequence is the %ins2 instruction, which is shared with the second gather sequence.

These sequences provide the following results:

- The result of the first gather sequence is <4 x i32> <i32 %0, i32 poison, i32 poison, i32 poison>, where %0 is inserted at index 0, and the remaining elements are poison values.

- The result of the second gather sequence is <4 x i32> <i32 %0, i32 %1, i32 %2, i32 poison>, where %0, %1, and %2 are inserted at indices 0, 1, and 2, respectively, and the remaining element is a poison value.

- The result of the buildvector sequence is <4 x i32> <i32 %0, i32 %v1, i32 poison, i32 %v0>, where %0, %v1, and %v0 are inserted at indices 0, 1, and 3, respectively, and the remaining element is a poison value.

6. SLP vectorizer tries to vectorize sequences of the comparison instructions (see Listing 6-11).

Listing 6-11. Vectorization of compare instructions.

```
# Process cmp instructions for reduction vectorization
for each cmp in cmp_instructions:
    if not is_vectorized(cmp):
        operands = get_operands(cmp)
        try_to_vectorize_reduction(operands)

# Sort cmp instructions and group by opcodes and constants
sorted_cmps = sort_and_group_cmps(cmp_instructions)

# Process sorted cmp slices for vectorization
for each slice in sorted_cmps:
```

```
    if slice_has_most_compatible_values(slice):
        try_to_vectorize(slice)

# Process remaining non-vectorized cmp instructions
remaining_cmps = get_non_vectorized_Cmps(cmp_instructions)
try_to_vectorize(remaining_cmps)
```

7. SLP vectorizer tries to gather GEPs and considers them for vectorization. The SLPVectorizerPass ::vectorizeGEPIndices function is responsible for collecting and analyzing GEP instructions to determine their suitability for vectorization. This function identifies GEP instructions that can be safely vectorized without violating dependencies or introducing illegal memory accesses (see Listing 6-12).

Listing 6-12. Vectorization of address (GetElementPtr) instructions.

```
# Remove unnecessary GEPs
remove all previously vectorized GEPs or GEPs with constant
indices.
remove GEPs, which have constant difference.

gather all indices;

try_to_vectorize(inidices);

extract inidices to form correct GEPs;
```

CHAPTER 6   LLVM SLP VECTORIZER

Reduction Analysis Phase

Horizontal reduction stands as a very important paradigm in vectorization, offering substantial performance gains in SIMD (Single Instruction, Multiple Data) architectures. This operation coalesces multiple elements within a SIMD vector, gathering them into a single scalar result. Its gain lies in its ability to perform computations across vector elements with remarkable efficiency.

In the realm of vector and SIMD Instruction Set Architectures (ISAs), many targets have incorporated specialized instructions tuned for horizontal reduction computations. These special instructions serve to optimize the reduction process, leveraging the full potential of the hardware.

Considering the RISC-V RVV extensions, it introduces a suite of vector reduction instructions, including

1. vred{u,s}{sum,max,min,and,or,xor}: These perform reduction operations (sum, max, min, and bitwise operations) on integer vector elements.

2. vfred{sum,max,min}: Specifically designed for floating-point reduction operations.

These instructions enable efficient horizontal reductions directly in hardware, significantly accelerating common computational patterns.

However, the absence of direct hardware support for horizontal reductions in an ISA does not disable optimization. Complex compilers can transform the algorithmic complexity from $O(n)$ in scalar code to $O(\log(n))$ in vector code. This logarithmic improvement stems from the smart application of divide-and-conquer strategies, often implemented as tree-based reduction algorithms.

For instance, consider a sum reduction on a vector of 8 elements:

CHAPTER 6　LLVM SLP VECTORIZER

1. Initial vector: [a, b, c, d, e, f, g, h]

2. First iteration: [(a+b), (c+d), (e+f), (g+h)]

3. Second iteration: [(a+b+c+d), (e+f+g+h)]

4. Final iteration: [a+b+c+d+e+f+g+h]

This approach requires $\log2(8) = 3$ iterations, as opposed to 7 additions in a linear reduction, resulting in the $O(\log(n))$ complexity.

Proficient exploitation of horizontal reductions can result in a significant performance enhancement, particularly in compute-intensive domains such as scientific simulations, computer graphics, and machine learning.

The LLVM compiler infrastructure's SLP vectorizer incorporates a sophisticated analysis mechanism specifically tuned for associative reductions. Associative reductions, in contrast to their ordered counterparts, offer the flexibility to perform calculations in any order. This property either preserves the result or introduces acceptable variations, particularly when dealing with floating-point operations under relaxed precision requirements (e.g., when the -ffast-math compiler flag is used).

The difference between associative and ordered reductions is significant:

1. Result Consistency. Ordered reductions constantly produce identical results, whereas associative reductions may provide slight result variations due to differing execution sequences.

2. Performance Characteristics. Associative reductions generally result in better performance and offer enhanced parallelization opportunities.

3. Precision Considerations. Ordered reductions maintain precision for non-associative operations, which is particularly critical for floating-point computations.

CHAPTER 6 LLVM SLP VECTORIZER

In its current implementation, the LLVM SLP vectorizer exclusively supports associative reductions. The incorporation of ordered reductions requires additional development to preserve the original order of reduced values.

The HorizontalReduction class serves as the cornerstone for reduction analysis and pattern matching within the LLVM framework. It encapsulates the logic required to identify reduction patterns in the intermediate representation of the code.

A key component of this class is the matchAssociativeReduction function. This function performs the initial analysis and verification to determine whether a specified instruction (referred to as Root) represents the root of a reduction operation sequence (see Listing 6-13).

Listing 6-13. Reductions analysis algorithm.

```
# Identify reduction kind based on the opcode of the Root
instruction
RdxKind = HorizontalReduction::getRdxKind(Root)

# Check if we can safely vectorize this reduction (is it
associative?)
if !isVectorizable(RdxKind, Root)
    return false

# Check if the type of the Root is vectorizable
if !isVectorizableType(Root.type)
    return false

# Initialize lists for potential reduction operations and
reduced values
potentialReductionOps = [Root]
reducedValues = []

# Process all potential reduction operations
```

```
while !potentialReductionOps.isEmpty()
    instruction = potentialReductionOps.pop()

    # Analyze each operand of the instruction
    for operand in instruction.operands
        # Check if the operand is a valid reduction operation
        if !isInstruction(operand) ||
           !matchesReductionKind(operand, RdxKind) ||
           !hasRequiredUses(operand, RdxKind)
            # If not, add it to the list of reduced values
            reducedValues.append(operand)
        else
            # If it is, add it to the list of potential
            reduction operations
            potentialReductionOps.push(operand)

# Sort reduced values for better reduction vectorization in
the future
# Sorting criteria: parent, value kind, compatibility
sortReducedValues(reducedValues)

return true
```

The success of the reduction identification process triggers the next phase of optimization. The compiler invokes the HorizontalReduction::tryToReduce function, initiating an attempt to vectorize the previously identified reduced values. The tryToReduce function implements algorithms to analyze the reduction pattern and determine whether vectorization is both feasible and beneficial.

During this process, the function considers various factors, including

1. The nature of the reduction operation (e.g., sum, product, logical AND/OR)

2. The data types involved in the reduction

CHAPTER 6 LLVM SLP VECTORIZER

3. The target architecture's vector capabilities
4. The potential performance gain versus the cost of vectorization

If the analysis determines that vectorization is advantageous, the method transforms the scalar reduction into a vector operation. This transformation typically involves

1. Grouping scalar operations into vector-width chunks
2. Replacing scalar instructions with their vector equivalents
3. Combining all vector operands into a single vector operand using reduction operation. This allows better utilization of the vector units and allows to reduce total reductions emission, which may be very expensive in terms of performance
4. Handling edge cases for reductions that don't evenly fit into vector widths (see Listing 6-14)

Listing 6-14. Vectorization of the identified reductions.

```
# Constants and limits
ReductionLimit = 4
RegMaxNumber = 4
RedValsMaxNumber = 128

# Calculate total number of reduced values
NumReducedVals = sum of good reduction values (either constants
or compatible instructions) in ReducedVals

# Check if vectorization ican be performed
```

```
if NumReducedVals < ReductionLimit and (identity reduction is
not enabled or all uniques):
    mark analyzed reduction roots
    return null

# Set up tracking structures for instructions, transformed
during vectorization of reductions
TrackedVals = initialize map for tracking values
ExternallyUsedValues = initialize map for externally
used values

# Get comparison instruction for min/max reduction
CmpInst = get compare instruction for min/max reduction if
applicable

# Initialize reduced values opcode and alternate opcode
States = initialize vectorization states for ReducedVals

VectorizedTree = null
CheckForReusedReductionOps = false

# Main loop for processing reduced values
for each OrigReducedVals in ReducedVals:
    Candidates = get and filter candidates from OrigReducedVals

    # Handle special cases (constants, shuffled extracts)
    if is constant values and allowed:
        process constant values
        continue

    # Determine reduction width and prepare for vectorization
    ReduxWidth = calculate appropriate reduction width

    # Attempt vectorization for different positions and widths
    while position < (NumReducedVals - ReduxWidth + 1) and
    ReduxWidth >= ReductionLimit:
```

CHAPTER 6   LLVM SLP VECTORIZER

```
        VL = get vectorized list from Candidates

        # Build and analyze the tree
        build tree for VL
        if tree is not suitable for vectorization:
            continue

        # Reorder the tree and gather externally used values
        reorder tree
        transform nodes in the tree
        gather externally used values
        compute minimum value sizes

        # Compute costs and check if vectorization is
        beneficial
        Cost = compute vectorization cost
        if Cost >= -SLPCostThreshold:
            emit optimization remark missed
            continue

        # Vectorize the tree
        VectorizedRoot = vectorize tree
        Save the vectorized result in the list

        # Update vectorized values count
        update count of vectorized values

        update position and reduction width
        AnyVectorized = true

    # Handle optimized reused scalars if applicable
    if optimized reused scalars and not AnyVectorized:
        process optimized reused scalars

# Finalize the reduction
```

```
if VectorizedTree exists:
    reorder operands of boolean logical operations if needed

    # Emit reduction code
    combine the vectorized instructions from the list
    ReducedSubTree = emit reduction for combined vector value

    # Update VectorizedTree
    VectorizedTree = update vectorized tree with ReducedSubTree

    finish reduction by processing extra reductions
    replace original reduction root with VectorizedTree
    cleanup original reduction operations
else if not CheckForReusedReductionOps:
    mark analyzed reduction roots

return VectorizedTree
```

Tree Building and Legality Checks Phase

After gathering and filtering the relevant instructions, the next stage in the SLP vectorization process is building the vectorization tree. This tree represents the relationships and dependencies between instructions, guiding the compiler in making informed decisions about vectorization.

The tree building procedure is implemented as a recursive pass, implemented in the BoUpSLP::buildTree_rec function. It begins by selecting a homogeneous and/or compatible heterogeneous root instruction from the pool of potential profitable candidates. The selection process considers factors such as the compatibility of incoming values, the nature of the instructions (avoiding ephemeral instructions used only in @llvm.assume intrinsics), and the profitability of building the node.

CHAPTER 6 LLVM SLP VECTORIZER

The profitability assessment is based on several criteria. The tree height is considered, with the maximum depth controlled by the -slp-recursion-max-depth option (default value is 12). If the tree is too small (less than the value specified in -slp-min-tree-size, default is 3) or the vectorization of the nest node leads to less profitable vector code, the node is deemed unprofitable. In such cases, the nest analysis is terminated, and an SLP tree node is constructed as a gather or buildvector node.

The tree building process may also result in a gather or buildvector node under other conditions. If the sequence consists of a single value splat (possibly mixed with undef or poison values), all constants, or values from different basic blocks, a gather or buildvector node is created.

Before proceeding with the actual vectorization, the compiler performs preliminary checks to determine if the group of instructions can be safely vectorized. The BoUpSLP::getScalarsVectorizationState function is responsible for this task. It examines each specific opcode and verifies that the instructions with that opcode are suitable for vectorization.

For example, the function checks that load instructions create a vectorizable sequence (nonatomic, nonvolatile, either consecutive, masked gather, or strided). It ensures that each instruction has a valid vectorization type and that store instructions are simple (nonatomic, nonvolatile, consecutive). In the case of call instructions, it verifies that they all invoke the same vectorizable function.

These preliminary checks serve as a safeguard, saving valuable compile time by identifying and filtering out instructions that are not suitable for vectorization before proceeding with the actual instruction scheduling and code generation (see Listing 6-15).

Listing 6-15. Legality checks and node building algorithm.

```
function buildTree_rec(VL, Depth, UserTreeIdx):
    if Depth >= RecursionMaxDepth or
        any value in VL is (ephemeral or broadcast or
        constant or
```

CHAPTER 6 LLVM SLP VECTORIZER

        instruction with non-matched parent
        block or
        has vector type or part of another
        (non-matching VL) node or
        part of reduction operations):
    create buildvector node
    return

if BasicBlock is unreachable or is catchswitch block:
    create buildvector node
    return

#Temporarily limitation, will be removed removed once full
non-power-of-2 number of elements is supported
if VL has non-power-of-2 unique elements:
    extend the list of scalars with poison values to the
    closest whole-register num of elements

if getScalarsVectorizationState(VL) ==
TreeEntry::NeedToGather:
    create buildvector node
    return

BSRef = BlocksSchedules[BB]
if BSRef is null:
    BSRef = create new BlockScheduling(BB)
BS = BSRef

Do not schedule, just check if the instructions are
schedulable
Bundle = BS.tryScheduleBundle(UniqueValues, this)
if Bundle is null:
    create buildvector node
    return

CHAPTER 6   LLVM SLP VECTORIZER

```
TE = newTreeEntry(VL, Bundle)
for I in range(number of operands):
    Operands = ValueList(number of unique values, Ith
    operand of each instruction)
    buildTree_rec(Operands, Depth + 1, {TE, I})
```

The compiler's vectorization process involves a critical step: verifying the legality of constructing vector nodes by assessing whether the source scalar instructions can be scheduled for concurrent execution. This assessment is implemented in the BoUpSLP::BlockScheduling::tryScheduleBundle function, which attempts to create a schedule bundle for the original scalar instructions and subsequently schedules them.

Scheduling, in this context, refers to the compiler's effort to consolidate source scalar instructions into a single execution unit, ensuring safe parallel processing. This process unfolds in two distinct phases. The initial legality scheduling phase doesn't schedule the instructions; instead, it evaluates the feasibility of grouping them for simultaneous execution. Instructions are deemed unschedulable if they depend on each other (one instruction is an operand of another instruction), have potential memory conflicts, or other control dependencies.

The tryScheduleBundle function initiates the construction of a scheduling block by incrementally adding the instructions to the block. Starting with a single instruction, it iteratively expands the scheduling block using the BoUpSLP::BlockScheduling::extendSchedulingRegion function. This expansion is implemented as a bidirectional, stepwise iteration, bounded by the ScheduleRegionSizeLimit parameter. This limit, controlled by the -slp-schedule-budget option (defaulting to 100,000 instructions), controls the maximum size of the scheduling region. The budget decreases with each added instruction; when exhausted, no further additions are permitted, and the entire group is classified as nonschedulable. This mechanism serves to cap the number of scheduling attempts, thereby optimizing compilation time.

Certain instructions may bypass this scheduling process. For instance, instructions used exclusively outside their basic block (and not involved in memory operations), or those with only non-instruction operands (or phi nodes), are always schedulable and can be processed more efficiently.

The scheduling evaluation begins by computing dependencies for each instruction in the bundle. The BoUpSLP::BlockScheduling::calculateDependencies function traverses the scheduling data associated with each instruction, reassessing its dependencies. This involves verifying that instructions within the same bundle don't form a def-use chain, checking for control dependencies, and identifying potential memory conflicts.

Control dependencies may arise from various sources, including memory barriers, fences, non-speculatable function calls, volatile memory accesses, or atomic operations. Memory conflicts can occur when memory regions are modified and subsequently accessed by other instructions within the bundle. The detection of any such conflict marks the instruction bundle nonschedulable, precluding safe vectorization.

Upon successful scheduling, the vectorizer proceeds to construct vectorized SLP nodes and recursively generates nodes for the operands, applying the same analysis process to each operand bundle.

This refined approach to instruction scheduling and vectorization enables compilers to optimize code execution while maintaining program correctness and safety (see Listing 6-16).

Listing 6-16. Instructions scheduling algorithm.

```
function std::optional<BoUpSLP::ScheduleBundle *> BoUpSLP::BlockScheduling::tryScheduleBundle(ArrayRef<Value *> VL, BoUpSLP *SLP, const InstructionsState &S)
  # Instructions with non-instruction operands or which are used only outside of their basic block do not need to be scheduled.
```

```
if all values are phi nodes or vector like
instruction(insert/extractelement) with the constant operands
or do not require scheduling
   return nullptr

for each instruction V in VL
   if V requires scheduling and not extendSchedulingRegion(V)
      return std::nullopt

ReSchedule =  any value in VL was previously scheduled or
scheduling region expanded
calculateDependencies()

if ReSchedule
  reset scheduling for the entire region

while region is not fully scheduled or instructions remain to
be scheduled
     schedule next instruction # schedule(), check if region
     is schedulable by checking scheduling of the next
     instruction

return final schedule bundle

function bool BoUpSLP::BlockScheduling::extendSchedulingRegion(
Value *V, const InstructionsState &S)
  if scheduling data exists for V
    return true

  # Scheduling data does not exist - need to create a new one
  and attach to the scheduling block.
  while not at end of BasicBlock
    if ++ScheduleRegionSize > ScheduleRegionSizeLimit
      return false
```

CHAPTER 6   LLVM SLP VECTORIZER

      expand scheduling block boundaries

   create and attach new scheduling data for V
   return true

function void BoUpSLP::BlockScheduling::calculateDependencies(ScheduleBundle &Bundle, bool InsertInReadyList, BoUpSLP *SLP)
   while unprocessed data exists for dependency calculation
      for each schedule data BundleMember from current to last in region
         if BundleMember has all valid dependencies
            continue

         # Handle def-use chain dependencies.
         if BundleMember is in region but not vectorized
            increment dependency counter for BundleMember
            if BundleMember lacks valid dependencies
               add BundleMember to dependency calculation list
         else
            for each user of BundleMember instruction
               if user is in region
                  increment dependency counter for BundleMember
                  if user lacks valid dependencies
                     add user to dependency calculation list

         # Handle the memory dependencies (if any).
         if memory operations between BundleMember and region end may alias
            increment memory dependency counter for BundleMember
            increment general dependency counter for BundleMember
            if BundleMember lacks valid dependencies
               add BundleMember to dependency calculation list

CHAPTER 6 LLVM SLP VECTORIZER

```
function void BoUpSLP::BlockScheduling::schedule(ScheduleEntity
*Data, ReadyListType &ReadyList)
  mark current schedule entity as scheduled

  for each schedule data BundleMember from the schedule entity
    # Handle the def-use chain dependencies.
    for each operand of BundleMember instruction
      if operand data has valid dependencies and is scheduled
        decrement unscheduled dependency count for BundleMember

    # Handle the memory dependencies.
    for each memory dependency of BundleMember
      if memory dependency data has valid dependencies and is
      scheduled
        decrement unscheduled dependency count for BundleMember

    # Handle the control dependencies.
    for each control dependency of BundleMember
      if control dependency data is scheduled
        decrement unscheduled dependency count for BundleMember
```

During this phase of compilation, another key analysis is performed: the reordering of commutative operands. This process allows the vectorizer to enhance the resulting vectorization outcome.

Consider, for instance, two addition operations in the intermediate representation, as shown in Listing 6-17.

Listing 6-17. Operands ordering mismatch.

```
%add0 = add i32 1, %mul0
%add1 = add i32 %mul1, 2
```

Here %mul0 and %mul1 are multiplication instructions.

Without operand reordering, the compiler would generate a vectorized node for the addition instructions, using two separate buildvector nodes: (1, mul) and (mul, 2). However, by implementing operand reordering, the compiler can produce a more efficient structure:

- A vectorized node for the addition operations
- A constant node containing (1, 2), which is cheap in many cases and for many targets
- A vectorized node for the multiplication operations

This reordering leverages the commutative property of addition, allowing the compiler to align similar operands across multiple instructions. The resulting structure is often more amenable to vectorization and can lead to a more efficient use of the vector instructions.

Furthermore, this optimization can reduce register pressure and minimize memory access operations, as it consolidates similar operations and constants. It also simplifies subsequent optimization passes, potentially enabling additional vectorization opportunities or constant folding.

While this example focuses on addition, the same principle applies to all commutative operations, including multiplication, bitwise AND, OR, and XOR. The compiler must, however, be cautious to preserve the original program semantics, especially in the presence of potential side effects or when dealing with floating-point operations where the order of operations can affect precision (see Listing 6-18 and listing 6-19).

Listing 6-18. Vectorization with and without operands reordering.

```
define void @test(ptr %p, i32 %v) {
  %mul0 = mul i32 %v, 2
  %mul1 = mul i32 %v, 3
  %add0 = add i32 1, %mul0
```

CHAPTER 6   LLVM SLP VECTORIZER

```llvm
  %add1 = add i32 %mul1, 2
  store i32 %add0, ptr %p
  %p1 = getelementptr i32, ptr %p, i64 1
  store i32 %add1, ptr %p1
  ret void
}

; without reordering phase
define void @test(ptr %p, i32 %v) {
  %mul0 = mul i32 %v, 2
  %mul1 = mul i32 %v, 3
  %bv0 = insertelement <2 x i32> <i32 1, i32 poison>,
  i32 %mul0, i32 1
  %bv1 = insertelement <2 x i32> <i32 poison, i32 2>,
  i32 %mul1, i32 0
  %add = add <2 x i32> %bv0, %bv1
  store <2 x i32> %add, ptr %p
  ret void
}

; with reordering phase
define void @test(ptr %p, i32 %v) {
  %bv = insertelement <2 x i32> poison, i32 %v, i32 0
  %splat = shufflevector <2 x i32> %bv, <2 x i32> poison,
  <2 x i32> zeroinitializer
  %mul = mul <2 x i32> %splat, <i32 2, i32 3>
  %add = add <2 x i32> %mul, <i32 1, i32 2>
  store <2 x i32> %add, ptr %p
  ret void
}
```

Listing 6-19. *Vectorization with and without operands reordering (assembly).*

```
# without reordering phase
test:                                   # @test
        slliw   a2, a1, 1
        addw    a1, a2, a1
        vsetivli        zero, 2, e32, mf2, tu, ma
        vmv.v.i v8, 1
        vslide1down.vx  v9, v8, a2
        vmv.v.x v8, a1
        li      a1, 2
        vslide1down.vx  v10, v8, a1
        vsetvli zero, zero, e32, mf2, ta, ma
        vadd.vv v8, v9, v10
        vse32.v v8, (a0)
        ret

# with reordering phase
test:                                   # @test1
        vsetivli        zero, 2, e32, mf2, ta, ma
        vid.v   v10
        vadd.vi v8, v10, 2
        vadd.vi v9, v10, 1
        vmadd.vx        v8, a1, v9
        vse32.v v8, (a0)
        ret
```

The compiler implements a sophisticated operand reordering mechanism in the BoUpSLP::reorderInputsAccordingToOpcode function, utilizing the VLOperands helper class. This class uses a greedy, three-pass optimization approach for operand reordering.

CHAPTER 6 LLVM SLP VECTORIZER

Initially, the SLP vectorizer identifies the lane least likely to require reordering using the VLOperands::getBestLaneToStartReordering function. This function relies on the Boyer-Moore majority voting algorithm to determine the most frequently used opcode across lanes. It also quantifies the number of reorderable instructions in each lane. The lane with the minimal number of instructions sharing the same or compatible opcode and the least number of reorderable operands is selected as the fixed, base lane for reordering.

The compiler then determines the optimal reordering strategy for each operand, supporting four primary strategies:

1. Same/Compatible Opcode Vectorization (most common)
2. Constant
3. Splat
4. Ordered Loads

The selection criteria for these strategies are as follows:

- Ordered Loads selected when the operand in the best lane is a compatible load instruction with the same parent basic block.
- Constant is chosen if the operand is a constant value.
- Splat is applied if the operand is a function argument, an instruction and/or a constant value selectable through reordering of other operands.
- Opcode is the default strategy for all other cases.

Following strategy selection, the compiler initiates a three-pass analysis and transformation process to reorder operands across lanes. This process may terminate early if perfect matching is detected or if no further reordering is possible.

During each iteration, the previously analyzed lane becomes the new base lane, facilitating the selection of compatible instructions in close proximity. The VLOperands::getBestOperand() function is used to estimate compatibility costs and determine the most suitable operand for a given lane/operand combination.

The cost estimation varies based on the selected strategy:

- For Constant strategy, it prefers constant value operands.

- For Splat strategy, it favors identical values or constants.

- For Ordered Load strategy, it attempts to construct consecutive, reversed, or strided load sequences (utilizing the LookAheadHeuristics helper class).

- For Opcode strategy, it seeks instructions from the same basic block with identical or alternate opcodes.

Throughout this analysis, the procedure tracks the number of unique values, considering nodes with power-of-2 unique values/instructions more profitable. Upon completion of this phase, the analysis and legality check are considered finalized.

Transformation Phase

The SLP vectorizer currently implements two main tree transformation approaches, complemented by additional analytical processes. These algorithms refine the intermediate representation and prepare it for efficient code generation.

1. Tree Nodes Reordering. This phase focuses on restructuring the tree to reduce the number of shuffles. It involves reordering operations and adjusting the tree topology to align similar operations across vector lanes. This can lead to more efficient code generation.

2. Target-Specific Tree Node Transformation. This phase adjusts the tree to the specific characteristics of the target architecture. It may involve replacing generic operations with architecture-specific intrinsics, or restructuring operations to better utilize the target's instruction set. This transformation is required for getting maximum performance from the target hardware.

In addition to these transformation phases, the compiler performs two important analyses:

1. External Vector Element Usage Analysis. This process identifies which elements of vector values are used outside the current vectorization context. This information is vital for determining the necessary extract operations and for optimizing the interface between vectorized and scalar code regions.

2. Minimal Bitwidth Selection Analysis. The compiler analyzes the data flow to determine the minimal bitwidth for each operation. This can lead to using narrower data types where possible, potentially allowing for more elements to be processed in parallel or reducing memory bandwidth requirements.

These phases and analyses create a more optimized intermediate representation and result in a better (and correct!) final code.

Tree Nodes Reordering

The SLP tree, constructed during the initial phase, may not achieve optimal configuration in its original form. Consequently, the compiler performs the optimization step: tree nodes reordering.

During the tree construction phase, the compiler makes initial decisions based on local information and heuristics. However, these decisions may not always lead to the most favorable global structure for vectorization. The reordering phase addresses this limitation by applying a more comprehensive analysis.

Listing 6-20. Unordered scalars example.

```
define i32 @test(ptr noalias %in, ptr noalias %inn, ptr noalias %out) {
  %load.1 = load i32, ptr %in, align 4
  %gep.1 = getelementptr inbounds i32, ptr %in, i64 1
  %load.2 = load i32, ptr %gep.1, align 4
  %gep.2 = getelementptr inbounds i32, ptr %in, i64 2
  %load.3 = load i32, ptr %gep.2, align 4
  %gep.3 = getelementptr inbounds i32, ptr %in, i64 3
  %load.4 = load i32, ptr %gep.3, align 4
  %load.5 = load i32, ptr %inn, align 4
  %gep.4 = getelementptr inbounds i32, ptr %inn, i64 1
  %load.6 = load i32, ptr %gep.4, align 4
  %gep.5 = getelementptr inbounds i32, ptr %inn, i64 2
  %load.7 = load i32, ptr %gep.5, align 4
  %gep.6 = getelementptr inbounds i32, ptr %inn, i64 3
  %load.8 = load i32, ptr %gep.6, align 4
```

CHAPTER 6 LLVM SLP VECTORIZER

```
  %mul.1 = mul i32 %load.3, %load.6
  %mul.2 = mul i32 %load.2, %load.5
  %mul.3 = mul i32 %load.4, %load.7
  %mul.4 = mul i32 %load.1, %load.8
  %mul.5 = mul i32 %load.4, %load.8
  %mul.6 = mul i32 %load.3, %load.7
  %mul.7 = mul i32 %load.1, %load.5
  %mul.8 = mul i32 %load.2, %load.6
  %sub1 = sub i32 %mul.1, %mul.5
  %sub2 = sub i32 %mul.2, %mul.6
  %sub3 = sub i32 %mul.3, %mul.7
  %sub4 = sub i32 %mul.4, %mul.8
  %r1 = add i32 %sub1, %sub2
  %r2 = add i32 %r1, %sub3
  %r3 = add i32 %r2, %sub4
  ret i32 %r3
}
```

In the scenario from Listing 6-20, the compiler constructs an initial SLP tree that contains three shuffled operations, which is not the best decision (see Listing 6-21 and Listing 6-22).

Listing 6-21. Unordered vectorized code (LLVM IR).

```
define i32 @test(ptr noalias %in, ptr noalias %inn, ptr noalias %out) {
  %1 = load <4 x i32>, ptr %in, align 4
  %2 = shufflevector <4 x i32> %1, <4 x i32> poison, <4 x i32> <i32 1, i32 2, i32 3, i32 0>
  %3 = load <4 x i32>, ptr %inn, align 4
  %4 = mul <4 x i32> %2, %3
  %5 = shufflevector <4 x i32> %1, <4 x i32> poison, <4 x i32> <i32 2, i32 3, i32 0, i32 1>
```

```
    %6 = shufflevector <4 x i32> %3, <4 x i32> poison, <4 x i32>
    <i32 2, i32 3, i32 0, i32 1>
    %7 = mul <4 x i32> %5, %6
    %8 = sub <4 x i32> %4, %7
    %9 = call i32 @llvm.vector.reduce.add.v4i32(<4 x i32> %8)
    ret i32 %9
}
```

Listing 6-22. Unordered vectorized code (assembly).

```
"test":                     # @test
        vsetivli        zero, 4, e32, m1, ta, ma
        vle32.v v8, (a0)
        vle32.v v9, (a1)
        vslidedown.vi   v10, v8, 1
        vslideup.vi     v10, v8, 3
        vmul.vv v10, v10, v9
        vmul.vv v8, v8, v9
        vslidedown.vi   v9, v8, 2
        vslideup.vi     v9, v8, 2
        vsub.vv v8, v10, v9
        vmv.s.x v9, zero
        vredsum.vs
        v8, v8, v9
        vmv.x.s a0, v8
        ret
```

Instead of accepting the initial tree with three shuffled operands, the compiler performs operand rotation within each tree node.

CHAPTER 6 LLVM SLP VECTORIZER

To efficiently manage the reordering process and minimize the number of reordering operations, the SLP vectorizer implements two distinct reordering procedures. The first one is Whole Tree Reordering. This global optimization strategy is implemented in the BoUpSLP::reorderTopToBottom() function. The process involves

1. Traversing the entire tree, node by node.
2. Collecting all reordering operations that would be necessary during code generation. This includes

    (a) Direct reorderings associated with vectorized nodes (e.g., from load or extractelement nodes).

    (b) Indirect reorderings from gather/buildvector nodes, which are affected by the reordering of vectorized nodes.

3. Calculating the number of each specific ordering across the tree.
4. Selecting the most often occurring order as the optimal configuration.
5. Reordering each node in the tree to align with this chosen order.

This global approach ensures a consistent ordering strategy across the entire tree, potentially eliminating many local shuffles and creating more uniform access patterns (see Listing 6-23 and Listing 6-24).

Listing 6-23. Reordered vectorized code (LLVM IR).

```
define i32 @test(ptr noalias %in, ptr noalias %inn, ptr noalias %out) {
  %1 = load <4 x i32>, ptr %in, align 4
```

```
  %2 = shufflevector <4 x i32> %1, <4 x i32> poison, <4 x i32>
<i32 3, i32 0, i32 1, i32 2>
  %3 = load <4 x i32>, ptr %inn, align 4
  %4 = shufflevector <4 x i32> %3, <4 x i32> poison, <4 x i32>
<i32 2, i32 3, i32 0, i32 1>
  %5 = mul <4 x i32> %2, %4
  %6 = mul <4 x i32> %1, %3
  %7 = sub <4 x i32> %5, %6
  %8 = call i32 @llvm.vector.reduce.add.v4i32(<4 x i32> %7)
  ret i32 %8
}
```

Listing 6-24. Reordered vectorized code (assembly).

```
test:                               # @test
        vsetivli        zero, 4, e32, m1, ta, ma
        vle32.v v8, (a0)
        vle32.v v9, (a1)
        vslidedown.vi   v10, v8, 3
        vslideup.vi     v10, v8, 1
        vslidedown.vi   v11, v9, 2
        vslideup.vi     v11, v9, 2
        vmul.vv v10, v10, v11
        vnmsac.vv       v10, v8, v9
        vmv.s.x v8, zero
        vredsum.vs      v8, v10, v8
        vmv.x.s a0, v8
        ret
```

In this specific example, the compiler's reordering algorithm encounters two distinct orders and must decide which one to apply globally. Let's break down the scenario and its implications:

CHAPTER 6   LLVM SLP VECTORIZER

1. Available Orders are a) <2,3,0,1> and b) <1,2,3,0>
2. Frequency of Occurrence.
    (a) Order <2,3,0,1> appears twice in the tree
    (b) Order <1,2,3,0> appears once
3. Decision Process. The compiler opts for the order <2,3,0,1> based on its higher number of occurrences. This decision aligns with the principle of minimizing the total number of required shuffles across the entire tree.
4. Optimization Result. By applying the chosen rotation order <2,3,0,1> globally, the compiler reduces the total number of required shuffles from 3 to 2. This represents a 33% reduction in shuffle operations.

The implications and benefits are

1. Reduced Instruction Count. Decreasing the number of shuffles from 3 to 2 directly translates to fewer instructions in the final code, potentially improving both code size and execution time.
2. Improved Vector Lane Utilization. The chosen order likely aligns more operations for efficient execution.
3. Simplified Dependency Chains. The new order may simplify dependency chains between operations, potentially allowing better instruction-level parallelism.
4. Register Pressure Reduction. Fewer shuffle operations generally mean less register-to-register movement, which can alleviate register pressure.

The second tree reordering approach, implemented in the BoUpSLP: :reorderBottomToTop(bool IgnoreReorder) function, implements a more granular strategy for optimizing the SLP tree. This method complements the whole-tree reordering by focusing on subtree-level optimizations. The key steps of this approach are

1. Bottom-to-Top Analysis. Unlike the top-to-bottom approach, this method starts from the leaf nodes of the tree and works its way up. This allows for more localized optimizations that can capture patterns that might be missed in a global analysis.

2. Subtree Isolation. Each subtree within the larger SLP tree is analyzed independently. This isolation allows for optimizations tailored to the specific characteristics of each subtree.

3. Reordering Decision. For each subtree, the algorithm determines the optimal rotation order based on the maximum number of occurrences of each order within that subtree. This localized decision-making process can lead to more tuned optimizations.

4. Recursive Optimization. After rotating a subtree, its root node becomes a leaf node for the next higher-level subtree. This recursive approach allows the optimization to propagate upward through the tree structure.

5. Flexibility with IgnoreReorder Parameter. The boolean parameter IgnoreReorder provides a mechanism to selectively apply or skip reordering in certain contexts, adding flexibility to the optimization process.

CHAPTER 6 LLVM SLP VECTORIZER

The key benefits of this approach include

1. Fine-grained Optimization. By focusing on subtrees, the compiler can apply more targeted optimizations that might be overlooked in a global analysis.

2. Adaptation to Local Patterns. Different parts of the tree may benefit from different rotation orders. This method allows for such localized adaptations.

3. Potential for Better Overall Results. In some cases, optimizing subtrees independently and then combining these optimizations can lead to better overall results than a single global optimization pass.

4. Handling of Complex Trees. For large, complex trees where a single global rotation might be suboptimal, this approach can provide more balanced optimizations.

By implementing both whole-tree and subtree reordering strategies, the SLP vectorizer demonstrates a sophisticated approach to tree optimization. This multilevel strategy allows the compiler to capture both broad patterns across the entire computation and nuanced, localized opportunities for improvement (see Listing 6-25 and Listing 6-26).

Listing 6-25. *Reordered vectorized code (LLVM IR).*

```
define i32 @test(ptr noalias %in, ptr noalias %inn, ptr
noalias %out) {
  %1 = load <4 x i32>, ptr %in, align 4
  %2 = load <4 x i32>, ptr %inn, align 4
  %3 = shufflevector <4 x i32> %2, <4 x i32> poison, <4 x i32>
  <i32 1, i32 2, i32 3, i32 0>
```

CHAPTER 6 LLVM SLP VECTORIZER

```
  %4 = mul <4 x i32> %1, %3
  %5 = shufflevector <4 x i32> %4, <4 x i32> poison, <4 x i32>
    <i32 2, i32 3, i32 0, i32 1>
  %6 = mul <4 x i32> %1, %2
  %7 = sub <4 x i32> %5, %6
  %8 = call i32 @llvm.vector.reduce.add.v4i32(<4 x i32> %7)
  ret i32 %8
}
```

Listing 6-26. *Reordered vectorized code (Assembly).*

```
test:                                   # @test
        vsetivli        zero, 4, e32, mf2, ta, ma
        vle32.v v8, (a1)
        vle32.v v9, (a0)
        vslidedown.vi   v10, v8, 2
        vslideup.vi     v11, v9, 3
        vslidedown.vi   v10, v8, 2
        vslideup.vi     v11, v9, 1
        vmul.vv v10, v11, v10
        vnmsac.vv       v10, v9, v8
        vmv.s.x v8, zero
        vredsum.vs      v8, v10, v8
        vmv.x.s a0, v8
        ret
```

This example illustrates the effectiveness of the bottom-to-top subtree reordering approach. Let's analyze the process and its implications in detail:

1. Initial Subtree Identification. The compiler first identifies a subtree centered around the multiplication operation: %5 = mul <4 x i32> %2, %4.

283

2. Operand Reordering. The compiler determines that reordering of the operands of this multiplication can eliminate the need for extra shuffle operations. This decision is based on the analysis of the operands %2 and %4, likely finding a more optimal alignment that reduces vector lane shuffling.

3. Subtree Root Reordering. After reordering the operands, the compiler also reorders the root of this subtree (the multiplication operation itself). This step is important for propagating the optimization upward in the tree.

4. Propagation to Parent Node. The optimization then affects the parent node in the tree: %4 = mul <4 x i32> %1, %3. This node is assigned a new order of <2,3,0,1>.

5. Shuffle Sinking. By applying this transformation, any necessary shuffle operations are effectively "sunk" closer to the root of the overall tree, reducing overall number of shuffles.

This transformation sets the stage for additional optimizations in larger trees. As shuffles are consolidated near the root, the compiler may find opportunities for better vectorization for deeper subtrees.

Target-Specific Tree Nodes Transformation

The target-specific tree node transformation pass, implemented in the BoUpSLP::transformNodes() function, is the phase in the SLP vectorizer's optimization pipeline, which is designed to apply architecture-specific optimizations to the SLP tree, tailoring the generated code to exploit unique features of the target hardware.

This function is currently focused on two primary transformations: first is the optimization of load/store operations followed by reverse sequences and the second is analysis of the loads across gather/buildvector nodes. The first pass transforms these patterns into strided loads/stores with a stride of -1, subject to two key conditions:

- The target architecture must support strided memory operations.

- The use of strided operations must be more efficient than the combination of consecutive loads/stores and a subsequent reverse shuffle.

This optimization is particularly beneficial for RISC-V architectures, where strided memory access patterns have been observed to outperform the alternative approach of consecutive accesses followed by data reversal. The transformation process involves several steps:

1. Pattern Recognition. The pass identifies sequences of load/store operations immediately followed by reverse operations in the SLP tree.

2. Profitability Analysis. A cost model evaluates whether the strided access pattern would be more efficient for the target architecture than the original sequence.

3. Tree Transformation. If deemed profitable, the pass modifies the tree, replacing the original nodes with new nodes representing strided memory operations.

While currently limited to this specific transformation, the pass provides an extensible framework for introducing additional target-specific optimizations. This design allows future enhancements to focus on evolving hardware capabilities across various architectures.

CHAPTER 6 LLVM SLP VECTORIZER

The implications of this optimization are significant:

1. Improved Memory Bandwidth Utilization. Strided access patterns can lead to more efficient use of memory bandwidth.

2. Reduced Instruction Count. By collapsing multiple operations into a single strided operation, the overall instruction count can be decreased.

3. Potential Performance Gains. For supported architectures, this optimization can result in noticeable performance improvements, especially in memory-bound scenarios (see Listing 6-27, Listing 6-28, and Listing 6-29).

Listing 6-27. Original scalar code (LLVM IR).

```
define void @test(ptr noalias %in, ptr noalias %out) {
  %1 = load i32, ptr %in, align 4
  %gep1 = getelementptr i32, ptr %in, i64 1
  %2 = load i32, ptr %gep1, align 4
  %gep2 = getelementptr i32, ptr %in, i64 2
  %3 = load i32, ptr %gep2, align 4
  %gep3 = getelementptr i32, ptr %in, i64 3
  %4 = load i32, ptr %gep3, align 4
  %gep4 = getelementptr i32, ptr %in, i64 4
  %5 = load i32, ptr %gep4, align 4
  %gep5 = getelementptr i32, ptr %in, i64 5
  %6 = load i32, ptr %gep5, align 4
  %gep6 = getelementptr i32, ptr %in, i64 6
  %7 = load i32, ptr %gep6, align 4
  %gep7 = getelementptr i32, ptr %in, i64 7
  %8 = load i32, ptr %gep7, align 4
```

```
  store i32 %8, ptr %out, align 4
  %ogep1 = getelementptr i32, ptr %out, i64 1
  store i32 %7, ptr %ogep1, align 4
  %ogep2 = getelementptr i32, ptr %out, i64 2
  store i32 %6, ptr %ogep2, align 4
  %ogep3 = getelementptr i32, ptr %out, i64 3
  store i32 %5, ptr %ogep3, align 4
  %ogep4 = getelementptr i32, ptr %out, i64 4
  store i32 %4, ptr %ogep4, align 4
  %ogep5 = getelementptr i32, ptr %out, i64 5
  store i32 %3, ptr %ogep5, align 4
  %ogep6 = getelementptr i32, ptr %out, i64 6
  store i32 %2, ptr %ogep6, align 4
  %ogep7 = getelementptr i32, ptr %out, i64 7
  store i32 %1, ptr %ogep7, align 4
  ret void
}
```

Listing 6-28. Vector code without/with target-specific transformations (LLVM IR).

```
; without target-specific transformation pass
define void @test(ptr noalias nocapture readonly %in, ptr noalias nocapture writeonly %out) {
  %1 = load <8 x i32>, ptr %in, align 4
  %2 = shufflevector <8 x i32> %1, <8 x i32> poison, <8 x i32> <i32 7, i32 6, i32 5, i32 4, i32 3, i32 2, i32 1, i32 0>
  store <8 x i32> %2, ptr %out, align 4
  ret void
}

; with target-specific transformation pass
```

CHAPTER 6 LLVM SLP VECTORIZER

```
define void @test(ptr noalias nocapture readonly %in, ptr
noalias nocapture writeonly %out) {
  %ogep7 = getelementptr i8, ptr %out, i64 28
  %1 = load <8 x i32>, ptr %in, align 4
  tail call void @llvm.experimental.vp.strided.store.v8i32.
  p0.i64(<8 x i32> %1, ptr align 4 %ogep7, i64 -4, <8 x i1> <i1
  true, i1 true, i1 true, i1 true, i1 true, i1 true, i1 true,
  i1 true>, i32 8)
  ret void
}
```

Listing 6-29. Vector code without/with target-specific transformations (Assembly).

```
# without target-specific transformation pass
test:                                   # @test
        vsetivli        zero, 8, e16, m1, ta, ma
        vle32.v v8, (a0)
        vid.v   v10
        vrsub.vi        v10, v10, 7
        vsetvli zero, zero, e32, m2, ta, ma
        vrgatherei16.vv v12, v8, v10
        vse32.v v12, (a1)
        ret

# with target-specific transformation pass
test:                                   # @test
        vsetivli        zero, 8, e32, m2, ta, ma
        vle32.v v8, (a0)
        addi    a1, a1, 28
        li      a0, -4
        vsse32.v        v8, (a1), a0
        ret
```

CHAPTER 6   LLVM SLP VECTORIZER

The second transformation, supported by the SLP vectorizer, is the analysis for the clustered loads. This transformation enhances the vectorization process by identifying and optimizing multiple groups of (consecutive) vectorizable loads within a gather/buildvector node.

The core idea behind this optimization is to construct separate vectorize nodes for each identified cluster of loads. During the vectorization phase, these distinct nodes are then merged into a single, more efficient long vector. The clustered loads transformation results in more efficient use of vector registers and fewer instructions overall. This optimization is particularly beneficial in scenarios involving complex data structures or when processing large arrays of data, as it can significantly reduce memory access operations and improve cache utilization (see Listing 6-30, Listing 6-31, and Listing 6-32).

Listing 6-30. Original scalar code (LLVM IR).

```
define void @test(ptr noalias %p, ptr %p1) {
  %l1 = load i16, ptr %p, align 2
  # part of first load cluster
  %gep1 = getelementptr inbounds i8, ptr %p, i64 2
  %l2 = load i16, ptr %gep1, align 2
  # part of first load cluster
  %gep2 = getelementptr inbounds i8, ptr %p, i64 16
  %l3 = load i16, ptr %gep2, align 2
  # part of second load cluster
  %gep3 = getelementptr inbounds i8, ptr %p, i64 18
  %l4 = load i16, ptr %gep3, align 2
  # part of second load cluster
  store i16 %l1, ptr %p1, align 2
  %geps1 = getelementptr inbounds i8, ptr %p1, i64 2
  store i16 %l2, ptr %geps1, align 2
  %geps2 = getelementptr inbounds i8, ptr %p1, i64 4
```

```
  store i16 %13, ptr %geps2, align 2
  %geps3 = getelementptr inbounds i8, ptr %p1, i64 6
  store i16 %14, ptr %geps3, align 2
  ret void
}
```

Listing 6-31. Vector code without/with clustered analysis (LLVM IR).

```
; without clustered loads transformation pass
define void @test(ptr noalias %p, ptr %p1) #0 {
  %gep2 = getelementptr inbounds i8, ptr %p, i64 16
  %13 = load i16, ptr %gep2, align 2
  %gep3 = getelementptr inbounds i8, ptr %p, i64 18
  %14 = load i16, ptr %gep3, align 2
  %1 = load <2 x i16>, ptr %p, align 2
  store <2 x i16> %1, ptr %p1, align 2
  %geps2 = getelementptr inbounds i8, ptr %p1, i64 4
  store i16 %13, ptr %geps2, align 2
  %geps3 = getelementptr inbounds i8, ptr %p1, i64 6
  store i16 %14, ptr %geps3, align 2
  ret void
}

; with clustered loads transformation pass
define void @test(ptr noalias %p, ptr %p1) #0 {
  %gep2 = getelementptr inbounds i8, ptr %p, i64 16
  %1 = load <2 x i16>, ptr %p, align 2
  %2 = load <2 x i16>, ptr %gep2, align 2
  %3 = call <4 x i16> @llvm.vector.insert.v4i16.v2i16(<4 x i16>
  poison, <2 x i16> %1, i64 0)
```

```
    %4 = call <4 x i16> @llvm.vector.insert.v4i16.v2i16(<4 x i16>
    %3, <2 x i16> %2, i64 2)
    store <4 x i16> %4, ptr %p1, align 2
    ret void
}
```

Listing 6-32. Vector code without/with clustered analysis (Assembly).

```
# without clustered loads transformation pass
test:                                           # @test
        mv      a3, a0
        lh      a2, 16(a3)
        lh      a0, 18(a3)
        vsetivli        zero, 2, e16, mf4, tu, ma
        vle16.v v8, (a3)
        vse16.v v8, (a1)
        sh      a2, 4(a1)
        sh      a0, 6(a1)
        ret

# with clustered loads transformation pass
test:                                           # @test
        addi    a2, a0, 16
        vsetivli        zero, 2, e16, mf4, ta, ma
        vle16.v v8, (a0)
        vle16.v v9, (a2)
        vsetivli        zero, 4, e16, mf2, ta, ma
        vslideup.vi     v8, v9, 2
        vse16.v v8, (a1)
        ret
```

CHAPTER 6 LLVM SLP VECTORIZER

Also, this transformation implements target-specific detection and vectorization of interleaved (or segmented, in terms of RISC-V vector extension) loads. As it was already described before, interleaved memory accesses typically occur when multiple arrays or fields of a structure are processed simultaneously. Interleaved accesses also arise in structures of arrays (SoA) representations, where elements of different arrays are stored in an interleaved layout.

The transformation pass identifies and optimizes interleaved access patterns by

- Detecting memory accesses with constant stride.
- Grouping them into interleaved load/store sets.
- Replacing multiple scalar loads with vector loads and shuffle operations, which later can be lowered in the codegen as segmented/interleaved loads.
- Generating target-specific instructions for hardware that supports interleaved memory accesses.

Listing 6-33 shows an example, where it may help.

Listing 6-33. Original code (LLVM IR).

```
@src = common global [8 x double] zeroinitializer, align 64
@dst = common global [4 x double] zeroinitializer, align 64

define void @test() {
%a0 = load double, ptr @src, align 8
  %a1 = load double, ptr getelementptr inbounds ([8 x double],
  ptr @src, i32 0, i64 1), align 8
  %a2 = load double, ptr getelementptr inbounds ([8 x double],
  ptr @src, i32 0, i64 2), align 8
  %a3 = load double, ptr getelementptr inbounds ([8 x double],
  ptr @src, i32 0, i64 3), align 8
```

```
  %a4 = load double, ptr getelementptr inbounds ([8 x double],
  ptr @src, i32 0, i64 4), align 8
  %a5 = load double, ptr getelementptr inbounds ([8 x double],
  ptr @src, i32 0, i64 5), align 8
  %a6 = load double, ptr getelementptr inbounds ([8 x double],
  ptr @src, i32 0, i64 6), align 8
  %a7 = load double, ptr getelementptr inbounds ([8 x double],
  ptr @src, i32 0, i64 7), align 8
  %res1 = fsub fast double %a0, %a1
  %res2 = fsub fast double %a2, %a3
  %res3 = fsub fast double %a4, %a5
  %res4 = fsub fast double %a6, %a7
  store double %res1, ptr @dst, align 8
  store double %res2, ptr getelementptr inbounds ([8 x double],
  ptr @dst, i32 0, i64 1), align 8
  store double %res3, ptr getelementptr inbounds ([8 x double],
  ptr @dst, i32 0, i64 2), align 8
  store double %res4, ptr getelementptr inbounds ([8 x double],
  ptr @dst, i32 0, i64 3), align 8
  ret void
}
```

With the support for interleaved/segmented loads, it can be transformed into this (Listing 6-34 and Listing 6-35).

Listing 6-34. Vector code with segmented memory analysis (LLVM IR).

```
@src = common global [8 x double] zeroinitializer, align 64
@dst = common global [4 x double] zeroinitializer, align 64

define void @test() #0 {
  %1 = load <8 x double>, ptr @src, align 8
```

```
%2 = shufflevector <8 x double> %1, <8 x double> poison, <4 x
i32> <i32 0, i32 2, i32 4, i32 6>
%3 = shufflevector <8 x double> %1, <8 x double> poison, <4 x
i32> <i32 1, i32 3, i32 5, i32 7>
%4 = fsub fast <4 x double> %2, %3
store <4 x double> %4, ptr @dst, align 8
ret void
}
```

Listing 6-35. Code with/without segmented memory analysis (Assembly).

```
# without segmented loads transformation pass
test:                                    # @test
# %bb.0:
        lui     a0, %hi(src)
        fld     fa5, %lo(src)(a0)
        fld     fa4, %lo(src+8)(a0)
        fld     fa3, %lo(src+16)(a0)
        fld     fa2, %lo(src+24)(a0)
        fld     fa1, %lo(src+32)(a0)
        fld     fa0, %lo(src+40)(a0)
        fld     ft0, %lo(src+48)(a0)
        fld     ft1, %lo(src+56)(a0)
        lui     a0, %hi(dst)
        fsub.d  fa5, fa5, fa4
        fsub.d  fa4, fa3, fa2
        fsub.d  fa3, fa1, fa0
        fsub.d  fa2, ft0, ft1
        fsd     fa5, %lo(dst)(a0)
```

```
        fsd     fa4, %lo(dst+8)(a0)
        fsd     fa3, %lo(dst+16)(a0)
        fsd     fa2, %lo(dst+24)(a0)
        ret

# with segmented loads transformation pass
test:                                   # @test
# %bb.0:
        lui     a0, %hi(src)
        addi    a0, a0, %lo(src)
        vsetivli        zero, 4, e64, m2, ta, ma
        vlseg2e64.v     v8, (a0)
        vfsub.vv        v8, v8, v10
        lui     a0, %hi(dst)
        addi    a0, a0, %lo(dst)
        vse64.v v8, (a0)
        ret
```

As SLP vectorizer continues to evolve, it can implement a wider range of architecture-specific optimizations, further bridging the gap between high-level code and efficient machine instructions across different hardware platforms.

External Uses Analysis

The External Uses Analysis phase is implemented in the BoUpSLP::buildExternalUses() function. This phase focuses on managing scalar values that have been vectorized but are still required in their original scalar form outside of the vectorized region.

It includes several required steps:

1. Identification of Externally Used Scalars. The compiler identifies scalar values that should become part of vector operations but still referenced by scalar instructions outside the SLP tree.

2. Extraction Candidacy. These identified scalars are considered candidates for extraction from their respective vector values. This approach ensures that the original program semantics are preserved while maintaining the benefits of vectorization.

3. Instruction Generation Planning. For each scalar requiring extraction, the compiler plans the insertion of appropriate extractelement instructions. These instructions will be used to retrieve the scalar values from their vector counterparts at the necessary points in the code.

4. Optimization of BuildVector Sequences. The analysis phase also examines whether externally used values are part of buildvector sequences. In such cases, the compiler evaluates if these values can be more efficiently accessed through shuffle operations rather than extractions.

The implications of this analysis are important:

1. Preservation of Program Correctness. By carefully managing externally used scalars, the compiler ensures that the vectorized code maintains the same functionality as the original scalar code.

2. Performance Tuning. The cost analysis for extractions allows the compiler to make informed decisions about when vectorization is truly beneficial, considering the overhead of scalar extractions. In some cases, this analysis may result in keeping the original scalar instruction rather than extractelement instruction. It may happen only if all operands of this instruction are scalar or must be extracted for other external uses and the cost of such scalar instructions is lower than the cost of the extractelement instruction.

3. Reduction of Extraction Overhead. By identifying opportunities to use shuffles instead of extractions, the compiler can often reduce the performance penalty associated with accessing individual elements of vector registers.

4. Improved Register Utilization. By carefully planning extractions and leveraging shuffles where possible, the compiler can optimize register usage, potentially reducing register pressure.

Minimal Bitwidth Analysis

The Minimal Bitwidth Analysis, implemented in the BoUpSLP::computeMinimumValueSizes() function, is a sophisticated optimization phase aimed at reducing the computational cost and improving the efficiency of vector operations. This analysis is particularly valuable for languages like C and C++, where default integer promotions often result in operations being performed on larger data types than necessary.

Key aspects of this analysis include

1. Tree Traversal. The pass iterates through the SLP tree nodes, focusing on identifying sign-extension (sext), zero-extension (zext), and truncation (trunc) operations. These operations serve as indicators of potential type size optimizations.

2. Minimum Type Size Determination. For each node, the compiler analyzes the actual data range to determine the smallest data type that can safely represent the values without loss of correctness.

3. Def-Use Chain Analysis. The compiler traverses the def-use chains within the tree, assessing the feasibility of propagating smaller data types through various operations while maintaining correctness.

4. Demanded Bits Analysis. Utilizing the computeKnownBits() function and demanded bits analysis, the compiler determines which bits of each value are used or significant in subsequent operations.

5. Profitability Assessment. The pass evaluates whether reducing the bitwidth for a given path or subpath in the tree is beneficial. This assessment considers factors such as

    - Reduction in vector register pressure
    - Elimination of unnecessary extension or truncation operations
    - The depth of the profitable transformation in the tree

6. Type Size and Signedness Assignment. For nodes where bitwidth reduction is deemed profitable and safe, the compiler associates the optimized bitwidth size and signedness information.

7. Optimization Application. The derived bitwidth information is utilized in subsequent phases, particularly during cost estimation and code generation, to produce more efficient vector code.

Implications and benefits of this analysis are

1. Improved Register Utilization. By operating on smaller data types where possible, the compiler can pack more elements into a single vector register, potentially increasing the degree of parallelism.

2. Elimination of Redundant Operations. By removing unnecessary extension and truncation operations, the compiler reduces the overall instruction count and computational overhead.

3. Enhanced Vectorization Efficiency. Many vector instruction sets offer higher parallelism for smaller data types, allowing more elements to be processed simultaneously.

4. Optimization of C/C++ Idioms. This analysis is particularly effective in optimizing C and C++ code, where integer promotions often lead to suboptimal use of larger types for operations that could be performed on smaller types (see Listing 6-36, Listing 6-37, and Listing 6-38).

Listing 6-36. Original code (LLVM IR).

```
@c = global [12 x i64] zeroinitializer
define i16 @test() {
entry:
  %0 = load i64, ptr @c, align 8
  %conv = trunc i64 %0 to i32
  %conv3 = and i32 %conv, 65535
  %conv4 = xor i32 %conv3, 65535
  %1 = load i64, ptr getelementptr inbounds ([12 x i64], ptr @c, i64 0, i64 3), align 8
  %conv.1 = trunc i64 %1 to i32
  %conv3.1 = and i32 %conv.1, 65535
  %conv4.1 = xor i32 %conv3.1, 65535
  %.conv4.1 = tail call i32 @llvm.umax.i32(i32 %conv4, i32 %conv4.1)
  %2 = load i64, ptr getelementptr inbounds ([12 x i64], ptr @c, i64 0, i64 6), align 8
  %conv.2 = trunc i64 %2 to i32
  %conv3.2 = and i32 %conv.2, 65535
  %conv4.2 = xor i32 %conv3.2, 65535
  %.conv4.2 = tail call i32 @llvm.umax.i32(i32 %.conv4.1, i32 %conv4.2)
  %3 = load i64, ptr getelementptr inbounds ([12 x i64], ptr @c, i64 0, i64 9), align 8
  %conv.3 = trunc i64 %3 to i32
  %conv3.3 = and i32 %conv.3, 65535
  %conv4.3 = xor i32 %conv3.3, 65535
```

```
  %.conv4.3 = tail call i32 @llvm.umax.i32(i32 %.conv4.2, i32
  %conv4.3)
  %res = trunc i32 %.conv4.3 to i16
  ret i16 %res
}
```

Listing 6-37. Vector code without/with minbitwidth analysis (LLVM IR).

```
; without minbitwidth analysis
define i16 @test() {
  %0 = call <4 x i64> @llvm.experimental.vp.strided.load.v4i64.
  p0.i64(ptr align 8 @c, i64 24, <4 x i1> <i1 true, i1 true, i1
  true, i1 true>, i32 4)
  %1 = trunc <4 x i64> %0 to <4 x i32>
  %2 = and <4 x i32> %1, <i32 65535, i32 65535, i32 65535,
  i32 65535>
  %3 = xor <4 x i32> %2, <i32 65535, i32 65535, i32 65535,
  i32 65535>
  %4 = tail call i32 @llvm.vector.reduce.umax.v4i32(<4 x
  i32> %3)
  %res = trunc i32 %4 to i16
  ret i16 %res
}

; with minbitwidth analysis
define i16 @test() {
  %0 = tail call <4 x i64> @llvm.experimental.vp.strided.load.
  v4i64.p0.i64(ptr nonnull align 8 @c, i64 24, <4 x i1> <i1
  true, i1 true, i1 true, i1 true>, i32 4)
  %1 = trunc <4 x i64> %0 to <4 x i16>
```

CHAPTER 6   LLVM SLP VECTORIZER

```
  %2 = xor <4 x i16> %1, <i16 -1, i16 -1, i16 -1, i16 -1>
  %3 = tail call i16 @llvm.vector.reduce.umax.v4i16(<4 x
  i16> %2)
  ret i16 %3
}
```

Listing 6-38. Vector code without/with minbitwidth analysis (Assembly).

```
# without minbitwidth analysis
test:                                    # @test
        lui     a0, %hi(c)
        li      a1, 24
        addi    a0, a0, %lo(c)
        vsetivli        zero, 4, e32, mf2, ta, ma
        vlse64.v        v8, (a0), a1
        lui     a0, 16
        addi    a0, a0, -1
        vnsrl.wi        v8, v8, 0
        vnot.v  v8, v8
        vand.vx v8, v8, a0
        vredmaxu.vs     v8, v8, v8
        vmv.x.s a0, v8
        ret

# with minbitwidth analysis
test:                                    # @test
        lui     a0, %hi(c)
        li      a1, 24
        addi    a0, a0, %lo(c)
        vsetivli        zero, 4, e32, mf2, ta, ma
        vlse64.v        v8, (a0), a1
        vnsrl.wi        v8, v8, 0
```

CHAPTER 6 LLVM SLP VECTORIZER

```
vsetvli     zero, zero, e16, mf4, ta, ma
vnsrl.wi    v8, v8, 0
vnot.v      v8, v8
vredmaxu.vs v8, v8, v8
vmv.x.s     a0, v8
ret
```

To view the tree in Grpahviz format you can use -view-slp-tree LLVM option, which outputs DOT file (see Figure 6-1).

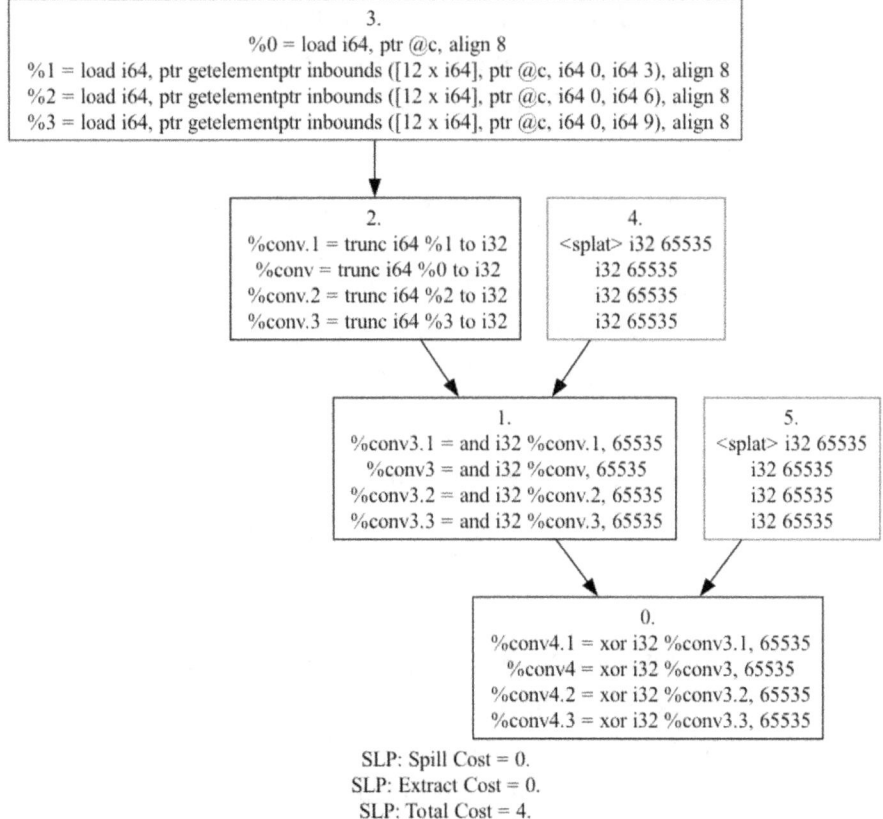

Figure 6-1. *SLP vectorized code graph*

CHAPTER 6　LLVM SLP VECTORIZER

Cost Estimation Phase

The Cost Estimation Phase is a critical component in the SLP vectorization process, implemented primarily in the BoUpSLP::getTreeCost function. This phase performs a comprehensive analysis to determine whether vectorization will yield performance benefits for a given code segment.

Key aspects of the cost estimation process include

1. Metric: Reciprocal Throughput. The vectorizer uses reciprocal throughput as its primary metric for cost estimation. This measure provides estimation into how quickly instructions can be executed, trying to consider factors like pipeline stages and execution unit availability.

2. Node-by-Node Cost Calculation. The estimator traverses the entire SLP tree, invoking BoUpSLP::getEntryCost() for each node, checks whether it's a gather/buildvector node or a fully vectorized node and calculates the cost appropriately.

3. BuildVector and Gather Sequence Analysis. Beyond basic instruction costs, the estimator performs an in-depth analysis of buildvector and gather sequences:

    (a) BuildVector Optimization. Instead of naively translating buildvector nodes into multiple insertelement instructions, the analyzer identifies opportunities to represent these as shuffle operations on existing vector values. This can significantly reduce the instruction count and associated costs.

CHAPTER 6   LLVM SLP VECTORIZER

(b) Gather Pattern Recognition. The estimator identifies complex gather patterns that can be optimized into more efficient operations such as strided loads, segmented loads, or masked gather operations.

4. External Scalar Uses Consideration. Some scalar values, despite being part of the vectorization candidate set, may need to remain in scalar form due to uses outside the vectorized region. The cost estimator accounts for necessary extractelement operations to maintain these scalar values.

5. Scalar Preference for Certain Instructions. For specific instructions like getelementptr, the estimator may determine it's more efficient to keep them in scalar form, especially when the base pointer is not vectorized or when all operands are scalar or must be extracted. This strategy can reduce the overall number of extractelement instructions.

6. Perfect Diamond and Partial Match Optimization. The cost estimation skips nodes that form a "perfect diamond match"—a scenario where a buildvector node exactly matches another vectorized or buildvector node. This optimization prevents redundant cost calculations for identical operations. Also, it can do partial match analysis, even if the matched instructions are parts of different vectorized (or even buildvector/buildvalue) nodes.

Checking carefully the trade-offs between scalar and vector execution, considering intricate instruction patterns, and accounting for architecture-specific nuances, the SLP vectorizer can make informed decisions about when and how to apply vectorization, ultimately contributing to the generation of highly efficient code for modern processors (see Listing 6-39).

Listing 6-39. Cost estimation algorithm.

```
for each tree_entry in SLP_tree:
  if tree_entry is a gather node and perfectly matches one of
  the nodes
    continue  # Perfect diamond match

 Cost += getEntryCost(tree_entry)

for each external_use in external_uses:
  if external_use.scalar is analyzed or is ephemeral value:
    continue # Already estimated or can be sfely skipped

  if external_use.user is insertelementinstr:
    if external_use.user is part of the buildvector:
      mark external_use.scalar as part of this buildvector
      mark external_use.scalar position in the mask
      continue

  if external_use.scalar is GEP and all operands are scalar or
  extracted already:
    continue # Original scalar GEP will be kept to avoid
    unneeded extractelementinst.
  Cost += extractelement instruction cost;

Cost += getSpillCost() # Add the cost of the potential spills
around function calls.

for each buildvector in buildvectors_with_external_scalars:
  Cost += cost of shuffle with the calculated mask
  Cost -= cost of each replaced insertelementinst from the
  buildvector

InstructionCost BoUpSLP::getEntryCost(entry):
  if tree_entry is the gather node:
```

CHAPTER 6   LLVM SLP VECTORIZER

```
    gather_cost = the cost of the buildvector of the
    unique values
    gather_cost +=  the cost of shuffle of the repeated values
    return gather_cost

  InstructionCost CommonCost = reordering cost (if any) +
  shuffle reused scalars cost (if any)
  return CommonCost + cost of the future vector
instruction(s) - cost of the original scalar instructions
```

Vector Code Emission Phase

If the cost estimation model shows that the vector code is more profitable than the original scalar code, the compiler generates vector code and removes old scalar code (see BoUpSLP::vectorizeTree).

At first, the original scalar instructions are scheduled, i.e., moved close to each other in each scheduling bundle (BoUpSLP::scheduleBlock). The compiler has already checked that the instructions are schedulable and can be moved according to bundles, so it knows this is a safe operation. This functionality reuses the functionality from the legality phase for checking that instructions are schedulable, and instead of checking, it performs actual scheduling and moves scalar instructions.

The next step is the actual vectorization. Here are the potential issues with inserting the new vector instructions. The SLP tree also may have cyclic dependencies, so the code emission tries to address this problem by splitting the code emission process. At first, it tries to emit the code for all initial non-PHI nodes. For PHI node, it just emits the empty PHI vector instruction, but does not follow the operands, i.e., the vectorization of the operands of PHI nodes does not occur. Then the vectorization for each PHI node is repeated, but now it already follows the operands and vectorizes them, if they were not vectorized yet. It allows to solve the issue with cyclic dependencies.

CHAPTER 6 LLVM SLP VECTORIZER

The next step is the vectorization of the postponed gathers. During the cost estimation phase, the compiler tries to identify the gather/buildvector nodes, which can be represented not as just insertelement instructions (forming gather/buildvector sequence), but instead can be represented as the series of shuffle instructions. This may happen if the original scalar instruction has several uses, which also gets vectorized. But operands of these vectorized uses are either in the different order, or only some of the operands match the other operands. Originally, such operands were vectorized in one of the operand nodes, then the extractelement instructions were generated for other uses values, which were part of the buildvector sequence. But instead, this extractelement + insertelement buildvector sequence might be represented as just a shufflevector of the previously vectorized value. This allows to improve performance of the vector code and reduce the total number of vector instructions.

But, when doing the actual vectorization, such dependencies are not preserved, and the dependent node might be vectorized earlier than the base node. The vectorization of such nodes is postponed and thus the compiler needs to vectorize them later. So, after two main vectorization phases, it runs through the list of the postponed nodes and vectorizes them, shuffling the vector instructions, being emitted for the base vectorized nodes.

The next step is the emission of extractelement instructions for each external use (i.e., the use of the vectorized scalar instruction outside of the SLP tree). It tries to reduce the number of emitted extractelements, checking if the pass already emitted this instruction for the scalar and is moving it, if necessary, instead of emitting a new one. If the external use is detected to be a buildvector sequence, it again tries to replace potential extractelement + insertelement with just shufflevector instructions.

Also, it tries to reduce the number of extractelement instructions. If all operands of the vectorized scalar instruction are also scalarized (they remain scalar after the vectorization or the compiler had emitted extractelement instructions for them already) and this instruction is cheaper than the extractelement instruction, it just copies the original

CHAPTER 6 LLVM SLP VECTORIZER

scalar instruction with the scalar operands. This is especially important for getelementptr instructions, since the scalar address calculations are cheaper for most of the platforms than just extractelement instruction. Scalar address can be effectively folded, while extractelement instruction requires data movement from vector unit to scalar and then special scalar register loading for preparing address (see Listing 6-40).

Listing 6-40. Vector code emission algorithm.

```
schedule all sheculed blocks
build the list of the new vector instructions insert points

for each node in slp_tree:
  if is_phi_node(node):
    generate_vector_stub(node)
  else:
    generate_vector_code(node)

for each postponed_node in postponed_nodes:
  generate_vector_code(postponed_node)

for each external_use in external_uses:
  if external_use.scalar is analyzed already:
    move previously emitted extractelement instruction to the
    correct position # If required, to preserve def-use chain
    continue

  if external_use.user is insertelementinstr:
    if external_use.user is part of the buildvector:
      mark the external_use.scalar as part of this buildvector
      mark external_use.scalar position in the mask
      continue

  if external_use.scalar is GEP and and all its operands are
  scalar or extracted already:
```

```
    clone external_use.scalar
    continue # Original scalar GEP will be kept to avoid
    unneeded extractelementinst

  generate extractelement instruction

for each buildvector in buildvectors_with_external_scalars:
  replace  buildvector by the shuffle instruction with the
calculated mask
  mark replaced insertelementinst for deletion
```

The SLP vectorizer in LLVM is still not mature enough and continues to see the enhancements to take advantage of new RVV features and to handle increasingly complex code patterns. This continuous development ensures that RISC-V processors with RVV can be effectively utilized across a wide range of high-performance computing applications. This includes (but is not limited by) support for segmented (and potentially, indexed) memory operations, native support for "non-power of two" scalar elements in the nodes, and other important features, like tree throttling.

Summary

In this chapter you learned

- The concept of Superword-Level Parallelism (SLP) vectorization, which identifies and combines independent scalar instructions in straight-line code into vector operations.

- The key objectives of SLP vectorization and how the SLP vectorizer in LLVM works as a bottom-up greedy algorithm, balancing performance gains with compilation efficiency.

- The main phases of the SLP vectorizer.

- How target-specific transformations (e.g., strided loads/stores, clustered loads, interleaved/segmented accesses) enhance SLP performance for RISC-V and other architectures.

- The role of operand reordering in aligning similar operations and reducing shuffle overhead.

- That SLP vectorization complements loop vectorization by handling patterns not visible at loop boundaries, enabling broader SIMD exploitation.

- LLVM's ongoing improvements to SLP, including better support for RVV features, segmented memory operations, and tree throttling, ensuring scalability for future workloads.

Index

A

Algebraic simplification, 154
Algebraic transformations, 155
Algorithm adaptation, 135
Alias analysis, 150
Alignment considerations, 242
AoS, *see* Array-of-structs (AoS)
Application Vector Length (AVL), 14, 17
Architecture-Aware optimizations, 117
Arithmetic combination, 147
ARM-based processors, 173
Array-of-structs (AoS), 197
Associative reductions, 255, 256
Attributes, 125
Autovectorization, 122
AVL, *see* Application Vector Length (AVL)

B

Backedge, 169
BFloat16 data type, 20
Bitwidth analysis, 237
Bottom-to-top subtree reordering approach, 283
Boyer-Moore majority voting algorithm, 272
Buildvalues sequence, 247–249
Buildvector sequences, 247–252, 262, 296, 304, 308

C

C/C++ language extensions, 46, 54
Clang, 2, 21–26, 96
    compilation pipeline, 26–29
    cross-compilation, 22
    lexical analysis, 26
    parsing, 27
    RVV-specific types, 44
    toolchain compilation, 22
    users, 38
Clang-based compilers
    loop hints, 59–91
    Open Multi-Processing (OpenMP), 91–122
Clang/LLVM compiler, 95
cmp, *see* Comparison instructions (cmp)
Code emission, 161
Code generation process, 43, 48, 90, 146, 157–167, 179

INDEX

Code vectorization, 136–138
Common Subexpression Elimination (CSE), 151, 155
Comparison instructions (cmp), 247
Compilation process, 182
Compiler directives, 91
Compile-time-known vector length, 73
Computational complexity, 147
Conditional vectorization, 103
Consecutive stores, 242, 243
Consistency, 51
Control dependencies, 185–187
Cost-aware optimization, 237
Cost estimation, 273
Cost estimation phase, 239, 304–307
Cost model, 154
CSE, *see* Common Subexpression Elimination (CSE)

D

DAG, *see* Directed Acyclic Graph (DAG)
Data alignment, 152
Data type, 135
Debugging mechanism, 217
Decision process, 280
Def-use chains, 298
Demanded bits analysis, 298
Dependency chain, 249
Deprecation, 38

Device offloading, 93
Directed Acyclic Graph (DAG), 159
Dual-loop structure, 189

E

Early-stage transformations, 154
EEW, *see* Effective Element Width (EEW)
Effective Element Width (EEW), 13
Efficient processing, 134
Environment variables, 92
EVL, *see* Explicit Vector Length (EVL)
EVL-based approach, 212
execute() member function, 230
Explicit Vector Length (EVL), 222, 231
External uses analysis phase, 295–297
Extractelement instructions, 308, 309
Extraction candidacy, 296

F

FastISel, 159
Fine-grained control, 89
Fine-grained optimization, 282
Fixed-length vector, 161
Fixed-length vector declarations, 48
Fixed-point types, 12
Fixed vectorization, 208
Fixed vectors, 161

Flattening, 149
Floating-point operations, 269
Floating-point reductions, 10
Fork-join model, 92
Function inlining, 152

G

Gather pattern recognition, 305
Gather sequences, 251, 304
GCC-based toolchains, 21
GetElementPtr (GEP) instructions, 240, 253, 254
Global Instruction Selection pass (GlobalISel), 159
GlobalISel, *see* Global Instruction Selection pass (GlobalISel)
Google Highway, 123

H

Hardware configurations, 95, 96
Hardware-software co-optimization, 43
Hardware-specific code, 2
High-level interface, 48
Homogeneous instruction sequences, 244
HorizontalReduction class, 256

I

IgnoreReorder Parameter, 281
Indexed operations, 137
Induction variable (IV), 222
Inlining heuristics, 152
InnerLoopVectorizer class, 227
Instruction combining, 147
Instruction generation planning, 296
Instruction set architecture (ISA), 1, 2, 6, 254
Instruction Simplification, 147
Instructions scheduling algorithm, 265–268
Interleaved accesses, 203–207
optimization, 197
Interleaved loads, 196
Intermediate representation (IR), 238, 240, 256, 268, 273, 275
Internal tool users, 39
IR, *see* Intermediate representation (IR)
ISA, *see* Instruction set architecture (ISA)
IV, *see* Induction variable (IV)

J, K

JIT components, 158

L

Language-specific constructs, 28
Legality checks, 262–264
Legality checks phase, 261–273
Length Multiplier (LMUL), 14, 15
LICM, *see* Loop invariant code motion (LICM)

INDEX

LLVM
    flexible abstraction, 141
LMUL, *see* Length
        Multiplier (LMUL)
Logical operations, 147
Loop-centric approaches, 234
Loop flattening, 149
Loop hints
    additional hints, 60
    codes, 60–62
    suggestions, 60
    transformation, 59
    vectorizable source code, 62–91
LoopInfo, 169
Loop invariant code motion
        (LICM), 148, 149
Loop multiversioning, 190, 195–201
Loop strength reduction (LSR), 153
Loop tail, 210, 211
Loop unrolling, 149
Loop vectorization, 128–135,
        184, 188
LoopVectorizationPlanner, 180,
        226, 229
Loop vectorizer, 169, 176, 189, 203
    architectures, 209
    canonical loop, 171
    designs, 178–182
    instruction classification,
        214, 215
    iteration count, 209
    iterative process, 217
    pass invocation, 171–173
    runtime, 210

    RVV-specific requirements, 230
    scalar remainder, 171
    vector factor, 213
    vectorization strategy, 212
        See also Low-level virtual
        machine (LLVM)
Lower-level programming
        techniques, 91
Low-level virtual machine
        (LLVM), 234
    analysis algorithms, 150
    code generation
        process, 164–166
    compiler, 255
    compiler coding, 234–237
    compiler framework, 1
    computational needs, 30, 31
    experimental features, 37–39
    extensions support, 32, 33
    features, 43
    fine-tuned, 208
    instructions, 144
    legality checks and
        analysis, 182–207
    mask vectors, 143
    memory dependence
        analysis, 151
    operations, 159
    RISC-V Vector Extension
        (RVV), 21–26
    SLP vectorization, 234
    SLP vectorizer, 237, 238
    target-independent code
        generator, 166

target-independent
    optimizations, 146
target-specific assembly, 26
target support, 156
toolchains, 30–43
type system, 142
vectorized code, 198–202
    See also Superword-level
    parallelism (SLP)
LSR, *see* Loop strength
    reduction (LSR)

M

Machine code optimizations, 161
MachineInstrs, 160
Mask types, 47, 48
Memory access efficiency, 134
Memory access operations, 289
Memory Bandwidth
    Utilization, 286
Memory-bound scenarios, 286
Memory dependence analysis, 151
Minimal bitwidth
    analysis, 297–304
Mixed-width operations, 13
Multicore architectures, 94
Multi-core processors, 91–122

N

Node building algorithm, 262–264
Node-by-node cost calculation, 304
Non-loop node, 169

Non-OpenMP code, 128
Nonvectorizable instructions, 183

O

OpenBLAS, 123
OpenHW Group, 41
OpenMP, *see* Open Multi-
    Processing (OpenMP)
OpenMP 5.2, 95
Open Multi-Processing (OpenMP),
    22, 91–122
    SiFive extension, 128–135
    Vector Function Application
        Binary Interface
        (VectorABI), 122–128
Operand reordering, 269, 270, 284
Optimization application, 299
Ordered reductions, 255, 256
Original scalar code, 286–288

P

Parallelism, 134
Partial match optimization, 305
Partial Redundancy Elimination
    (PRE), 151
Pattern disruption, 155
Performance implications, 134
Performance tuning, 90, 297
PHI nodes, 183, 245, 247, 307
Portability, 43, 135
Post-vectorization, 227
#pragma clang loop, 89

INDEX

PRE, *see* Partial Redundancy Elimination (PRE)
Predication inefficiencies, 90
Profile-based approach, 32
Profiling-driven tuning, 135
Profitability assessment, 262, 298
Proof-of-concept demonstration, 38
Propagation, 148
Proposed format usage, 117–121
Pseudo instructions, 162

Q

Qualcomm, 41, 42

R

Ratification, 6, 37, 38
RAW, *see* Read-after-write (RAW)
Read-after-write (RAW), 185
Reassociation, 148
Reciprocal throughput, 226
Recursive optimization, 281
Reduced instruction count, 280, 281
Reduced Instruction Set Computer (RISC), 2
Reduction analysis phase, 254–261
Reduction pattern identification, 247
Reduction patterns, 244
Reduction roots analysis, 247, 248
Redundant operations, 299

Register utilization, 297
Reordered vectorized code, 278, 279, 282, 283
Reordering algorithm, 279
Reordering decision, 281
Reordering operations, 278
Reordering strategy, 272
Return instructions (rets), 246
RISC, *see* Reduced Instruction Set Computer (RISC)
RISCVInsertVSETVLI, 163
RISC-V Vector Extension (RVV), 1, 166, 188
   abstraction, 144
   architectural elements, 8
   assembly-level elements, 158
   builtins, 54–57
   clang, 21–26
   code generation, 142, 157–167
   code representation classes, 157
   collaborative approach, 4
   common profiles, 5, 6
   computing platforms, 3
   extension, 7
   extension mechanism, 4
   first-class citizens, 142
   future-proofing, 8
   generated versions, 127, 128
   key features, 146
   language extensions, 43–56
   LLVM, 21–26
   masking modes, 16
   mask registers, 17, 18
   open source software, 136

optimizations, 146–156
optimization strategy, 211
optional extensions, 3
performance, 96
primary mechanisms, 144
processor status, 3
profiles, 5
scalable vector
    types, 141, 142
scientific computing, 19
SEW/LMUL representation,
    142, 143
standard extensions, 3
support status, 33–36
target-agnostic intrinsics, 146
target-independent
    algorithms, 158
vector extension, 8–20
vectorization, 84, 212
vector masking, 16
vector predication (VP),
    145, 146
vector reduction
    instructions, 254
vector-scalar addition, 19
vscale factor, 142
Rivos, 42
Root instruction, 249
Root node identification, 240
Runtime library routines, 92
RVV, *see* RISC-V Vector
    Extension (RVV)
RVVEmitter, 53

S

Same-width operations, 12
SAXPY principles, 22–24
Scalable parameter, 79
Scalable vector, 47, 141
Scalable Vector Extension (SVE), 141
Scalable vectorization, 208
Scalar code, 254, 286–290
Scalar loop remainder, 176
Scalar preference, 305
Scalar reduction, 258
Scalar Replacement of Aggregates
    (SROA), 151
Scheduling, 264, 265
Selected Element Width (SEW), 13,
    15, 116, 128, 129
SelectionDAG, 159, 161
Semantic analysis, 27
SEW, *see* Selected Element
    Width (SEW)
Shared-memory parallel
    programming, 94
Shuffle sinking, 284
SiFive clang-based
    toolchain, 128–135
SIMD, *see* Single Instruction,
    Multiple Data (SIMD)
simdlen/safelen, 111
Single Instruction, Multiple Data
    (SIMD), 6, 97–122
Single user, 249
SLP, *see* Superword-Level
    Parallelism (SLP)

INDEX

SLP vectorization, 146, 154
SoA, *see* Structures of arrays (SoA)
SROA, *see* Scalar Replacement of Aggregates (SROA)
SSA, *see* Static Single Assignment (SSA)
Stack space, 160
Standard Vector Instructions, 144
Static Single Assignment (SSA), 22
Store instructions, 262
   analysis, 243, 244
   description, 240
   memory locations, 241
   vectorizer, 242
Store-to-load forwarding, 151
Store vectorization process, 241, 242
Strategy selection, 272
Stride analysis, 242
Strided load recognition, 237
Strided memory operations, 202
Structures of arrays (SoA), 197, 292
Suboptimal vectorization, 91
Subtree isolation, 281
Subtree reordering strategies, 282
Subtree root reordering, 284
Superword-Level Parallelism (SLP), 233, 273
   reduction analysis phase, 254–261
   vectorization, 233, 234
   vectorizer, 233, 237, 238
      analysis phase, 240–254
      designs, 238, 239 *See also* Transformation phase
SVE, *see* Scalable Vector Extension (SVE)
Synchronization mechanisms, 95

T

TableGen, 50, 51
Tail elements, 17
Tail handling, 53
Target description interfaces, 157
Target independence, 22
Target-independent algorithms, 158
Target processor, 79
Target specification, 30
Target-specific detection, 292
Target-specific information, 146–156
Target-specific instructions, 292
Target-specific tree node transformation, 274, 284–295
TargetTransformInfo (TTI), 156, 166
Task-based parallelism, 93, 95
Task group, 7
Terminal operations, 246
T-HEAD Extensions (Alibaba), 39, 40
Threshold-based inlining, 153
Toolchain compatibility, 43
Top-to-bottom approach, 281

Trade-offs, 153
Transformation, 222–226
Transformation phase, 239
    external uses analysis phase, 295–297
    external vector element usage, 274
    minimal bitwidth analysis, 274, 297–304
    target-specific tree nodes, 284–295
    tree node reordering, 275–284
    tree topology, 274
    vector code emission phase, 307–310
Tree building procedure, 261–273
Tree node reordering, 275–284
Tree transformation, 285
TripCount check, 173
tryScheduleBundle function, 264
TTI, *see* TargetTransformInfo (TTI)
Type definitions, 45, 46
Type system, 44

U

Unordered scalars, 275
Unordered vectorized code, 276–278
User-defined functions, 123

V

Value operand analysis, 242
Value parameter, 68
Vector arithmetic operations, 9
VectorABI, *see* Vector Function Application Binary Interface (VectorABI)
Vector code emission phase, 239, 307–310
Vector code without/with clustered analysis (LLVM IR), 289–292
Vector code without/with target-specific transformations, 286–288
Vector cryptography, 11
Vector extension
    loop hint optimizations, 59–91
    OpenMP, 91–122
Vector factor (VF), 156, 213
Vector fixed-point instructions, 11
Vector Function Application Binary Interface (VectorABI), 122–128
Vectorizable instructions, 183, 184
Vectorization, 1, 2, 179, 212, 237, 248, 257, 261, 307, 308
    candidates, 179
    of compare instructions, 252, 253
    efficiency, 299
    extractelement instructions, 308
    identified reductions, 258–261
    interleaved accesses, 196
    legality, 183
    opportunities, 241
    parameters, 68–91, 128
    phases, 289

Vectorization (*cont.*)
  RVV, 84
  superword-level parallelism
      (SLP), 233, 234 (*see also*
      Superword-Level
      Parallelism (SLP))
  support, 96
  transformations, 183
  tree building
      procedure, 261–273
  with and without operands
      reordering, 269, 270
Vectorized code, 173–182
Vectorized function, 125, 126
Vectorizer
  analysis phase, 240–254
  characteristics, 246
  computation, 245
  exhaustive analysis
      techniques, 239
  key phases, 238, 239
  PHI nodes, 244, 247
Vector length (VLEN), 14, 16
Vector length (VLMAX), 175, 212
Vector-length agnostic (VLA), 9, 90,
      178, 222, 231
Vector mask, 11
Vector masking, 17
Vector operation, 242
Vector Plan Recipes (VPRecipes),
      178, 180, 215, 231
Vector Plans (VPlans), 207, 215,
      217, 221–225
Vector predication (VP), 145, 146
Vector reduction
      operations, 10, 237
Vector register class, 163
Vector Register File (VRF), 13
Vendor extensions, 39
Vendor-Specific Support, 51
Ventana Micro Systems, 40
VF, *see* Vector factor (VF)
VLA, *see* Vector-length
      agnostic (VLA)
VLEN, *see* Vector length (VLEN)
VLOptimizer pass, 163, 167
Void-type instructions, 246
VP, *see* Vector predication (VP)
VPBasicBlock, 181
VPBlockBase, 181
VPCanonicalIVPHIRecipe, 222
VPDef, 181
VPInstructions, 178, 181
VPlan-based vectorization, 179, 180
VPlans, *see* Vector Plans (VPlans)
VPRecipeBase, 180
VPRecipes, *see* Vector Plan Recipes
      (VPRecipes)
VPRegionBlock, 181
VPUser models, 181
VPValue, 181
VRF, *see* Vector Register File (VRF)

W, X, Y, Z

WAR, *see* Write-After-Read (WAR)
WAW, *see* Write-After-Write (WAW)
Write-After-Read (WAR), 185
Write-After-Write (WAW), 185

GPSR Compliance

The European Union's (EU) General Product Safety Regulation (GPSR) is a set of rules that requires consumer products to be safe and our obligations to ensure this.

If you have any concerns about our products, you can contact us on

ProductSafety@springernature.com

In case Publisher is established outside the EU, the EU authorized representative is:

Springer Nature Customer Service Center GmbH
Europaplatz 3
69115 Heidelberg, Germany